ULTIMATE

QUILTING

BIBLE

COLLINS & BROWN

ULTIMATE

Marie
Clayton

QUILTING

A Complete
Reference with
Step-by-Step
Techniques

BIBLE

For David, who always believed in me and gave me space to do my own thing.

contents

introduction   6

getting started   10
quiltmaking basics   34
wholecloth and strippy quilts   66
pieced quilts   84
appliquéd quilts   178
embellished quilts   208
folded quilts   230

glossary   248
resources   251
acknowledgements   252
index   253

introduction

Quilting, in all its forms, is one area of sewing that has remained consistently popular over the last few decades. At a time when more and more people were giving up on making their own clothes and other household items, there were still those who made quilts in all their many forms. Today, now that dressmaking and running up simple curtains, cushions and other soft furnishings has become trendy once more, quilting is being discovered by even more sewers than ever.

The traditional definition of a quilt is a textile made from two layers of fabric with a layer of padding in between, the whole held together with stitching or ties through all the layers. Modern quilts are not necessarily made as bedcovers – many are intended as wall hangings for display. But even this is not a new idea – in the Middle Ages quilts and tapestries were often hung on walls to provide extra insulation and cut down draughts.

The art of patchwork, or piecing, has become so firmly entwined with that of quilting that for many people the two terms are interchangeable, even though a quilt can be made without piecing, and piecing can be done without quilting the finished result. Appliqué techniques are also often used to decorate quilts, and folding, or otherwise manipulating fabric in various ways, can be used to create three-dimensional effects.

This book aims to cover all the basic techniques that are used in making a quilt, whatever kind you might wish to create. The first chapter, Getting Started, has details of the basic sewing equipment and what it is all used for, so you can make an informed decision about what to buy and how to choose the right sewing machine. Following on from this are the basic stitches you will use time after time, explained with helpful step-by-step diagrams. The different types of fabric are covered in brief, with information on their characteristics, so you learn what to look for and what not to choose. A section on colour and pattern will help you design your quilt, by explaining how these might work together. This section also covers how to set up a practical working area and looks at how you can store materials and equipment safely and conveniently.

The second chapter, Quiltmaking Basics, looks at the different techniques of quilting by hand and machine, and the techniques you will need to construct a finished quilt. Each of the following chapters covers a different type of quiltmaking tradition: Wholecloth and Strippy Quilts, Pieced Quilts, Appliquéd Quilts, Embellished Quilts and Folded Quilts. As well as providing an introduction to any special techniques needed for that type of quilt, each of these chapters looks at some of the most traditional and well-loved designs. As well as step-by-step diagrams, each chapter also includes any relevant templates needed for the designs featured. Finally, a glossary of quiltmaking terms completes the book, making this a one-stop resource that you will return to time and time again.

If you are new to quilting, you will find all the basic techniques you need in this book. If you are a more experienced quilter, hopefully you will find something new and different to try – and this book will also be a useful source of reference for some of the less common techniques. Happy quilting!

Marie Clayton

quiltmaking: a short history

Quilts have been made for centuries in many cultures around the world. In cold climates, the earliest types of quilting developed because of a need for warmth – several layers of fabric were warmer than one, and it was practical to hold them together with stitching, so quilting was born. In countries with a hot climate, quiltmaking was a way of recycling worn fabrics to give them a new lease of life, or to create protective clothing, or to decorate wall hangings to keep out draughts or insects.

Quiltmaking around the world

Although many people think of quiltmaking as being a Western tradition, it also features in the history of other cultures around the world, particularly in the Middle East and Asia. In Bengal, old saris are layered together and stitched with kantha embroidery to make light coverlets. In Japan sashiko – intricate stitching, usually in white thread on dark blue fabric – was developed both to reinforce worn clothing and to create warm, padded garments for workmen, and a form of patchwork in strips, known as yosegire, was used to decorate clothing, hangings and screens.

Often, quilts incorporated other decorative work such as appliqué, embroidery or piecing. In the deserts of Egypt, beautiful appliqué was used to embellish hangings and cushions in the tents of nomadic tribes. In South America, reverse appliqué was used to decorate clothing and on the opposite side of the world, in China, it was used for household items and ceremonial textiles.

Quiltmaking in Europe

In the West, one of the earliest recorded uses of quilted fabric was for the padded garments that were worn underneath metal armour for both comfort and protection by Crusaders returning from the Middle East in the eleventh and twelfth centuries. The idea of quilting fabric was soon picked up by needlecrafters in Italy, France, Germany and Britain, who adapted it for other uses. Quilting was often used to make bedding and quilted clothing after the big freeze hit Europe in the fourteenth century, and the earliest surviving European bed quilts are three trapunto (stuffed) quilts, all made in Sicily during the late fourteenth century.

By the late seventeenth and early eighteenth centuries, beautifully quilted clothing and bedcoverings had become a normal part of life among the upper and middle classes across Europe – quilted petticoats for women and waistcoats or tunics for men were particularly popular. By the early nineteenth century, quilting was an established art in France, Sweden and Germany, with similar patterns often developing independently in more than one country.

Quiltmaking in Britain

In Britain, two distinct forms of quiltmaking developed: the rich commissioned finely detailed, labour-intensive decorative work, which was most probably stitched by members of one of the professional guilds of embroiderers; the poor had their own form of quilting, making warm and practical bedcovers and clothing. Strong traditions of quilting developed in particular areas of Britain, notably in Wales and in Durham and Northumberland in the north-east of England. Both men and women could earn a living as quilters, either as village needlecrafters, who lived locally and usually also made clothes and did other sewing work, or as itinerant quilters – often men – who went from farm to farm to make quilts in return for their keep. Quilting was frequently a family affair, with the techniques and the patterns being handed down, or friends would gather together to work on opposite sides of the same quilt.

In the late nineteenth century there were also professional quilt-markers, or quilt-stampers, who would mark the pattern on a quilt top with a blue pencil, ready for the owner to quilt over the lines. The tops could be bought ready-stamped, or an owner could provide her own top and specify the pattern required. Quilt-stampers used both templates and freehand drawings to mark the patterns and certain designs became typical in different areas.

Quiltmaking in America

Quilting first arrived in America with the settlers from Europe, but it soon developed its own distinct styles and traditions. American quiltmakers increasingly began to use blocks to construct their quilts – they were more portable for settlers on the move, and could easily be stored until enough had been made for a complete quilt.

Both appliqué and piecing techniques could be used to make blocks, and existing designs were adapted and new ones developed. The lack of easily available cloth meant that makers had to use what they could find around them: old blankets, worn-out dresses and feed sacks. The quilting bee, when women could get together to gossip and pass on news as they stitched, was valuable not only for social reasons but also because it allowed an exchange of sewing skills. The pinnacle of American quilting was perhaps in the nineteenth century, when every household needed a good stock of quilts, both for warmth and to create a makeshift bed for visitors. Every girl of marriageable age had a hope chest, filled with at least a dozen quilt tops – it was considered unlucky to finish the quilt before an engagement had been announced.

As well as the mainstream of American quilting, various other types of quiltmaking also developed in North America. Hawaiian quilts are worked using a distinctive form of appliqué to make strongly graphic, symmetrical designs. African slaves, who were taught sewing to make quilts for the plantation owner's house, developed the techniques using African symbols and motifs to make quilts for their own cabins. Many Native American tribes also picked up the quiltmaking tradition, using the ceremonial traditions of their tribe.

The Amish are perhaps the best-known quilters in the world. The 'Plain People' are descended from a sect of Anabaptists, who travelled to the New World from Germany in the 1720s. They formed very private and self-contained communities, which even today do without most modern conveniences such as electricity. Many of them are farmers, working the land with horses and mules, or by hand. They use and recycle anything they consider essential, and do without anything considered frivolous or unnecessary. The women cook and sew, making household linens and clothes for both children and adults, recycling fabric left overs into quilts. Amish clothing is never made from patterned fabric, always plain: trousers, jackets and dresses are in dark colours – usually black, dark grey or navy – while children's clothes and shirts are sometimes made using bright colours. This gives Amish quilts quite a distinctive look, with the bright scraps glowing like jewels against sombre, dark backgrounds. The Amish originally developed quilting patterns learnt from their non-Amish neighbours – who were known as the 'English' no matter where they came from – into their own characteristically simple designs, which were worked with great skill and precision. Today, although they have hand- or treadle-operated sewing machines for dressmaking, the quilts are always stitched by hand.

Quiltmaking today

After manufactured items of bedlinen became widely available in most countries, quiltmaking became less of a necessity and more of an outlet for creative expression, but it always retained its popularity in many areas of the world. Modern quiltmakers have developed a whole range of new skills, and quilting by machine is now accepted as being an art form in its own right. With the recent resurgence in the practice of traditional skills, even more stitchers will turn to quilting as a way of showcasing their sewing techniques – and perhaps to create an heirloom for generations to come.

getting started

One of the joys of quiltmaking is that you really don't need very much special equipment and for many centuries the most beautiful pieces of work have been created just with fabric, scissors, needle and thread. However, there are now many items on the market that will save you time and make some parts of the process much less laborious than before.

measuring and marking tools

You may already have many perfectly adequate tools for measuring and marking in your sewing box or on your desk, but if you buy some special items, they will certainly make your life easier when creating patchwork or quilting.

Water-soluble pen

Use on washable fabrics only. The pen marks can be removed with water when no longer required.

Air-soluble pen

Marks made with this pen will fade over time on exposure to the air. Not suitable if your project will be worked on over several months, as the marks may fade too soon.

Chalk pencil/ tailor's pencil

Comes in a range of colours and often has a stiff brush at one end for removing the chalk marks when no longer required.

Lead pencil

Useful for drawing shapes on pattern paper, but not ideal for fabric unless used on the wrong side.

Tailor's chalk

Available in a range of colours and in different shapes. Marks can be brushed away easily when no longer needed.

Chalk wheel

A more up-to-date version of tailor's chalk, filled with chalk dust. Also available in a range of colours.

Tracing wheel

Use with dressmaker's carbon to transfer design lines to fabric – but the marks may be difficult to remove, so use these for designs that will be hidden by stitching.

Eraser

To remove pencil marks on paper or fabric – usually more successful on paper.

Tape measure

A standard tape measure that shows both metric and imperial is most useful. Avoid fabric tapes, which can stretch over time.

Compass

For drawing out straightforward circles and simple curves.

Seam gauge

A useful piece of equipment that will help you to produce seams of an even depth, but is also great for measuring borders accurately.

Plastic ruler

A clear plastic ruler will allow you to see the fabric beneath. Don't use it as a straight-edge for cutting, as it may become damaged.

Metal ruler

A metal ruler is best if you need to make a cut by drawing a craft knife along a straight-edge. These come in a range of lengths and in metric, imperial or both.

T-square

One of the essential items for achieving right-angled corners when making blocks that need to fit together perfectly.

Flexible curve

An essential item for achieving unusual curves, as it can easily be twisted and bent to exactly the right shape.

Protractor

Used for measuring angles – the type for school students is perfectly adequate.

Adjustable set square

Ideal to measure and mark lines at a wide range of angles and to achieve right-angled corners. Available in a range of sizes.

Tracing paper

Essential for copying and transferring shapes to cardboard, or for creating your own designs and motifs.

Squared or isometric graph paper

Handy for templates, planning out a design, or when working out different setting patterns.

Marking and measuring

Test the marker on a spare piece of fabric first to see if it will show up, and also to find out whether the marks can be removed easily.

In most quiltmaking – and piecing particularly – accurate cutting and measuring is vitally important for good results. Take your time at this stage to prevent problems later.

cutting tools

Although you can manage with just a sharp pair of good scissors, there is other equipment available that will speed up the cutting process considerably – as well as ensuring that the cuts you make are more accurate.

Thread scissors

A small pair of scissors with sharp points is ideal for snipping thread and for fine-detail fabric cutting. Alternatively, there are special thread clippers that are ideal for both right- and left-handed people.

Paper scissors

These should be kept solely for cutting paper patterns and templates, which can blunt the blades. You would not, therefore, use them on fabric. However, they can be used on synthetic wadding (batting).

Fabric scissors

Any scissors used for fabric must be very sharp with long blades. Never use fabric scissors to cut anything else, as they will soon become blunt.

Looking after your tools

Scissors and rotary cutters must be very sharp, so check the blades regularly. Keep the guard on the blade of a rotary cutter when it is not in use.

Store cutting mats flat or hang them up – don't roll them or they may develop a permanent curve. Mats can also be damaged by heat, so keep them out of direct sunlight.

Keep pins in a pincushion or plastic box – a metal pin box may lead to rust. Discard any rusty or blunt pins as soon as you spot them, since they will damage fabric.

Seam ripper

Ideal for unpicking seams quickly if you need to correct mistakes.

Rotary cutter

The rotary cutter will cut through several layers of fabric in one go, making it much easier to cut accurate shapes for patchwork. There are several different types on the market, so try a couple out for ease of use before you buy.

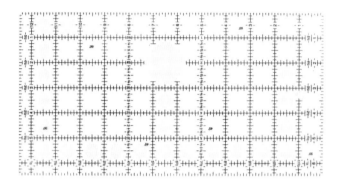

Quilter's rule/ rotary ruler

Most quilters have a selection of these rules, which come in many shapes and sizes – including rectangles, squares and triangles. Check that the markings are accurate and match along all edges. Markings are available in different colours, so choose one that is clear against your cutting mat.

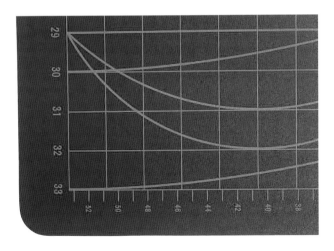

Self-healing cutting mat

Essential for use with the rotary cutter – gives a good cutting surface and at the same time will protect your worksurface. Usually, one side is marked with a grid and the other is plain. The grid is handy for lining up fabric and ruler, but don't use it as a measure. Mats come in many sizes and it may be worth having a large one for general use and a small one that is more portable.

Software for quilters

There are various special software programs available for quilters. A basic program will allow you to choose a block from a library of set designs and colour it in using a range of standard colours; you can then arrange different blocks on screen to make up a quilt design, changing the orientation of the blocks, adding sashing and borders and adjusting colours until satisfied with the result.

Some programs allow you to scan in your own fabrics, so you can see how a particular fabric will look in a block. There are also programs for sizing and printing out templates for standard blocks, and for quilting stitch patterns.

Try to arrange a demonstration of the software program to make sure it will do exactly what you need it to, and check the system requirements before buying to ensure that the software you have chosen is compatible with your computer.

templates and stencils

Manufactured templates or stencils may seem expensive, but they offer a high degree of accuracy and a basic selection will last for years. For special projects, you can also make your own.

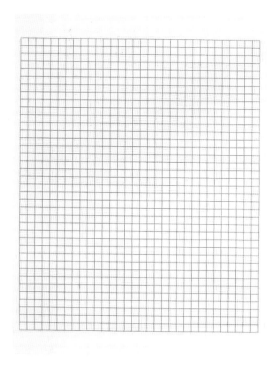

Template plastic and cardboard

Use these for making your own templates and stencils. Cardboard is adequate for single usage, but choose plastic for multiple usage as it will hold its shape better.

Craft knife

The best thing for cutting template plastic and cardboard – don't use paper scissors.

Freezer paper

This is coated with plastic on one side so it can be ironed on to fabric and later removed without leaving a trace. It is ideal for appliqué templates and English paper piecing.

Quilting stencil and patchwork template

Quilting stencils are usually made of translucent plastic and ideal for large projects. For smaller projects, just transfer the design using appropriate marking tools. For the patchwork template, choose either a double unit – one solid piece for backing papers and marking seam allowances, and one piece with a cut-out window so you can view motif positioning – or a multi-sized unit with 5mm (¼in) gradations.

Quilter's quarter

A length of acrylic that can be used to add a perfect 5mm (¼in) seam allowance around any straight-sided template.

Quarter wheel

A small brass wheel with a central hole. Place a marker in the hole and roll the wheel around any shaped template to add a perfect 5mm (¼in) seam allowance.

sewing tools

The sewing tools used for quilting are the same as those used for general sewing. Much can be done by hand, but on large projects a sewing machine can be quicker for all or some of the work.

Needles

There are many types of handsewing needle available, but quilters mainly use 'sharps' (ordinary sewing needles) for general sewing and piecing, and 'betweens' for quilting.

Pins

Any type of pin is suitable, but you can buy special quilter's pins, which are longer than normal in order to go through several layers of fabric. Pins with a large coloured head are often easier to see.

Safety pins

These are ideal for holding the layers of a quilt together while it is being quilted – they provide much more security than using straight pins, which might slip out.

Thread

Ordinary sewing thread to match the fabric (cotton for pure cotton, polyester for polycotton) is fine for piecing. It can also be used for quilting; however, special pre-waxed quilting thread is stronger, although it is not available in such a wide range of colours.

Thimble

Many sewers do not like using a thimble, but for quilting by hand it will prevent pricked fingers – even if you don't use it for anything else. There is a wide range of types, so experiment until you find a comfortable one.

Needle-threader

When using fine thread and small needles, a needle-threader will save you time and frustration.

Embroidery thread

For embellishment and for embroidery on some types of quilt, proper embroidery thread is the best thing to use. It is stranded, so you can use one or more strands depending on how thick you want the stitch to be.

Hoops and frames

These hold fabric taut while you quilt or embroider by hand. Available in a wide range of sizes and types, from a small hoop to a floor-standing table frame.

basic hand stitches

There are some hand stitches that you will use time and again when working patchwork and piecing. In some cases it is much easier and quicker to handstitch pieces together than to use a machine. As well as the stitches described here, you will also use hand-quilting stitch (page 40).

Running stitch

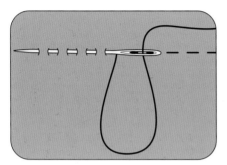

Used to join flat layers of fabric, or as a decoration. Tacking (basting) – to hold layers together temporarily – is a version of this with longer stitches.

Take the needle in and out of the fabric several times, making a small stitch each time to create a row of even and evenly spaced stitches. Pull the thread through gently until it is taut, but not too tight, then continue stitching as before.

Backstitch

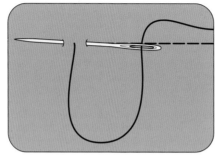

Used to join flat layers of fabric in a secure way, or as a decoration. From the front the stitches run end to end like machine stitching.

Bring the needle through the fabric to the right side, then insert it a short distance behind where it came out and bring it up through the fabric the same distance ahead. Each subsequent stitch begins at the end of the previous stitch and the needle comes up again an equal distance ahead, so the stitches are the same size.

Slipstitch

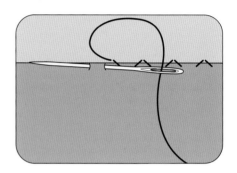

Used to join two folded edges together, or a folded edge to a flat piece, so that the stitches are almost invisible.

Bring the needle up through the folded edge of one side, take a tiny stitch through just one or two threads in the opposite layer or fold, then insert the needle back into the fold of the first layer. Slide the needle along inside the fold a short way, then repeat the sequence.

Whipstitch

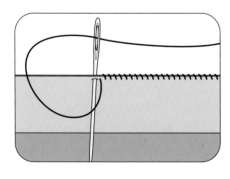

Another stitch used to join two folded edges. It is also known as oversewing or overcasting.

Insert the needle at a slight angle through the edges of both folds, picking up one or two threads on each edge. Pull the thread all the way through, then repeat the stitch. Whipstitch is usually worked from left to right, but there is no particular reason why it shouldn't be worked the other way if it feels more comfortable – as long as you are consistent.

Handstitching

Start with a length of thread about 60cm (24in) long – if any longer it may tangle after being pulled through the fabric a few times.

Always buy good-quality thread: cheap thread breaks easily when you are working or after the quilt is completed.

Tacking (basting)

Tacking, or basting, is a temporary method of holding layers of fabric together until they are stitched permanently together, either with a seam or by quilting. For quiltmaking, tacking can be done either with large running stitches, with rows of safety pins, or even by using a special spray adhesive.

Tacking (basting) techniques

When thread-tacking, use a bright thread in a contrasting colour to the fabric, so the stitches can be seen easily when you come to remove them. Make the tacking stitches large, but not absolutely gigantic or they will not hold the layers in alignment with each other.

Tacking (basting) for quilting

Tacking holds the layers of a quilt together while it is being quilted. A bagged quilt should be tacked after the bagging has been completed (see page 59).

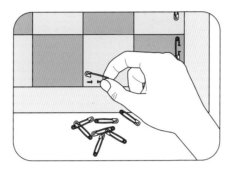

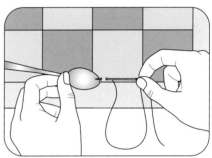

1 Always tack (baste) from the centre outwards. On a large quilt, additional rows of tacking should be spaced around 10cm (4in) apart. Place the different layers on top of one another, as described on page 59, and smooth out any creases. To pin-tack, pin the layers together with rustproof safety pins at intervals of approximately 10cm (4in).

2 To thread-tack (thread-baste), take large running stitches through all the layers, again at intervals of approximately10cm (4in). Be careful not to gather the fabric as you stitch and do not pull the layers out of alignment. You can use the tip of a small spoon to lift the point of the needle to save your fingers.

Tacking (basting) spray

This is a type of spray-on adhesive, which holds layers of fabric together for quilting but washes out easily. Make sure you follow the manufacturer's instructions and work in a well-ventilated area.

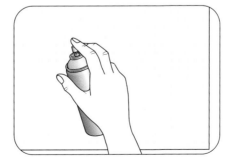

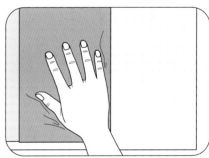

1 Lay the wadding (batting) on a flat surface and spray lightly all over with tacking (basting) spray. Lay the backing fabric on top, right side up, and smooth it over the area carefully.

2 Turn the whole thing over and spray the other side of the wadding. Layer and smooth the quilt-top fabric over the wadding, right side up. The fabric layers are now ready for quilting.

using a sewing machine

A sewing machine is not essential for quiltmaking, but it will certainly make many tasks much quicker and easier. You can use any sewing machine for most stitching, but some modern machines are specifically designed for the needs of quilters.

Understanding your sewing machine

All sewing machines have certain features in common, but details will almost certainly vary between models. Study the machine's manual and experiment with its functions on fabrics of different composition and different thicknesses. Always test the machine on the fabric you will be using for a project before you begin work in earnest.

Choosing a sewing machine

If you plan to free-motion machine-quilt (see page 47), you will need a machine in which the feed dog can be lowered or covered.

When working on a large quilt, it is useful to have a machine with an extension table that can be attached to the side of the machine to support your project properly.

The larger the throat space between the needle housing and the other side of the machine, the easier it will be to machine-quilt large quilts.

Troubleshooting

If the thread keeps breaking, make sure the machine is correctly threaded – particularly through the tension plates – and that the spool is able to turn easily to release thread.

Check the tension – it may be set incorrectly for the fabric and thread you are using.

Check the needle – a damaged or blunt needle can not only damage the thread but also cause the machine to skip stitches. If the needle is new, make sure that you are using the right size and type for the thread.

Always use good-quality thread – cheap or old thread breaks easily. If you are experiencing thread problems, try a different thread on a scrap piece of fabric to see if it performs better.

If the stitches appear uneven, try lifting the presser foot and then re-threading the machine. Many machines are designed to be threaded with the presser foot in the 'up' position, so the thread will feed through the tension plates correctly.

Try not to stitch over pins, even if they are at right angles to the stitching line. If the tip of the needle does catch on a pin, it can blunt or bend the needle, or even throw the timing of the sewing machine off.

Thread tension

For a perfect stitch, the tension between top and bottom thread must be equally balanced. On most modern machines, you can only adjust the tension for the top thread. Do this by turning the tension wheel or dial at the front or top of the machine.

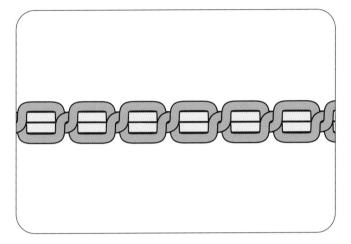

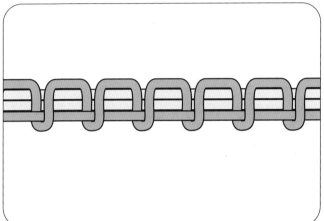

1 If the stitch is perfectly balanced, the two threads interlink in the middle of the layers of fabric and the stitch looks exactly the same on both sides.

2 If the bottom thread is too tight, the bottom thread will lie in a line with the loops of the top thread showing over the top. Tighten the tension to correct this.

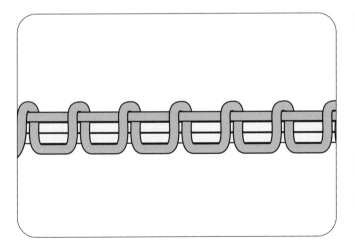

3 If the top thread is too tight, the top thread will lie in a line with the loops of the bottom thread showing over the top. Loosen the tension to correct this.

Useful feet

There are various special feet available for most sewing machines, which you might wish to consider buying if you plan to do a lot of quilting. The names given here may vary slightly from those given by different manufacturers.

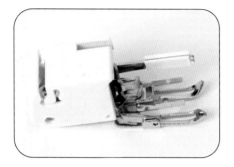

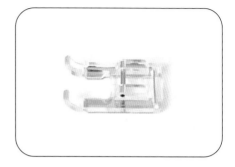

Walking foot
When sewing several layers, the bottom layer will tend to move along slightly faster than the top layer because it is being moved directly by the feed dog. This can cause the layers to shift apart, leading to puckered lines of stitching when machine-quilting. A walking foot prevents this by drawing the top and bottom layers of fabric along at the same speed.

Quarter-inch quilting/ patchwork foot
This measures exactly 5mm (¼in) from the point of the needle to the inner edge of the foot, to allow you to sew a seam allowance quickly and accurately. It may have a guide on it to prevent the fabric from going past the edge. It is sometimes known as a 'little foot'.

Appliqué foot
A clear, hinged foot, which allows the sewing underneath to remain clearly visible. It is also easy to manoeuvre when sewing appliquéd pieces or doing machine embroidery.

Bobbin holder

When free-motion quilting, many quiltmakers adjust the tension on the bobbin holder to make the stitches look right. Some manufacturers state that if you change the bobbin tension, it invalidates the warranty on the machine. So either buy a special bobbin holder set to the appropriate tension, or buy a second bobbin holder to adjust as required and keep the factory-set one for other sewing.

Ditch quilting foot
A foot with an extended guide that helps you to remain in the seam while the machine stitches.

Open-toe, free-motion quilting foot
A foot with the front removed, which makes it easier to see what is happening when doing free-motion sewing (see page 47).

Sewing machine needles

There was one type of needle available for early sewing machines – the only choice a purchaser had was in size – but nowadays there is such a wide variety of needle types that it can be hard to determine which one to use. The factors to take into account are the fabric being sewn, the thread used (for example, metallic or embroidery), and the type of stitch being worked (for instance, quilting or stitching seams). When you are doing ordinary – not decorative – sewing, the type of fabric determines the shape of the needle's point and the weight of the fabric determines the size of the needle.

Fabric type	Thread	Needle type	Needle size UK/US
Delicate: Tulle, chiffon, fine lace, organza	Fine mercerized cotton, fine synthetic thread, silk	Universal	9/65
Lightweight: Batiste, organdie, jersey, voile, taffeta, crêpe, chiffon, velvet, plastic film, silk	Medium mercerized cotton, synthetic thread, silk	Universal, Microtex or sharp	11/75
Medium weight: Gingham, percale, piqué, linen, chintz, faille, satin, fine corduroy, velvet, suiting, knits, deep-pile fabrics, vinyl	Medium mercerized cotton, cotton, synthetic thread, silk	Universal	14/90
Medium-heavy: Gabardine, tweed, sailcloth, denim, furnishing fabrics, synthetic leather	Heavy-duty mercerized cotton, cotton, synthetic thread	Universal, denim, Microtex or sharp	16/100
Any fabric: Machine quilting	Medium cotton, synthetic thread, silk	Quilting, stippling	14/90
All weights: Decorative topstitching, machine embroidery	Silk or synthetic decorative thread	Topstitching, embroidery	16/100
Any fabric: Free-motion machine quilting	Medium cotton, synthetic thread, silk	Spring	14/90

pressing

The pressing of seams and blocks as you work is a basic part of any quiltmaking project. With certain fabrics, you will be able to press open simple seams with your finger (see page 48), but at some point you will need an iron and an ironing board.

Iron

A steam iron is the best choice, as this gives you the option of dry-pressing or steam-pressing. Don't get water on fabrics that should be dry-cleaned, as the resulting watermarks may be very difficult to remove.

Ironing board

An ordinary domestic ironing board is fine for most pressing tasks during the construction of a quilt. If you need to press a large finished quilt, try laying it out on a thick blanket on the floor or on a large table, or on a clean sheet over the mattress of a double bed. There are extra-large ironing boards available for quilters, which may be worth investing in if you plan to do a lot of quilting.

Ironing and pressing

'Press' means just that – use the weight and heat of the iron. Don't drag the iron along a seam, particularly if the fabric has been cut on the bias, as you may stretch the piece out of shape.

If you use fusible webbing or interfacing, do make sure you don't get adhesive on the sole plate of the iron. Use a pressing cloth or a sole plate cover.

Be aware of the fabric type before you iron it. Durable fabrics, such as cotton, can take a fairly high temperature, which will make the task much easier. However, heat can damage delicate fabrics, so use a lower temperature when ironing synthetic fabrics or blends. Use a pressing cloth on synthetics and wool to avoid marking them.

Synthetic wadding (batting) is particularly sensitive to heat. If a steam iron is used, the wadding can get damp and may not dry out properly, causing it to rot or deteriorate over time. Try dry-ironing the main area of the quilt and then gently spray any stubborn creases with a small spray bottle of distilled water. This minimizes the risk of causing damage to the wadding.

Quilts with appliquéd patterns, delicate embroidery work or other embellishments should be treated with particular care. Be careful not to catch any corners of fabric on the iron and be aware that a hot iron can quickly burn embroidery thread, and melt plastic beads or sequins.

A useful technique for ironing delicate quilts is to place a cotton sheet on top and iron through it. This ensures a gentler transfer of heat.

With vintage or antique quilts, it may be better to get a professional with experience of handling such quilts to do the pressing for you.

a working place

In an ideal world, we would all have an entire room for quiltmaking, with layout space and lots of storage. Most quilts take some time to complete, and having to pack them away each time you finish working and get them out when you want to begin again is a waste of valuable quilting time! Unfortunately, for most of us a whole room dedicated to quilting just isn't possible – so here are some tips to make the best of your working area.

Storage and lighting

Luckily, there is a wide range of storage options available, allowing you to make a convenient workplace that can be as temporary or permanent as you choose. Don't forget the importance of lighting – it is much easier to sew well in a good light.

Table lamp

A flexible lamp that can be positioned to shine where you need extra light is the best option. There are also daylight lamps that are very useful if the colour-matching of fabrics is particularly important, and for embroidery and other coloured handstitching work.

Fabric storage

As you build up a good stash of fabric, you will need somewhere to store it all. Plastic see-through crates with a lid are one good option, as they will allow you to see what you have without unpacking the entire crate, and they can be stacked to take up less room. Alternatively, soft plastic storage bags on a frame are good, and can be folded away flat when not in use.

Quilt blocks storage

Finished blocks and blocks under construction need to be kept flat. There are special totes, boxes and bags available from several manufacturers; with these you can carry blocks around with you without them getting creased or damaged.

Small sewing equipment

There are many types of storage available for small pieces of miscellaneous sewing equipment. Again, a transparent type is usually best so you can see at a glance what you have. Choose a type with separate compartments or drawers, so the different items can be kept apart.

Sewing thread

Over time, you will soon build up a stock of different coloured spools of thread. A storage box will keep the spools neat and stop the ends tangling together. If your sewing machine uses the large cones of thread, there are racks available to store the different colours on.

Bobbins

Your sewing machine will probably only come with one or two bobbins, but it is worth buying more and filling them with a stock of the colours you use most often. A bobbin storage box will keep them neat and tidy.

General storage

A closet will conceal crates, boxes and sewing machine – everything is kept together but out of sight.

Practical working

Try to find a convenient corner where you can keep all your equipment and work without disrupting the rest of the household.

If your workroom has an alternative function, such as spare bedroom or dining room, install suitable storage so that projects and equipment can be stored away tidily when not in use.

You will need electrical outlets nearby for sewing machine and iron.

Make sure your chair and sewing table are at a suitable working height – you should be able to reach what you are working on without stretching, and your wrists should be level at a height between your waist and chest.

Before you begin working, put all the equipment you will need close at hand.

about fabric

The best fabric for quilting is woven neither too tightly nor too loosely: if it is tightly woven it is hard to quilt through, and if it is too loose it will fray easily. In general, a natural fabric is better than a synthetic one, preferably something that is easy to fold and press.

Cotton

Pure cotton fabric is the ideal medium for quilting, because it is very easy to fold, presses well, feels good to handle as you work, and can be washed without any problems. Cotton is available in a wide range of colours and patterns and in many different weaves and textures.

Wool

Wool has been used since quilting began – because it makes a warm quilt for cold climates. The best type of wool fabric for quilting has a smooth and lightweight weave – textured weaves tend to conceal quilting stitches. Wool is widely available in a range of solid colours and in woven patterns, but is also occasionally printed.

Linen

Linen is more expensive than cotton and frays more easily, so it can be difficult to handle. It also creases very quickly and can be difficult to press. It comes in a range of weights, mostly with a textured finish, and in plain colours and printed patterns.

Fabric preparation

Choose fabrics that are a similar type and weight – unless a contrast is part of the decorative effect.

Wash each colour separately in hot water before you begin. This will preshrink the fabrics and highlight any with unstable dye. Discard any fabrics that bleed – you don't want them spoiling the finished quilt the first time it is washed.

Press the fabric, ideally while it is still damp, to achieve a smooth, crease-free finish.

If possible, arrange the fabric by colour, since this will make it easier to find the right piece when you are planning your design.

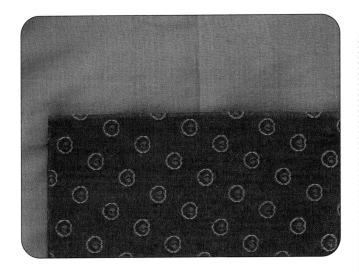

Silk

Silk can be used to make the most beautiful quilts – the play of light over different surfaces changes colours and brings a whole new dimension to the design. Silk is available in a wide variety of weights and in every colour of the rainbow, and it is easy to press and pleasing to work. However, it is very slippery and frays very easily, so it is not the best choice for detailed work or for the inexperienced quilter.

Fabric grain

Woven fabric is made up of two threads: the warp, or lengthways threads, which are the long threads strung the length of the loom; and the weft or widthways threads, which cross the warp threads under and over, backwards and forwards, across the width of the loom. At each edge of the fabric there is generally a more tightly woven strip, known as the selvedge, which stabilizes the edges. If you pull a fabric straight in the direction of the warp or the weft, it tends not to stretch and to remain quite stable. However, if you pull at a 45° angle diagonally across the fabric – a direction described as 'on the bias' – the fabric will stretch quite readily however tightly it is woven. Edges cut on the bias are prone to stretch out of shape and must be handled with extreme care.

Synthetic fabrics

Many synthetic mixes are quite suitable for quilting, but they are often not as pleasing to work as a natural fabric. Make sure any synthetic is easy to fold and press, not too slippery, and can be pinned and stitched without retaining marks. The big advantage of synthetic fabrics is that they are often much easier to wash – there is no shrinkage or other problems.

Unusual fabrics

If the quilt is to be used as a wall hanging or other decorative piece, rather than a bedcover, a range of unusual fabrics can be used. Velvet, brocade, organdie, satin and heavily textured fabrics have all been used to great effect in such quilts. Crazy quilts are traditionally made of scraps of luxury fabrics, usually with embroidery, beading and other embellishments added.

colour

When planning the design of a quilt, it's useful to understand a little about colour theory and know the effect produced when certain colours are placed next to one another. The simplest way to understand the relationship between different colours is to look at the basic colour wheel.

Obviously, fabrics come in a much wider range of shades, tints and tones than those shown on the colour wheel, but if you know the principles of colour mixing, you will begin to understand how to use colour to get the effect you want.

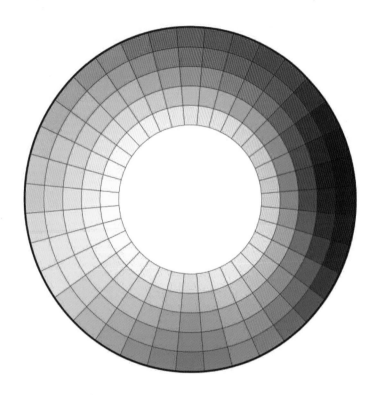

Primary, secondary and tertiary colours

The primary colours, or 'pure' colours, are those that cannot be obtained by mixing other colours: red, blue and yellow. Secondary colours are obtained by mixing two primary colours in equal amounts: red + blue for violet; blue + yellow for green; yellow + red for orange. Tertiary colours come between primary and secondary colours: red-violet, violet-blue, blue-green, green-yellow, yellow-orange, orange-red.

Combining colours

It can be a matter of trial and error working out the best combination of colours from those you have available – experiment and move the different elements around before actually stitching them together.

Don't forget to step back and judge the overall effect of the colours from a distance, as well as viewing them from close up.

Complementary colours

These colours are opposite each other on the colour wheel. Used together in the same quilt, they have a lively, spirited feel that makes an impact.

Analogous colours

These colours are next to one another on the colour wheel. When used together in the same quilt they create a harmonious, tranquil effect.

Accent colours

An accent colour is one that is used in quite small quantities to lift or to add punch to a design.

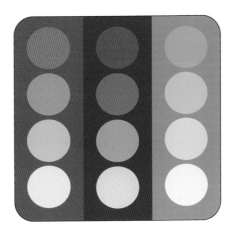

Neutrals

Neutrals don't appear on the colour wheel and include black, grey, white and sometimes brown and beige. They all go together and can be layered, mixed and matched. No single neutral colour will dominate over another.

Tones, tints and shades

A single colour can come in various tones (grey added), tints (white added) and shades (black added). Using varying tones/ tints/ shades of a colour – or the same tone/ tint/ shade of different colours – will create a design that works together well as a whole, with no one element standing out from the rest.

Visual effects

Red, orange and yellow – all colours associated with fire – are called warm colours. Blue, green and violet are more reminiscent of ice, snow and water, so they are called cool colours. When warm and cool colours are used next to one another, the warm colours will appear to advance, while the cool colours will appear to retreat – an effect to bear in mind if you are trying to achieve a three-dimensional look. You can get the same effect by using dark and light – light colours will appear to advance, while dark ones will retreat. When trying to create a balanced feel, remember also that a shape in a light fabric will appear bigger than an identically sized shape in a much darker fabric.

pattern

Although some most exciting quilts have been made solely using plain fabrics, patterned fabric can add an extra dimension to a design. Plain and patterned fabrics can quite easily be used in the same quilt – even in the same block, since they often bring out the best in each other. And a plain area of fabric in a highly patterned quilt is the ideal place to display a quilted motif.

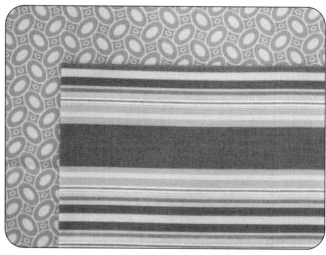

Floral patterns

Perhaps the most widespread design on printed cotton fabrics is the repeating small flower – in the UK known as sprigged cotton and in the US as calico. Floral patterns may be simple two-colour prints, or may contain many different colours. The larger flower prints more commonly known as chintz are the basis for broderie perse (see page 199).

Geometric patterns

These include all kinds of stripes, checks and dots. Small geometric patterns can be used just for their colour value, while bigger and bolder designs make more of a statement. There is no reason why geometric and floral designs should not be combined in the same quilt, as long as there is some other element that coordinates the overall design.

Choosing patterns

In general, small-scale patterns work best, particularly when piecing. However, for techniques such as broderie perse (see page 199ß), large motifs are required.

Quilting will show up less well on patterned fabric than on plain, so don't plan a complex quilting design on patterned blocks.

When using patterned fabric to make small squares or geometric shapes, you must cut very accurately (particularly with a repetitive geometric pattern, such as little dots or flowers) – if you go slightly askew it will be very obvious.

Make sure you cut all patterned pieces the same way up. There is nothing worse than finding out that you have cut pieces on their side or upside down and there is no more material left.

When buying patterned fabric, check that the pattern is correctly on the grain. If lines aren't running parallel or the fabric is cut off-square, look for another bolt or choose a different fabric.

Texture pattern

Some fabrics have a design that is woven in, which may be a small repeating motif, a textured stripe or a weave design. These can be great in small quantities, to add texture to a quilt, but remember that a texture may clash with the quilting design, or cause it to vanish entirely.

Scale

In general, small prints work best in quiltmaking, particularly in piecing – but large prints can give interesting and unusual results (a very successful and easy quilt can be made by simply quilting around the edges of a large, printed design). Prints in several different scales, used together, will add a lively feel to a design.

Combining prints

When combining different prints, try to follow a theme or the quilt may start to look uncoordinated. For instance, you may choose to use lots of different prints and plains in the same basic colour; here the colour is the coordinating factor. Or you may choose lots of multicoloured fabrics that all have one or two colours in common, or are all a similar colour value. If you find choosing difficult, a good way to start is to buy ready-selected fabric packs, which have been combined to work well together. Bear in mind that it is sometimes hard to judge the colour value of florals and large prints, because it can change across the fabric – cut a shape in one area and you get a very light colour value, cut in another and you get a dark one. A quick way to find a suitable area is to take a piece of cardboard and cut a window in it the size of the finished block; move this around the fabric to view small areas at a time and then make a decision.

Pre-cut fabric bundles

Pre-cut fabric packs are available in many different sizes with the most popular listed below. Generally, they require no prewashing.

Fat quarters: This is about a quarter of a yard. Instead of being cut in a narrow strip across the full width of the fabric, the yard is cut in half down its length and then each half is cut in half again across the width to give four oblongs of fabric usually around 45 x 55cm (18 x 22in). Fat eighths (measuring approx 23 x 55cm/9 x 22in) are also available.

Layer cakes™: Collections of fabric squares measuring approx 25 x 25cm (10 x 10in).

Charm packs: Collections of fabric squares measuring approx 13 x 13cm (5 x 5in). Mini charm packs (approx 6.5 x 6.5cm/ 2½ x 2½in) are also available.

Jelly rolls™: Strips of fabric cut approx 6.5cm (2½in) wide by the width of the fabric.

wadding and backing

Wadding, known as batting in the US, is an integral part of a quilt. It forms the middle layer and its original purpose was to make the quilt warm. The cloth that forms the bottom layer of the quilt, hiding its construction, is called the backing.

Wadding

Old quilts often feature worn-out blankets or otherwise unusable fabric (or sometimes discarded quilts) as a layer of wadding. These days, manufactured wadding is sold by length from a roll or in standard cut sizes. Most wadding is synthetic – usually polyester, or a polycotton mix – but it is also possible to buy cotton wadding and even pure silk or wool versions. In general, wadding is white, but it is also available in dark grey and black.

Polyester wadding

This type of wadding does not shrink, can be machine-washed and is quick to dry, and is not susceptible to moths or mildew. It is lightweight and inexpensive, and available in many lofts (thicknesses). However, it does have a tendency to work its way out through the weave of the fabric – called 'bearding', and does not offer 'breathability' as natural fibres do. It is fine for both hand and machine quilting; the higher lofts are good for tied quilts.

Cotton wadding

Cotton wadding is ideal for small projects and is fairly easy to work with to achieve an even look when quilted, although novice quilters may find it is rather dense. It is washable, but will almost certainly shrink by 3–5 per cent and so should be pre-washed otherwise it can cause the quilt to pucker after washing. It may take some time to dry. Cotton wadding is fine for both hand and machine quilting.

Silk wadding

Silk wadding is light, warm and flexible and drapes beautifully. It is ideal for silk quilts and clothes, and can be hand-washed but may shrink very slightly. It is not widely available and can be expensive, and will be damaged by exposure to strong sunlight. It is fine for both hand and machine quilting.

Wool wadding

Wool gives warmth and insulation, absorbs moisture and disperses excess heat well. It is significantly thinner than other

types of wadding, but retains its loft well. Follow cleaning instructions carefully, as wool wadding may not be washable. It is fine for both hand and machine quilting.

Polyester cotton wadding

The cotton adds 'breathability' to the polyester, and helps to resist fibre migration, while the polyester makes the wadding easier for novice quilters to work. This type of wadding is washable but may shrink slightly so ideally it should be pre-washed. It has a fairly good drape and is fine for both hand and machine quilting.

Fusible wadding

This is good for small projects, eliminates the need for tacking (basting), and there is no need to pre-wash. However, it comes in a limited range of sizes and may be hard for a novice quilter to work. It is best used for machine quilting.

Wadding loft

Thin, lightweight wadding is ideal for quilts that will be used as wall hangings or displayed in other ways. It is also easier to produce small, even stitches over the whole quilt if the needle and thread only have to go through a thin layer of wadding. Heavier wadding, with a higher loft, is more suitable for tied quilts and comforters. The higher the loft of the wadding, the less well it will drape.

Backing

Backing is the material layer on the reverse of a quilt that hides all the construction seams inside, and also the term denoting the act of adding that layer of fabric to the quilt.

Types of backing fabric

Many people spend a lot of time organizing the fabric for the quilt top but don't think too much about the backing. Plain white fabric is the most popular type of backing, but it will show every quilt stitch – which may not be great if your quilting is not perfect. A more interesting alternative would be to use the most dominant colour in the quilt top or to match the quilting thread, which would also camouflage less than perfect stitching. A simple print will also hide stitching details – but a very bright design or powerful print may overpower the design of the quilt top.

Reversible quilts

If you coordinate the backing fabric with the quilt top, and the stitching on the reverse of the quilt is as neat as on the front, the quilt can easily be reversible. For the backing fabric for a reversible quilt, you might choose to use a material that you love, but that only features slightly in the quilt top. It is even possible to back the entire quilt with a second quilt top, making a fully two-sided quilt – but be aware that the additional seams will make this harder to hand-quilt.

Choosing a wadding

The specification for the wadding in a project will quote the recommended distance between quilting stitches. If you exceed this, the wadding may shift and bunch up over time.

You can combine reasonably large pieces of left-over wadding from previous quilts to use for a new quilt. For very large quilts, joining pieces of wadding is also essential. Butt the strips together and join with herringbone stitch. Do not overlap the strips as this will give a double thickness in some areas, which will be much more difficult to quilt.

quiltmaking basics

In this chapter you will find all the basic stitches and the general techniques required for hand quilting and machine quilting, as well as the construction techniques for putting a quilt together. There are also some further techniques that are specific to different types of quilt at the start of each appropriate chapter.

hand quilting

For many centuries, quilts were stitched by hand, and what was originally intended as a practical method of holding layers of fabric together for warmth has developed over the years into a decorative art form. Many special techniques have been developed along the way.

Using templates

Quilting designs are often transferred to quilt top fabrics by using a template. Templates can be purchased, or you can make your own in cardboard or special template plastic. There are some quilting designs on pages 76–83.

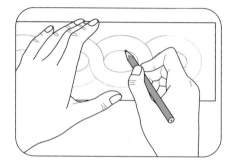

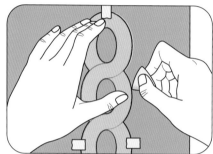

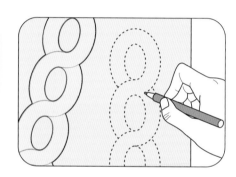

1 Trace the design and transfer it to thin cardboard or to a piece of template plastic. Carefully cut out the inner areas and around the outer edge to create the template.

2 Fix the template to the fabric with masking tape, and draw around it to mark out the shape. If the fabric is a dark colour, use a light marker such as tailor's chalk.

3 There are many different marking tools: here a pencil is being used on light-coloured fabric. See pages 12–13 for some alternative marking tools and always use a method that can be erased.

Marking straight lines

Quilting does not have to be in complex curved lines – sometimes, straight lines are needed for a design. There are several ways to mark these.

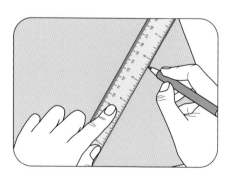

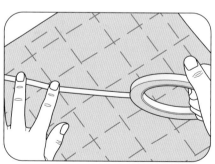

1 Use a ruler and a suitable marker. Measure out the position of the lines and then draw them directly on the fabric.

2 Low-tack masking tape can also be used to mark straight lines. Do not leave it on the fabric for too long as it may leave a sticky residue.

Using tissue paper

It can be quilt difficult to transfer intricate designs with a template or a ruler, but tissue paper is ideal for this. When tacking (basting), position the knots at the end of the thread on the right side of the fabric, so they are easy to remove later.

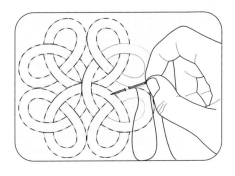

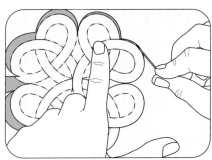

1 Draw the design on tissue paper, then pin it to the fabric. Work small tacking (basting) stitches along the lines in contrasting thread.

2 When you have finished stitching, run the point of the needle along each line. This will make it easier to pull the tissue paper away.

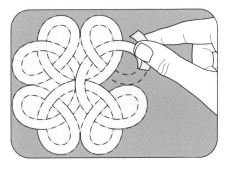

3 Tear the tissue paper away gently, working along the outside lines first. Be careful not to loosen the tacking (basting) stitches at this stage.

4 When the tissue paper has been removed, the design is easy to see. Quilt along the lines of tacking (basting) – you can remove them as you work, or when you have finished.

Learning to hand-quilt

You need to push the needle through the fabric with a thimble, otherwise you will very quickly have sore fingers. Some quilters wear thimbles on both upper and lower hands.

It is very difficult to understand the concept of quilting through all three layers unless you have seen it being done, so try to get someone to demonstrate the technique.

The needle will lie almost flat against the quilt as it is rocked downwards, and become almost vertical when rocked upwards again.

A common fault, when learning, is that stitches on the back of the quilt are too small – or missing. The thread may be falling off the needle as you rock it to bring it back up through the layers. Try to keep the needle as vertical as possible as you begin and end each stitch. Don't have the quilt pulled too taut in the hoop or quilting frame – you need some slack so the needle can manoeuvre.

The aim is to have small stitches, but work at having even stitches at first – small stitches will come with practice. See also page 40.

Using perforated patterns or a tracing wheel

Another method of transferring intricate designs is to use a perforated pattern, which you can easily make yourself; alternatively, use a pattern with dressmaker's carbon and a tracing wheel. Remember that chalk lines may brush away easily, so don't use chalk for large designs that will be worked on over time.

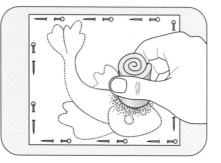
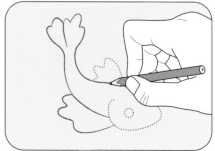

1 To make a perforated pattern, draw the design on sturdy paper. Place the paper on a soft surface, such as an ironing board or folded fabric. Pierce along the lines: use a pin or needle, or machine-stitch with the needle unthreaded, or run a tracing wheel along them.

2 Place the paper on the final fabric piece and go over the perforations with chalk powder or pounce (see page 249) on a small brush or rolled piece of felt. If using dressmaker's carbon, place it between the pattern and the fabric, and run the tracing wheel carefully along all the lines.

3 For a more permanent design, go over the lines with a pencil or water-soluble pen.

Enlarging designs

To reduce or enlarge a design by hand, use different sized grids.

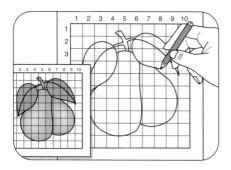

1 Draw a square grid over the design. To enlarge the design, draw a grid with larger squares; to reduce it, draw a grid with smaller squares. Redraw the lines of the image in the new grid, square by square.

Transferring designs

If you photocopy a design to enlarge or reduce it, check that it hasn't distorted, as photocopying machines often stretch or reduce an image slightly in one direction.

A lightbox will make it easier to trace over a design, but if you don't have one, try using a window against the light, or a bright light placed under a glass table.

Knots

To secure the end of the thread when you begin stitching, make a knot at the end. There are two quick methods of doing this.

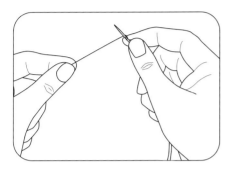

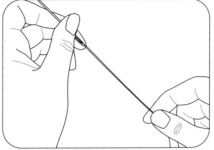

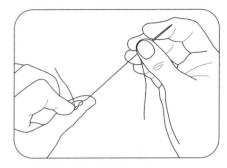

1 **Method 1**
Hold the threaded needle, with the point upwards, between your thumb and index finger. Wind the end of the thread around the point of the needle twice, holding it tightly in place against the needle with your index finger.

2 Holding the loops securely between the index finger and thumb, slide them down the needle and then continue on down the thread itself to form a knot at the end of the thread.

1 **Method 2**
Hold the threaded needle in your right hand, pressing against the eye of the needle so the thread cannot slip out. Take the other end of the thread in your left hand and use your right hand to bring the thread right around the tip of the index finger to cross over the thread end. Use your left thumb to roll the end through the loop and off your finger into a knot.

Knots when quilting

When you are working quilting stitch, the knot at the end of the thread should be hidden within the wadding (batting) layer and not visible on either the top or bottom of the quilt.

Insert the needle into the backing about 1cm (½in) away from where you want to start. Pass the needle through the wadding layer, bringing the tip out at your starting point on the top. Now pull the needle and thread until the knot is on the surface of the backing fabric, then tug gently until the knot pops through the backing.

At the end of a line of quilting, bury the knot within the wadding layer again. Hold the thread

5cm (2in) above the quilt top and wrap it around the threaded needle twice. Pull the needle to tighten the knot – ideally, the knot should be about 5mm (¼in) from the quilt top. Hold the thread out of the way so you can see the hole made by the last stitch.

Insert the needle back into the last stitch hole and travel about 1cm (½in) in the wadding layer, then come up through the top and pull until the knot is lying against the top layer. Tug to pop the knot into the wadding layer. Cut the thread close to the top, taking care not to snip into the fabric of the quilt.

Quilting stitch

Quilting stitch is a hand-quilting stitch that looks very similar to running stitch, but is not done in exactly the same way – it takes practice to master it perfectly. It is most efficient when you use a rocking, up and down motion to execute the stitches, working to put several on the needle before pulling the thread through. See the tip box on page 37.

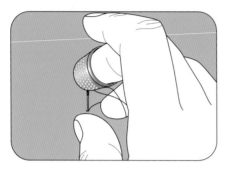

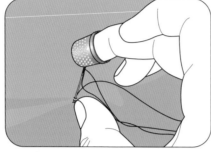

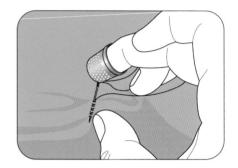

1 Hold the needle between your index finger and thumb and place the other hand under the quilt, with the tip of the index finger where the tip of the needle will come through. With the needle almost vertical, push the tip down through the layers until you can feel it with the index finger beneath. The moment the tip comes through the fabric, stop pushing.

2 Slide the index finger on the hand beneath the quilt upwards, to push the quilt up, and at the same time rock the eye of the needle down towards the quilt top. Use the thumb of the hand holding the needle to gently press down on the quilt just ahead of the next planned stitch, and at the same time push the needle forward with the end of your finger until the tip comes through the surface of the quilt top to the length of the next stitch.

3 Rock the needle back up into an almost vertical position, until the tip is in the fabric, again with the index finger of the hand beneath the quilt ready to feel for the tip of the needle. Keep repeating this sequence until you have several stitches on the needle, then pull the thread right through and begin the sequence again.

Travelling

If you have finished quilting a section, but have lots of thread left in the needle and want to start a new area close by, you can 'travel' within the wadding (batting). If you want to travel more than 2.5–5cm (1–2in), start afresh.

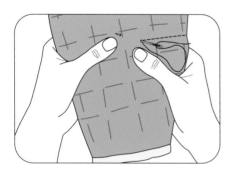

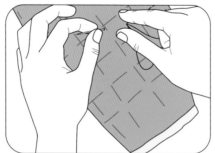

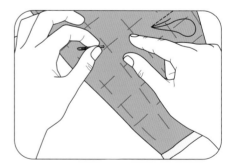

1 Bring the point of the needle up through the quilt top about half a needle length away from where you finished quilting, towards where you want to begin again. Don't pull the needle all the way through.

2 Holding the tip of the needle, and leaving the eye between the quilt layers, turn the needle around so the eye is pointing towards where you want to begin stitching.

3 Push the needle, eye first, towards the new stitching area and bring it out at the exact point you want to begin stitching. You can either bring it out eye first or tip first – whichever is easier.

Ways to quilt

There are several standard ways of quilting a piece of work, and you can choose whichever method suits the design best. Some pieces may even have several methods combined.

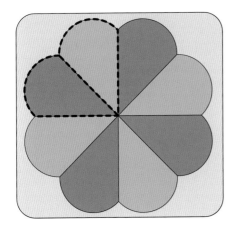

In-the-ditch
Simply stitch within the seam lines of a pieced pattern, or work exactly around the outline of a piece of appliqué. There is no need to mark the quilting pattern, since you work along stitching that already exists; with this method the quilting will, however, be nearly invisible.

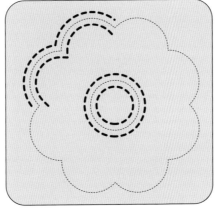

Outline
Outline quilting is similar to in-the-ditch quilting, but the stitching is positioned around 5mm (¼in) away from the seam line, appliqué edge or motif. It can be worked inside or outside the lines, or even both, and there is often no need to mark a pattern.

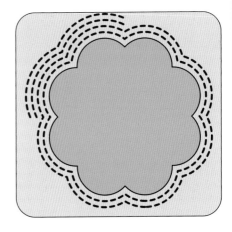

Echo
With this method, you stitch around the outline of an appliqué piece or motif as for outline quilting, but then keep repeating the shape of the outline in lines of stitching at close intervals, radiating outwards to fill the background. Marking will keep the lines and spacing even.

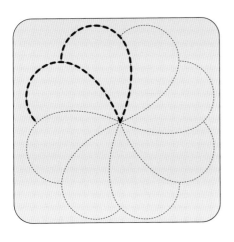

Motif
Marking is essential for this technique. Each individual motif is marked on to the quilt top in outline, and then you simply quilt along the lines. The marking lines are usually hidden under the stitching, but to be safe, use an erasable method.

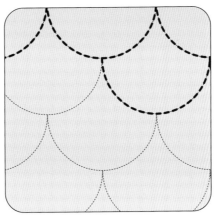

Filling grids or patterns
An all-over grid or pattern fills the background with texture. The pattern can be used to create a secondary design that is not related to the piecing or appliqué design of the quilt top. Marking is essential – but use an erasable method.

Stippling
Stippling is a method of working small, random stitches across a background area, in different directions and spaced apart, to create a simple texture that will make plain areas of the quilt stand out. Marking is not required.

Cording

Cording is also sometimes known as Italian quilting and is a variation of trapunto. It was widely used in the seventeenth and eighteenth centuries and was also very popular in the 1920s. Choose a design with strong outlines, as only these lines will be raised. You can use string, yarn or special quilting wool to form the cord.

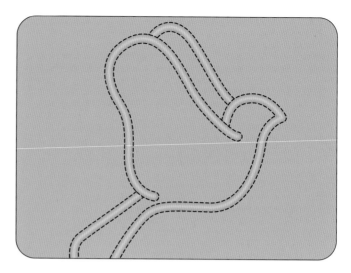

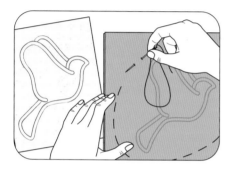
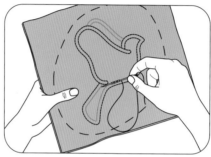

1 Trace the outlines of the design as a double row of parallel lines on the area of the quilt to be corded. Tack (baste) a square of loosely woven cloth, such as cheesecloth or muslin (gauze), to the back of the quilt top, behind the motif you want to cord.

2 Work a small running stitch along both lines of the outline, stitching right through both layers to create a channel. You can use a matching or contrasting thread, depending on the effect you want to achieve.

3 Thread a blunt-ended tapestry needle with a length of yarn or cord. Working from the back, slide the needle through the back layer only and into the channel. Thread the yarn down the channel – you can probably work round very shallow curves, but otherwise you can bring the needle out through the backing fabric and then in again.

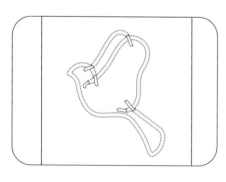

4 On the front, the lines of the outline will be raised. To make sure the cording won't pull out, leave a small end of yarn protruding from the back layer as you start and finish cording each section – the quilt will be layered with wadding (batting) and backing as normal, so ends will not be seen. Remove the tacking (basting) stitches when the quilt is ready for quilting.

Trapunto

Trapunto is sometimes called stuffed or dimensional quilting, as areas of the design are stuffed from behind to raise them up into a relief. Choose the quilting design with trapunto in mind – you will need defined shapes that will work visually as raised areas.

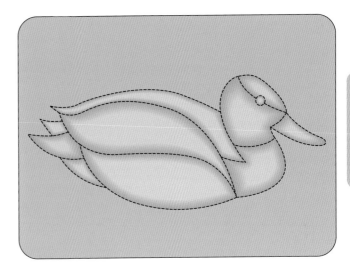

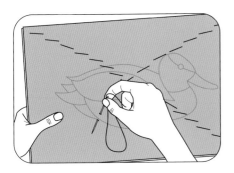

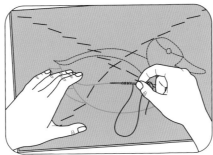

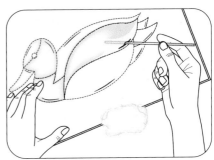

1 Trace the outlines of your chosen design on to the quilt top. Tack (baste) loosely woven cloth, such as cheesecloth or muslin (gauze), to the back of the quilt top, behind the areas of motif that you want to stuff.

2 Work outline quilting along the lines of the motif, stitching right through both layers. You can use a matching or contrasting thread, depending on the overall design of the quilt.

3 Working from the back, make a small slit through the back cloth only, in a segment you want to stuff. Slide small pieces of wadding (batting) into the segment, working them into any corners or points with a chopstick or other blunt point. Repeat on any other areas you want to stuff.

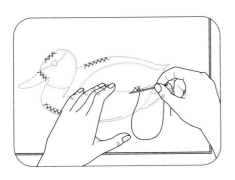

4 Stitch the slits in the back layer closed, using herringbone stitch (see page 215) or cross stitch (see page 213). Use thread to match the colour of the back cloth, so the stitching is unobtrusive. When all the stuffing has been inserted, the quilt top is ready for wadding (batting) and backing.

Utility quilting

There are many different forms of utility quilting – the name covers tied quilts and big-stitch quilting as shown below and opposite, and techniques such as the Japanese sashiko (opposite below) and the Eastern kantha (opposite below) and ralli quilts (see page 250). The advantage of all these techniques is that a very large area can be worked in the minimum amount of time. Many of them will give a quilt an attractive folk art look, which goes well with many traditional designs – and also with some modern ones. These techniques also allow the wadding (batting) to retain maximum loft, so they are great for use with heavyweight wadding to create a really puffy quilt.

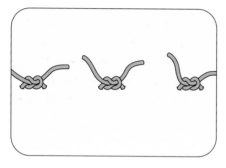

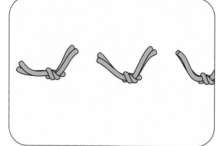

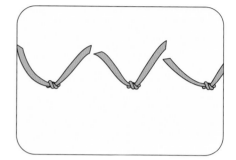

Simple tie

Quilt ties are often made in thick thread, but you can also use sturdy embroidery floss. Thread a needle and take it through the quilt top to the back, then back up again near the entry point. Tie the ends in a reef (square) knot. You can also take a double stitch before knotting the ends, which can make the tie more secure.

Decorative tie

Novelty threads can be used to tie quilts, and can be left loose if they don't fray. Work them in the same way as the simple ties. If you don't want any loose ends on the front of the quilt, tie the threads at the back instead.

Ribbon tie

Thin ribbon makes an attractive quilt tie. Choose one designed for ribbon embroidery, as it will be narrow enough to go through the eye of the needle. Use a sharp needle, or it will not go through the quilt layers.

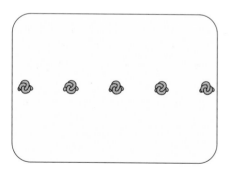

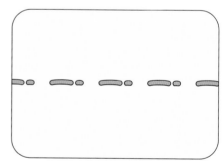

French knot

Knots such as this are an unobtrusive method of securing the quilt layers, particularly if they are worked in matching thread. At the back of the quilt you will only see a tiny stitch, while on the front there will be a small knot. See page 213 for how to work a French knot.

Cross stitch

Any type of embroidery stitch can be used to quilt. Cross stitch can add an extra decorative element to a quilt design, and give it an attractive folk art look. See page 213 for how to work cross stitch.

Methodist knot

Very simple to work, the Methodist knot is simply a very long running stitch followed closely by a much shorter one. The pairs of stitches are spaced an equal distance apart, and can be worked to create an interesting textured pattern on the quilt.

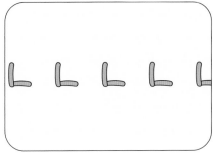

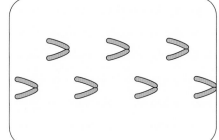

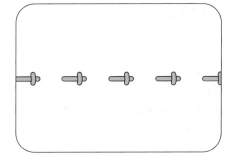

Half-buttonhole stitch

This L-shaped stitch is just a single buttonhole stitch worked on its own, with the next stitch taken some distance away. Many embroidery stitches can be varied in this way. See page 215, blanket stitch, for how to work a buttonhole stitch.

Crow's foot

This is another part-stitch: crow's foot is the individual parts of fly stitch spaced apart to create an attractive row of sideways V-shapes, like bird tracks across the quilt. See page 214 for how to work a fly stitch.

Mennonite tack

A variation on cross stitch, the Mennonite tack has a long, horizontal stitch and a short vertical placed across it at one end, instead of two equal stitches crossing diagonally. See page 213 for how to work cross stitch.

Sashiko

Sashiko was not originally intended as a quilting technique – it started out in Japan as a method of mending and reinforcing workmen's clothes. Traditionally, sashiko is most often worked in a thick white thread on indigo fabric, in a range of geometric designs or stylized motifs based on plants and animals.

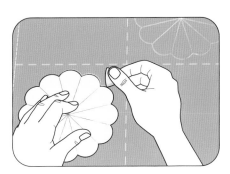

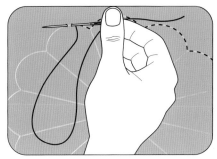

1 Transfer the design to the top fabric, using a suitable method (see pages 36–38). Layer the top and the interlining fabric – sashiko does not necessarily need a layer of wadding (batting).

2 Thread a needle with sashiko or embroidery thread and stitch along the outline of the design. Sashiko stitches are larger and spaced more widely apart than those used when quilting; stitches and the spaces between should be even.

Kantha

Originating from Bangladesh and West Bengal, kantha is a technique based on recycling – fabrics from old garments in precious silks and muslins (gauze) were layered and stitched together with a simple running stitch worked in motifs or patterns. Kantha uses bright colours to create animals, people, plants, and abstract or geometric designs.

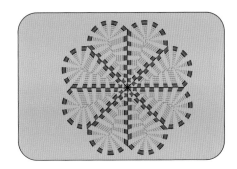

1 Layer the top with interlining fabric and backing, or use several layers of thin fabric. Trace out the design on the top layer using tracing paper and carbon. Stitch the outline and then fill in the design with running stitch, leaving very little space between lines. You can also create different patterns with the running stitch.

machine quilting

Machine quilting appeared with the advent of the sewing machine. Initially, machine stitching on a quilt marked out the maker as having the funds to own a scarce and expensive piece of equipment. As sewing machines became more affordable and common, machine quilting quickly became a poor cousin to hand quilting. However, in the last few years special machines designed for quilting have appeared, so now well-worked machine quilting can be every bit as attractive as a piece of hand work – and can be completed much more quickly.

Straight lines

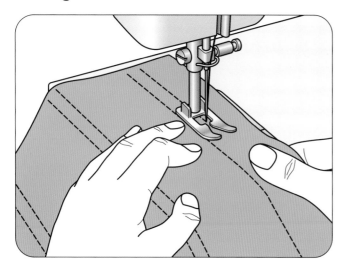

If you are working in straight lines, you can either mark the full design on the quilt top, or just mark the first line and then use the foot as a guide to space the following lines an equal distance away. If the lines are spaced more widely apart, use a special bar that fits on the sewing machine to measure out the distance.

Curved lines

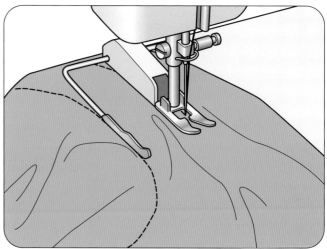

Concentric curved lines can also be marked, or you can stitch the first one and then follow it with a special bar to space the next and following lines. Curved lines in a motif must be marked in some way: see pages 36–38 for some marking techniques.

Meander stitch

Meander or free-motion quilting is the machine-stitch version of stippling, which adds texture to a background.

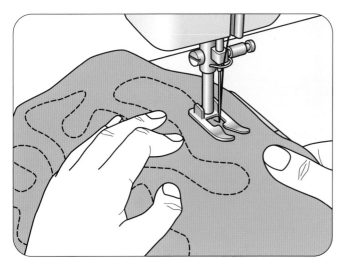

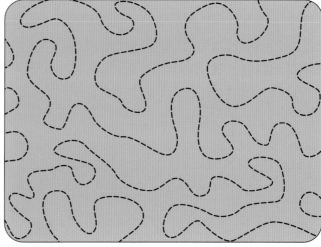

 1 The feed dogs on the sewing machine are dropped or covered, allowing the quilter to move the quilt top around under the needle to stitch in a random design.

2 Ideally lines should not cross, so work on small areas at a time and plan the general layout first.

Rolling

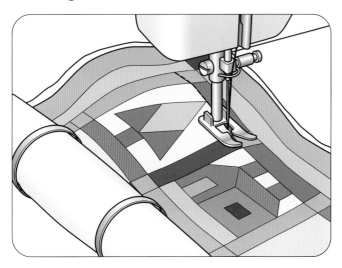

A domestic sewing machine will generally not have a large sewing area, so to make a big quilt more manageable, roll up the edges around the area you are working on and secure the rolls with quilt clips. (Bicycle clips make a good substitute for quilt clips.)

Working on a large quilt

If you start quilting at one edge, you will have the whole area of the quilt lying to one side and pulling as you work, which will make it hard to manoeuvre. Start at the middle and work outwards instead – this will also make sure that any fabric take-up caused by the stitching process will be distributed much more evenly.

A small table or ironing board next to the machine table will also help support a large quilt.

Machine quilting is probably the best option for any quilt that will be laundered frequently.

constructing a quilt

The majority of quilt tops are made up of smaller elements, and there are several ways in which these can be joined into a whole. Once the quilt top has been created, it needs to be made up into a finished quilt by adding the wadding (batting) – the middle layer – and the backing.

Blocks

A quilt block is a single unit, usually square, which can be joined together with many others to make up the top of a quilt. A block can either be a plain spacer unit, a pieced design using a number of pieces of fabric, an appliquéd motif on a background fabric, or even a folded fabric unit. The way blocks are arranged in a quilt top is called the setting pattern. Quilt blocks that are incorporated with their corners pointing up and down are described as set 'on point'.

Pressing for accuracy

Your accuracy in piecing will be much better if you take a bit of time to press each quilt block as you make it. This is an extra step, but it helps make sure the quilt blocks will fit together as they should. An unpressed seam may have just a very, very tiny amount of fabric caught up in it, but if the block contains several seams, this tiny amount can add up, creating distortions and making the block smaller than it should be. This may not matter too much if all the blocks are identical anyway, but if they vary in design and number of seams, you will end up with inaccurate sizes and blocks that don't match their neighbours.

Finger-pressing

Seams used to join patchwork pieces do not need to be thoroughly pressed in the early stages of construction.

Pressing with an iron

Long or intricate seams are easier to press with an iron, and the quilt should also be carefully pressed before it is quilted.

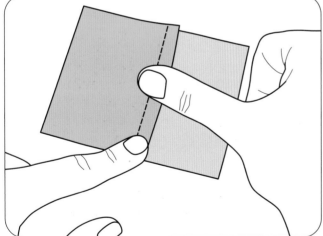

1 With the seam facing upwards, press down the seam allowance with your finger or thumb so that it lies flat. For a slightly sharper crease, run the edge of your fingernail down the seam line but be careful not to stretch the fabric.

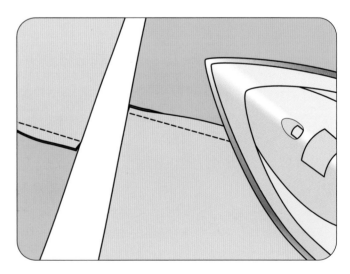

1 Set the iron to the correct temperature for the fabric you are using. With the seam facing upwards, press down with the iron until the seam allowance lies flat.

Joining blocks

After individual blocks have been made and pressed, they all need to be joined together in some way. There are various standard ways to do this, but an almost endless variety of designs can be created. When joining blocks directly to each other, start by joining all the blocks into strips – you can either work in columns down the quilt (below top), or in rows across (below bottom). Then join up the strips to make the finished quilt. This is a much more efficient way of working than adding one block at a time to an increasingly large and unwieldy quilt. Before you begin, plan your setting pattern (see page 50). It's a good idea to lay out all the blocks on a flat surface and stand back to judge the overall effect before you begin sewing.

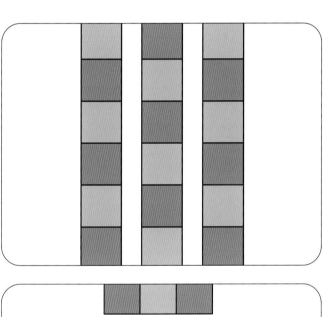

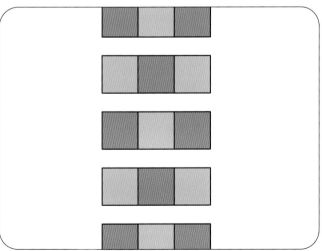

Squaring up blocks

Blocks intended for the same quilt may have been worked on over some time, or may have been collected from different sources, so they may not be identical. For best results, before you begin joining blocks together, check that they are all the same size and that they all have the same 5mm (¼in) seam allowance. Make sure all the corners are square and that the sides are straight.

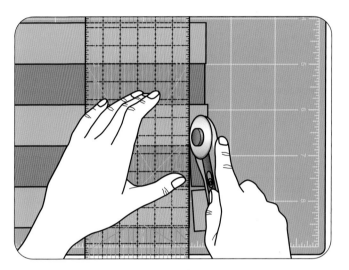

Block sizes

If some of the blocks are the wrong size, it is almost certainly because the seam allowances are not exactly 5mm (¼in). If you can't adjust the size of a block easily, there is no alternative but to remake it, taking greater care, so that all the seam allowances are correct.

If some blocks are only slightly too large, you might be able to trim them down. Trim equally on each side so the design will still be centred.

When blocks are much too small, you could add a border all around to bring them up to the right size. If the block design is asymmetrical, you may be able to get away with adding a border to only one or two sides.

Setting patterns

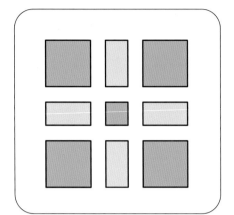

Spacer blocks

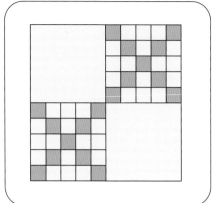

Sampler quilts

A sampler quilt is a collection of different block patterns made up into one quilt. It's considered a good starter quilt for beginners, as they can begin with the easiest block and progress to the more difficult. The different blocks usually cover a number of quilting techniques, and often include both piecing and appliqué. A sampler quilt will look much better if all the different blocks use the same coordinating fabrics, or are based on the same range of colours.

'Setting' is the term that refers to the way you put separate blocks together to create a complete quilt. You may have many blocks in an identical design, or a mixture of plain, pieced or appliquéd blocks that must be placed together in a logical way. If the blocks are set block to block – or joined directly to each other – many different secondary patterns can often be created: see pages 103–07 and 161 for some examples. Alternatively, individual blocks can be set with lines of sashing between them (see page 52), which is a way to eke out a limited number of blocks into a somewhat larger quilt. When quilt blocks are put into a quilt with their corners pointing up and down – in a diamond shape – they are described as being set 'on point'.

Spacer blocks, sometimes called setting squares – or setting triangles if they are triangular – are secondary blocks set between those of a much more complicated design. Spacers are often plain – offering an ideal surface to display quilting stitch designs – but may be pieced in a very simple way. They are used to set off the main blocks, to space them out visually, and sometimes to bring an element of cohesion to a quilt if the decorated blocks all look very different. Adding lots of plain spacer blocks is also a great way to stretch a small number of decorated blocks so there are enough to make up a complete quilt. Remember that spacer blocks should be of the same type and weight of fabric as the other elements used in a quilt top.

Block orientation

If the quilt is to be used on a bed, you may need to consider which blocks will come across the top and which will hang down at the sides and the end. With some block designs, the orientation will not matter, but others may need to be orientated so you view them the correct way up when the quilt is on the bed.

If you are working with many different block designs, consider their relationship to each other. Place similar blocks on each side of the quilt and odd, one-off designs down the centre.

To check whether there is any imbalance in the overall effect, look at the arrangement through half-closed eyes, standing as far back as possible.

Sashing

'Sashing' refers to the strips of fabric used to separate blocks within a quilt top. Not all quilts have it, but it can be a good way to unite a design if the blocks used have clashing colours, or if they are very disparate designs. Plan the sashing layout before you begin, trying out the blocks in different combinations to achieve the best effect.

Sashing designs

There are several ways to lay out sashing, so you can choose the one that best fits in with the design of your blocks.

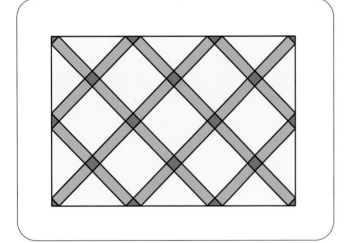

1 Plain trellis with the blocks set square. The sashing in one direction runs right across the quilt unbroken; in the other direction, the lines intersect. The unbroken lines of sashing can either run down the quilt or across it.

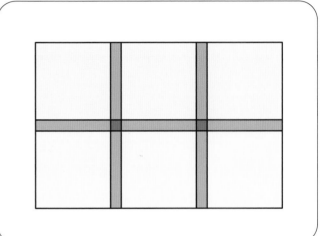

2 An alternative way of handling the point where the sashing lines intersect is to put in a corner square or cornerstone. This can be in the same or a contrasting fabric.

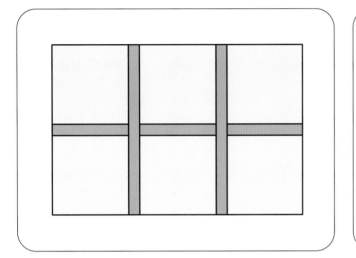

3 You can also set the trellis on the diagonal for blocks that are set on point (see page 50). The lines of sashing can either intersect or have cornerstones.

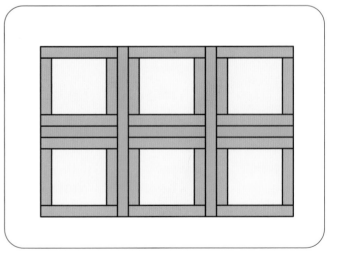

4 Individual blocks can be framed before they are sashed. Again, the sashing can intersect or have cornerstones.

Joining blocks with sashing

The simplest way to add sashing is to incorporate sections of it between the appropriate blocks as you work. Plan your order of work before you begin.

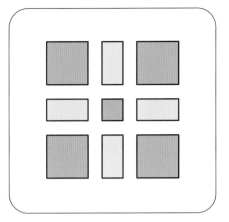

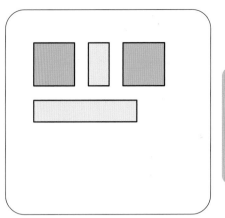

1 When measuring the width of strips of sashing before cutting, work out the width and then add a 5mm (¼in) seam allowance to both sides. The length of a strip between a pair of blocks will be exactly the same as the width of the blocks, including the seam allowances. A cornerstone, if used, will have all four sides the same length as the width of the sashing strips, including the seam allowances.

2 If there is an unbroken strip of sashing running across, work out the length required by measuring the finished size of a block (without seam allowances) and multiplying this measurement by the number of blocks needed. Then measure the finished width of the intersecting sashing strip (without seam allowances), and multiply this measurement by the number of intersecting sashing strips required between blocks. Add these two measurements together, then add a 5mm (¼in) seam allowance at each end.

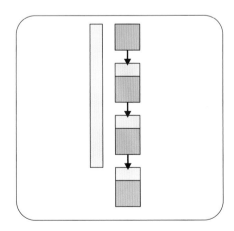

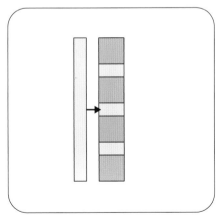

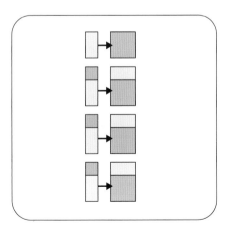

3 To join the sashing, first add an intersecting sashing strip to the top side of each block.

4 Join the blocks into a row, then add the continuous strip of sashing down one side of the row.

5 If you are using cornerstones, follow step 3. Then add a cornerstone to one end of each remaining strip of sashing. Stitch this strip of sashing, plus cornerstone, to one side of each block. Join the blocks in a row.

Borders

The final touch for the top of a quilt is to add a border. The border can be plain or pieced and can be undecorated or have a quilted, embroidered or appliquéd design. You can also have multiple borders in toning or contrasting fabrics. The border should be a little wider than any sashing, for visual balance.

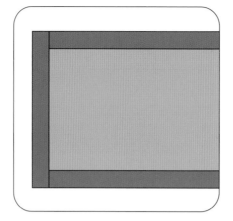

Straight border

The simplest border is a straight border, made of a strip of fabric on each side of the quilt. Add the first two strips on opposite sides of the quilt first, then the two strips at either end. Usually, the shortest ends run across the longer (as shown here), but sometimes the longer sides run across the shorter.

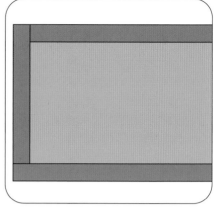

Continuous border

A continuous border runs around the quilt, overlapping at the ends in sequence. Cut the borders the length of the side, plus the width of the border. Apply the first strip at one side, leaving the extra length protruding at one end. Work around the quilt, adding each new strip across the end of the previous one. When you get back to the beginning, continue the stitching on the line of the first seam to catch the end of the last strip.

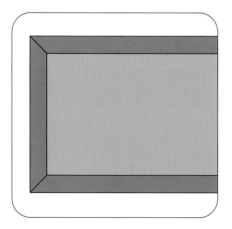

Mitred border

With a mitred corner, the two borders meet at the corner at a 45° angle and the angle must be precise. There are several ways to make a mitred border, but the method given alongside is one of the easiest. First, cut each border the length of the side plus two border widths.

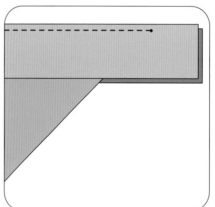

1 Centre and stitch a border to each side, starting and finishing 5mm (¼in) from the end in each case. Press the borders flat, with the seams towards the border and the excess border at the corners overlapping. Fold the quilt at 45° through one corner, with right sides together and aligning the edges of excess border sections.

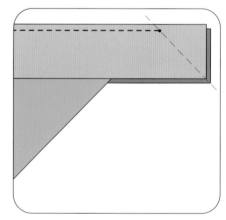

2 Beginning at the point where the side lines of stitching end, stitch across the border at 45°, in line with the diagonal made by the folded edge of the quilt. Trim away the excess fabric, open out the quilt and press the mitre seam open.

Cornerstones/ corner squares

Cornerstones (also known as corner squares), in a contrasting fabric, add an extra feature to a quilt top.

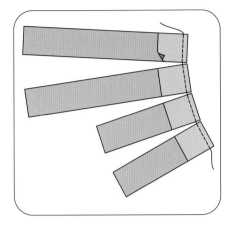

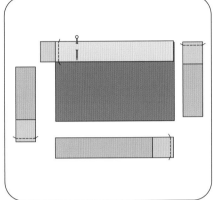

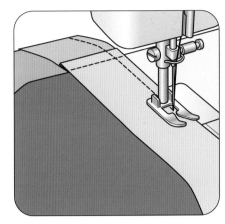

1 Cut the cornerstones with their sides the same measurement as the width of the border strip. Stitch a cornerstone to one end of each strip. Press seams to one side.

2 Place the first strip along the edge of the quilt, right sides together, with the cornerstone overhanging the end. Begin stitching 10cm (4in) from the cornerstone and continue to the end of the border.

3 Place the next border strip with the cornerstone at the end of the border just sewn. Stitch the seam, then carry on adding the remaining border strips in the same way, working around the quilt clockwise.

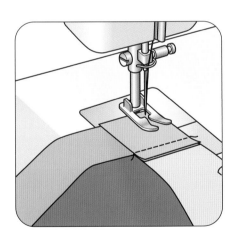

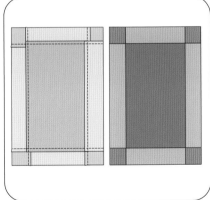

4 At the end, stitch the last border strip to the overhanging cornerstone and complete the first seam you made.

5 Press the seams to one side – in some places the construction of the border will dictate which way the seams can be pressed. On the front of the quilt, the border will have perfect contrast squares in each corner.

Pieced border

Borders can be pieced in numerous ways. Plan the design carefully at the corners – it is best if all four corners match. If repeating units in the border and the quilt itself do not relate to each other, you can add a plain inner border between the two.

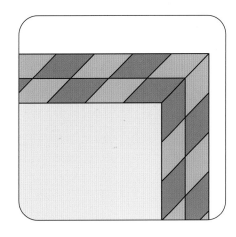

Seminole chevrons – for instructions on how to make Seminole chevrons, see pages 118–20.

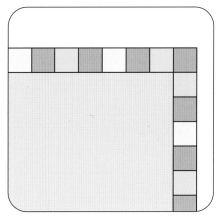

Squares – for instructions on how to make Squares, see pages 124–25.

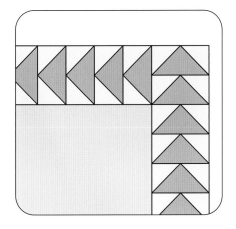

Flying Geese (side border) – for instructions on how to make Flying Geese, see page 74.

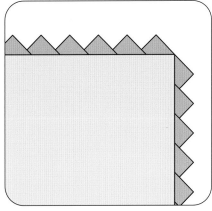

Prairie Points – for one of the ways to make the shapes, see page 247.

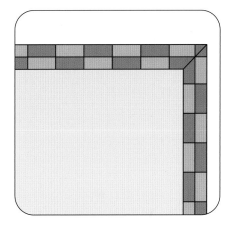

Four-Patch Rectangles– for instructions on how to make Four-Patch, see pages 124–25.

Designing a border

When choosing what type of border to have, consider the design of the quilt itself – the border should complement or add to the overall design, not overshadow it. If the quilt top is very complex, it may be better to opt for a plain border.

The width of the border needs to be in scale with the rest of the design – if it is too narrow it may look skimpy, and if it is too wide it could look clumsy. If you need a very wide edging, think about having both an inner and an outer border.

Adding wadding (batting) and backing

The wadding is the middle layer of the quilt sandwich – without it the quilt is not technically a quilt. For information on the different types of wadding available and what they are most used for, see page 32. The backing is the bottom layer of the quilt sandwich.

Wadding (batting)

Use light-coloured wadding with light fabrics, and dark wadding with dark fabrics. Wadding is available in a range of weights, from light to heavy, so choose a suitable type depending on the use of the final quilt. The wadding should be cut bigger than the quilt top – a little extra all round will allow for any pull or movement during the quilting process.

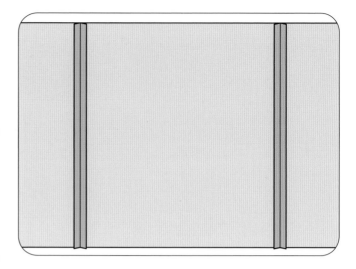

Backing

You may need to join more than one length of fabric to make up the backing. Pay attention to where the seams fall; it is better to have one full width in the centre of a quilt and two half-widths (or less) on each side, than to have the seam falling in the middle of the quilt. Plan out the piecing of the back if you do need to join several widths of fabric – you may use less fabric if you place the seams horizontally rather than vertically.

Preparing wadding (batting)

To help prevent bearding – a situation in which the wadding fibres migrate through the quilt top and form a fuzz on the surface – pre-wash fabrics using a quality fabric softener and dryer sheet. Quilt using a mercerized or coated thread. Apply beeswax to the thread or spray it (and/or the quilt layers) with a silicone spray for fabrics; this will also help prevent thread breakage.

Take the wadding out of its packaging and lay it out flat overnight before use. This will allow any folds or creases to drop out.

For more information on wadding types and how to choose between them for a particular project, see page 32.

If you pre-wash the wadding, make sure that it is completely dry and properly aired before using it for the quilt. If it is still damp when it is enclosed in layers of fabric, it will take a long time for the moisture to escape.

Preparing backing fabric

If the quilt top fabrics have been pre-shrunk, pre-shrink the backing too.

In general, the backing fabric should be the same weight and composition as the majority of the fabrics used for the quilt top.

Before you cut the backing, consider if you will be using backing fabric to bind the edge of the quilt (see binding methods on pages 60–65). If so, you need to allow extra fabric.

Always cut the backing slightly larger than the quilt top anyway, to allow for fabric taken up during the quilting process.

Trim off the selvage before using the backing fabric, as it is more tightly woven than the rest of the fabric and can cause puckered seams.

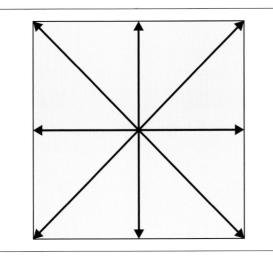

Tacking (basting)

To minimize the possible slippage of the layers in any one direction, begin tacking in the centre of the quilt, working out towards the edges. Rows of tacking should be spaced around 10cm (4in) apart, and should run horizontally, vertically and, on a large quilt, also diagonally.

When tacking a large quilt, sometimes the layers will tend to slip against each other – particularly if you are working in a small space so cannot lay the whole quilt flat. If this is a problem, try tacking the backing to the wadding (batting), and then tacking the quilt top on in a separate step. It is more work, but it will give you better control over the relationship between the different layers.

Bagging

Bagging is the process of joining the layers of the quilt together around the outside edges with right sides together, then turning the quilt right side out. This means the edges are finished and there is no need for binding. Bagging should be carried out before the quilt is quilted.

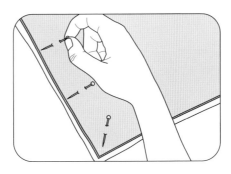

1 Lay the wadding (batting) out flat, and place the quilt top, right side up, on top of it. Place the backing fabric on this, right side down, as the final layer. Smooth out any wrinkles and pin or tack (baste) the layers together.

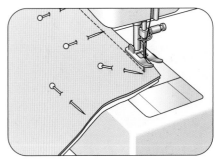

2 Pin and then stitch around the outside edges. When you reach a corner, stop the machine the width of the seam allowance away from the edge. Leaving the needle down in the fabric, lift the presser foot.

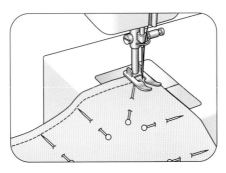

3 Swivel the fabric around the needle by 90°, to point along the next line to stitch. Lower the presser foot and begin stitching the seam. Leave a gap of around 15–30cm (6–12in) in one side, depending on the size of the finished quilt.

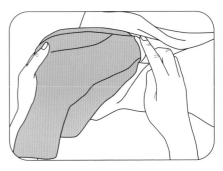

4 Trim seams to remove excess fabric, grading layers if necessary, and snip across corners close to the stitching. Turn the quilt right side out through the gap. Turn the raw edges under and slipstitch the gap to close.

Binding

If a quilt has been bagged it will not need binding, but if not, the raw edges will need to be finished off. Binding is carried out after all the quilting has been completed. Binding strips are usually cut on the straight grain, but if the quilt has scalloped edges or other curves, you will need to cut the binding on the bias.

Single binding

Single binding is fine for a quilt that will only be displayed – it uses less fabric than double binding, but will not protect the edges of the quilt as well as a double binding would. A single binding is usually quite narrow, and can be made in a contrasting or a toning colour to the border of the quilt.

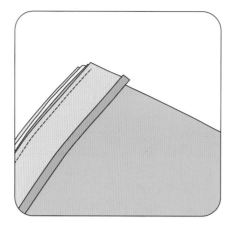

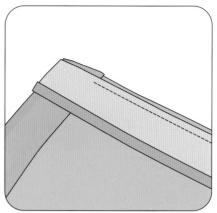

1 Cut four strips of binding the lengths of each side of the quilt and twice the width you want the binding to be, plus 1cm (½in) for seam allowances.

Along one long edge of each strip, press a 5mm (¼in) width of fabric to the wrong side. At each corner of the quilt, measure in 5mm (¼in) from the edges and make a small mark. Place a binding strip down one edge of the quilt top, with right sides together and raw edges aligned – the folded edge of the binding should be towards the inner part of the quilt. Stitch in place between the corner marks only.

2 Fold the attached strip of binding up out of the way and pin a new strip along the next edge as before. Stitch between the marked corner points again, being careful not to catch the edge of the first strip as you begin sewing. Repeat for the remaining two strips.

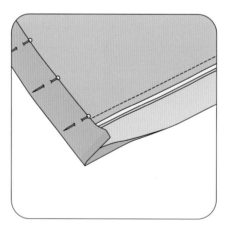

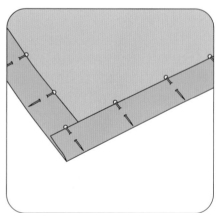

3 Fold the binding over to the back of the quilt, concealing the raw edges. Pin in place along the length of the side.

4 At the end of each strip, fold in the raw edges and square the corners. Pin in place and then slipstitch the binding to the backing along the fold line made in step 1, and at each corner.

Double binding

Double binding, also sometimes known as French-fold binding, is much stronger than single binding, so it is more suitable for quilts that will be heavily used and laundered frequently.

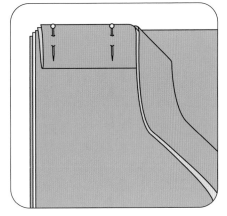

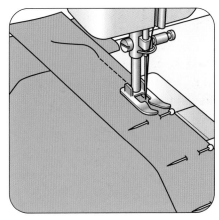

1 Cut four strips of binding the lengths of each side of the quilt and four times the width you want the binding to be, plus 1cm (½in) for seam allowances. Fold the strips in half lengthways and press. At each corner of the quilt, measure in 5mm (¼in) from the edges and make a small mark. Place a binding strip down one edge of the quilt top, with right sides together and raw edges aligned – the folded edge of the binding should be towards the inner part of the quilt. Stitch in place between the corner marks only.

2 Follow steps 2–4 for Single Binding, starting with the two raw edges of the binding aligned with the raw edge of the quilt and the fold to the inside edge.

Cutting straight-grain binding fabric

You may decide to cut binding from along the length of your fabric, to minimize joins. However, the threads on the warp, or lengthways, grain of fabric tend to run very straight and parallel to the selvedge edge. This means that if there is a weak thread that breaks, the split could travel the entire length of the binding. The weft, or widthways, threads do not tend to run so straight across the fabric, so if you cut the binding this way, any broken threads will cause a much shorter split. The fabric is also slightly more stretchy in this direction, which will help if binding around shallow curves.

Continuous binding

If you want to bind the edges of the quilt with a continuous strip of binding, you will probably need to join several strips to get the full length. Continuous binding can be single or double binding – just cut the strip to the appropriate width – but the diagrams here show single binding.

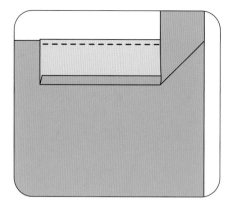

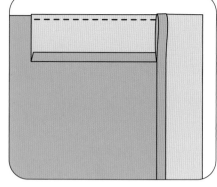

1 Beginning in the centre of an edge, place the binding strip along one edge of the quilt top, with right sides together and raw edges aligned – the folded edge of the binding should be facing towards the inner part of the quilt. Stitch to the first corner mark on the quilt, then backstitch to secure. Remove the quilt from the machine. Fold the binding upwards on a diagonal line and finger-press in place.

2 Then fold the binding strip down to align it with the next edge to be worked, holding the diagonal fold made in step 1 in place with your finger. Begin stitching again down the new edge, starting at the top folded edge of the binding. Repeat at all four corners.

Binding

Binding can be very narrow or quite wide, in either a plain or a patterned fabric. You can use one of the fabrics already in the quilt or something totally new. It's usually best to choose the binding fabric when the quilt is finished, as it can be difficult to judge the effect before this.

Spread out the quilt and try quite long strips of different lengths of fabric along the edge to see how they might look. Try out several options before making a final decision.

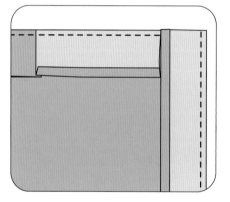

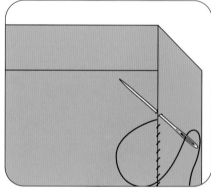

3 When you reach your starting position, fold the last 1cm (½in) of the binding over and slide it under the raw edge of the first section of binding.

4 Turn the binding to the back of the quilt, and slipstitch the folded edge to the backing fabric as before. At each corner, fold the excess binding into a neat mitre and slipstitch in place.

Making bias strip for binding

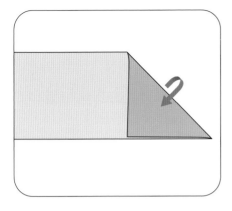

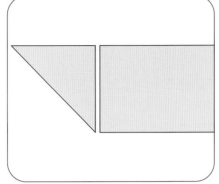

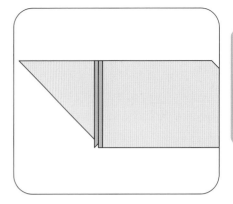

1 Fold the crossways grain of the fabric to the straight lengthways grain – the easiest way to do this is to make sure the end of the length is straight on the grain and then fold it down to line up with the selvedge. The diagonal fold is the true bias.

2 Cut along the fold line, then take the triangle of fabric you have just removed and add it to the other end of the piece to make a parallelogram shape.

3 Stitch the triangle to the edge and press the seam open. Mark a series of lines, parallel with the cut edge, set apart by twice the width you want the binding to be. So if you want a binding 2.5cm (1in) wide, space the lines 5cm (2in) apart.

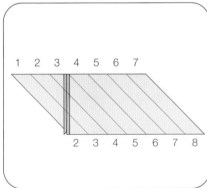

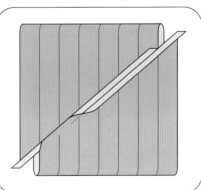

4 Number the bands along the top edge with an air-erasable marker. On the bottom edge, mark the end of band 1 as '2', then carry on to mark '3', '4' etc.

5 With right sides together, bring the edges round and match the numbers so '2' lines up with '2', '3' with '3', and so on. The first and the last numbers will not match up with anything. Stitch to join the pieces, leaving a 1cm (½in) seam allowance, which will create a tube of fabric. Cut along the marked line, which will now run around the tube in a continuous spiral from top to bottom.

Displaying quilts

To make a hanging tube for display, cut a fabric strip about 10cm (4in) deep by the width of the quilt (seamed if necessary) and hem the ends; fold it in half lengthways, right sides facing, and sew it into a tube. Turn the fabric tube right side out and handstitch it along its length (both top and bottom edges) on the reverse of the quilt, just under the binding. Slide a non-wooden rod through the hanging tube and suspend the rod from the ceiling using wire, or support it on brackets fixed to the wall.

Joining bias strips

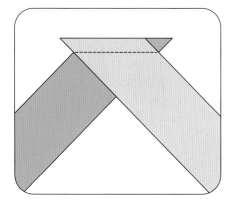

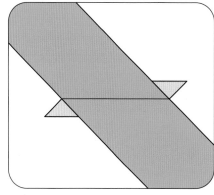

1 If you need to join two strips of bias binding, do it before you fold the edges over. Pin the strips with right sides together – they will run at right angles to each other. Stitch together, leaving a 1cm (½in) seam allowance.

2 Press the seam open – remember that if the bias strip has a pattern you should try to match it on the seamline, not on the cut edges. Trim off the protruding points and fold over a 5mm (¼in) width of fabric to the wrong side along both edges.

Bias binding maker

When you have cut the bias strip you can use it as it is, but you may want to fold both edges towards the middle and press them in position. A bias binding maker will make this easier – it turns the edges over, ready to iron, as you pull the strip through it.

Edge-to-middle binding

With this technique, the edges of the backing and the top are folded over to the middle of the quilt. Therefore there will not be a narrow line of different fabric showing on either the back or the front of the quilt.

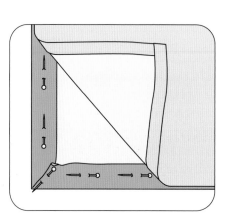

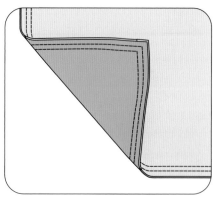

1 Fold the backing fabric over the edge of the wadding (batting) and pin. Fold the edge of the quilt top under and tuck inside the quilt.

2 Pin and then stitch all around the quilt, 5mm (¼in) from the edge. Run a second line of stitching 5mm (¼in) from the first.

Back-to-front binding

If you do not want to use a separate piece of binding fabric, the edges of the backing fabric can be folded over on to the front of the quilt to cover the raw edges – this is also sometimes known as self-binding.

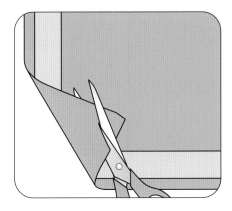
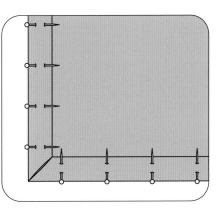
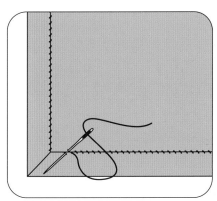

1 Cut the backing fabric bigger than the quilt all around by the width of the binding desired plus a 5mm (¼in) seam allowance. Fold the seam allowance over to the wrong side all around and press, folding a mitre in each corner. Trim the wadding (batting) to the same size as the quilt top.

2 Fold the backing fabric over to the front of the quilt. Bringing the backing over to the front of the quilt adds a sense of cohesion to the design. You can also work this technique in reverse, bringing the quilt top around to the back, if you prefer.

3 Pin the backing fabric in position along all four edges, then stitch in place by hand, or by machine. Slipstitch the mitres at each corner.

wholecloth and strippy quilts

Wholecloth quilts are a uniform piece of fabric, while strippy quilts are created in alternating strips of different fabrics that each run the length of the quilt. The beauty of these quilts mainly comes from the design and texture created by the quilting stitches, rather than from the way different fabrics are placed.

wholecloth

When creating a wholecloth quilt, the overall quilting design is generally made up of a series of smaller motifs or borders. Here are the steps for one motif, but the entire design needs to be carefully planned out on the quilt top before you begin to stitch. The techniques described here are illustrated for hand quilting, but will be basically the same for machine quilting.

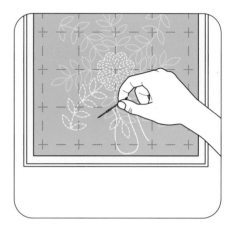

1 Place the motif pattern on a lightbox, put the fabric on top and trace the pattern on to it, using a suitable marker for the fabric. Alternatively, use one of the techniques for transferring a design shown on pages 36–38.

2 Layer the backing fabric, wadding (batting) and top fabric, then pin to hold in place. Tack (baste) across the area to be quilted, working the central vertical and horizontal lines first and then moving out towards the edges. On a large quilt, you may need to tack diagonally too.

3 Cut a length of quilting thread and start to hand-quilt outwards from the centre, as described on page 40. Try to keep the stitches evenly spaced and of equal sizes, and as small as you can manage. Alternatively, if the design is suitable, you could quilt it by machine.

4 Remove the tacking (basting) threads when all the quilting is complete, just leaving the outer line to hold everything together until you are ready to finish the outer edges. See pages 60–65 for binding techniques.

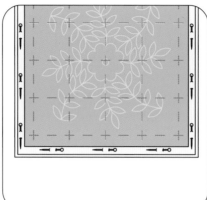

Quilting patterns

Traditional designs for wholecloth quilting drew upon a vast quilting pattern library that was often inspired by nature – although plant forms were often fanciful with very little botanical accuracy.

Many wholecloth quilts feature a central medallion design, with elaborate corner motifs, intricate borders and some form of infill grid, all created purely in quilting stitches.

When the quilting design is symmetrical, you only need to draw up one-quarter or one section, then just repeat it.

Cording and trapunto (see pages 42 and 43) can be used to create areas of higher relief in the design.

Although traditionally stitched entirely by hand, long-arm quilting machines are ideal for wholecloth quilting, since they can move easily across the entire surface of a quilt, guided accurately by hand.

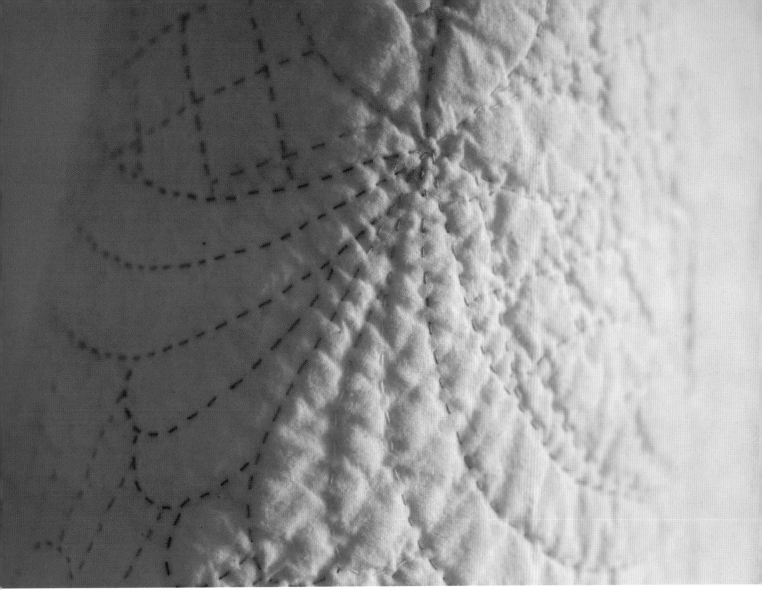

Medallion quilts

Medallion quilts were a later development of the wholecloth quilt widely made in Britain, and more particularly in Wales. A medallion quilt has a very defined central medallion, often square in shape, surrounded by at least one border; often, it has a series of borders. The central medallion could be a contrasting fabric, pieced or appliquéd.

Medallion quilts were also made across the Atlantic and in the nineteenth century, printed cotton handkerchiefs were often used as the central medallion in both Britain and America.

French traditions

In France, three main types of quilt developed: Matelassage, a type of wholecloth quilt where the top fabric is often sateen or high-quality printed or embroidered cotton, with a coarse backing fabric. Piqûre de Marseilles comes from the Marseilles area and has a top of fine plain cotton or silk, very richly quilted with areas of cording or stuffing to make the design stand out in relief.

Boutis (a Provençal word meaning 'stuffing') quilts are made in a similar way to piqûre de Marseilles, but the motifs are larger and boutis quilts are always reversible.

strippy

On a traditional strippy quilt, there is generally an odd number of strips – usually five, seven or nine. The strips can be two contrasting colours, patterned and plain, or plain and pieced. Construction is simple and a strippy quilt can be made larger or smaller by varying strip widths. The quilting design on the plain strips is often quite complex, but any linear design is suitable.

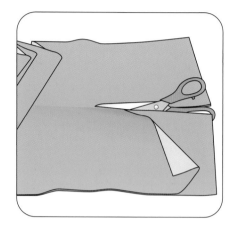

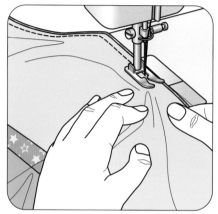

1 Use a plain fabric and a patterned or contrasting fabric. Fold both pieces of fabric along the lengthways grain at 20cm (8in) intervals and press. Cut the fabric into equal strips along the fold lines. You need at least four plain strips and three patterned or contrasting strips, depending on the size of the finished quilt.

2 Join the strips together along their long edges using 5mm (¼in) seams, alternating the colours. Press the seams towards the darker fabric. Add wadding (batting) and backing as described on page 58, using the edge-to-middle binding on page 64.

3 Transfer the quilting design to the strips of fabric, using one of the methods described on pages 36–38. If you are using patterned and plain fabric, you could quilt only the plain strips. If you have used two contrasting plain colours, you could use a different quilting design for each colour of strip.

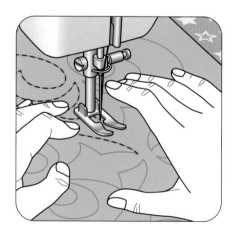

4 Machine- or hand-quilt the quilting design down each of the marked strips. You can also quilt in the ditch down the edge of each strip (see page 41).

Strippy design

A strippy quilt is a good way of making the most of an expensive fabric, by alternating it with a less expensive one. Make sure both are a similar weight and composition.

In some antique strippies, the individual strips were quilted before being joined, perhaps because working or storage space was limited.

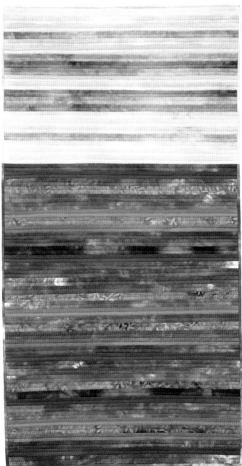

Amish Bars

The Amish Bars design is a version of the traditional strippy quilt, possibly originally inspired by strippies made by non-Amish British neighbours who had brought the design from England. The strips, or bars, are generally in two or three alternating colours all cut to the same width. Sometimes bars may be pieced and the borders may also have pieced corner squares. Traditionally, Amish quilts always have a border – sometimes two, wide and narrow – and use plain colours, set against black or grey.

Amish design

Traditional Amish quilts were made in plain, dark colours, set against black – the fabrics used were from worn-out dresses and men's suits. Quilts made commercially for sale by the Amish use a wider range of colours, but are still quite distinctive.

1 Cut the fabric strips for the bars approximately 12.5cm (5in) wide and 140cm (56in) long, or to the width and length required for the size of quilt you wish to make. For a basic Bars design you will need at least two colours, used alternately, to make up an odd number of bars.

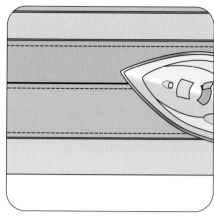

2 Join the strips together along their long edges, using 5mm (¼in) seams, then press the seams towards the darker fabric.

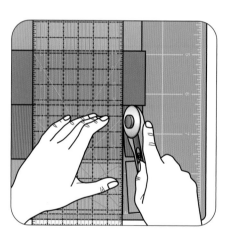

3 Trim off the edges of the bars at each end, so the central panel is square, using a rotary cutter and ruler on a cutting mat.

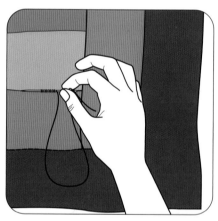

4 Add borders, wadding (batting), backing and binding as described on pages 54–57, and 60–65. Quilt in the ditch (see page 45) down the edge of each bar.

Split Bars

The Split Bars design is a variation of the basic Bars design shown opposite; it has thin lengthways strips on either side of alternate main bars. This is another design that is often made by Amish quilters. For a different look, the narrow strips can simply alternate with wide ones.

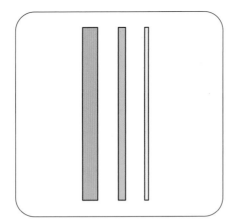

1 Cut six wide strips from fabric A; five strips one-third the width in fabric B plus 1cm (½in) seam allowance; and ten strips one-third the width of A plus 5mm (¼in) seam allowance in fabric C.

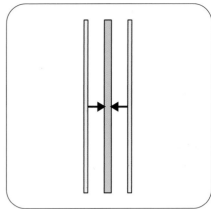

2 With a 5mm (¼in) seam, join one fabric strip C on either side of each fabric strip B. Press the seam towards the darker fabric.

Strengthening thread

When hand-quilting, the thread will be pulled through several layers of fabric numerous times, and this will cause a great deal of wear and tear on the thread. Hard-wearing special quilting thread is available, but not in a wide range of colours. However, any cotton or polyester thread can be strengthened by sliding it through a block of beeswax or by using a thread strengthener, such as Thread Heaven for example.

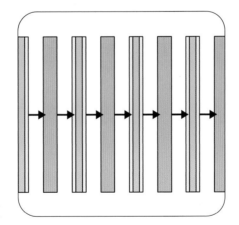

3 Alternate each fabric strip A with a C/B/C strip. Join the strips with a 5mm (¼in) seam.

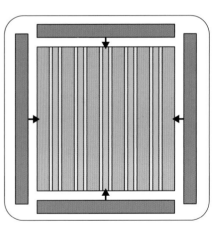

4 Add a border on all four sides, then add wadding (batting), backing and binding as described on pages 58 and 60–65.

Flying Geese Bars

The Flying Geese block is always twice as wide as it is high.
The diagram here will give you four Flying Geese units. Make
enough to create five bars of the finished quilt.

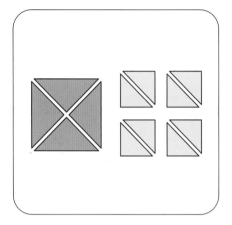

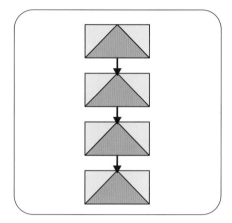

1 Cut one square in fabric A the size
of the finished width of the block
plus 3cm (1¼in). Cut this diagonally into
four triangles. Cut four squares in fabric B
the height of the finished block (i.e. half
the width) plus 2cm (⅞in). Cut each small
square diagonally into two triangles.

2 Using 5mm (¼in) seams, sew a
triangle in fabric B to the top two
angled sides of the triangle in fabric A.
Press the seams to one side. Repeat for
the other four sets.

3 Stitch each Flying Geese block to
the next one, using 5mm (¼in)
seams. Press the seams to one side.
Repeat until you have the length of bar
you need.

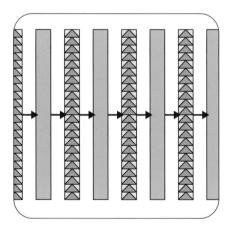

4 Join the Flying Geese bars
alternately to plain bars, and
then add a border on all four sides.
Complete with wadding (batting), backing
and binding as described on pages 58
and 60–65.

Mennonite quilts

The Mennonites are a similar religious group to the Amish; both were
originally descended from Swiss and Dutch Anabaptists who arrived
in the New World in the 1720s. The Mennonites also make distinctive
and beautiful quilts, but they are less strict than the Amish so they
sometimes use printed, tartan and striped fabrics, as well as appliqué
and embroidery.

Chinese Coins

The Chinese Coins design is a type of bars quilt in which alternate bars are pieced in scraps of fabric. Make at least five pieced bars for the finished quilt.

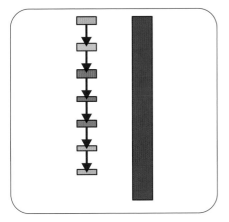

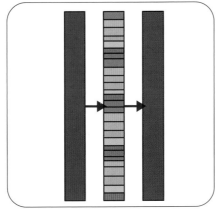

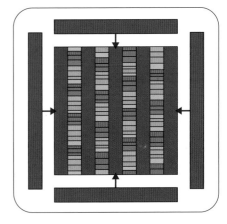

1 Cut six bars in plain fabric. Cut strips of different fabrics the same length as the width of the bar, and in varying widths. Stitch the small strips together in random order along the long edges using a 5mm (¼in) seam allowance. Press seams to one side.

2 Make at least five bars, all in random-width stripes. Stitch one plain bar alternately to the striped bar, using 5mm (¼in) seams. Press all the seams to one side.

3 Add a border on all four sides. Complete with wadding (batting), backing and binding as described on pages 58 and 60–65.

Variations

The Chinese Coins design does not have to be made in many multicoloured fabrics. It can be assembled from just two or three different colours, but random-height strips are essential.

Using scraps

A Chinese Coins project is great for using up all those narrow pieces of brightly coloured fabric from your stash that are not wide enough to cut into other shapes. It is very easy to sew, since it only requires straight seams. The plain bars offer an ideal place for more complex quilting designs.

templates

There are so many different quilting stitch templates that it is impossible to give a comprehensive selection here, but some of the more traditional designs are illustrated. These can be combined in an almost limitless selection of ways to make a very wide range of quilting designs.

Grids

Copy these designs to the size you require.

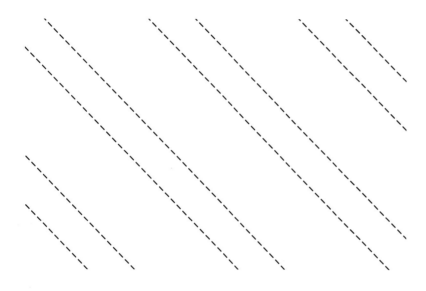

Diagonal Lines

Diamond Trellis

Basketweave

Diagonal Outwards

Diagonal Inwards

Clamshell

Hexagon

Steps

Wine Glass

Chevron

Borders

Copy these designs to the size
you require.

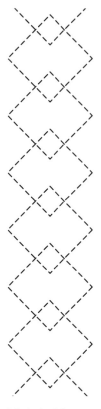

Interlocked Squares

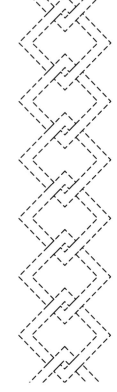

Double Interlocked Squares

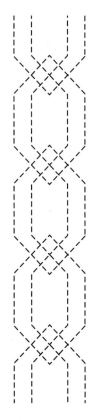

Interlocked Hexagons

Diamond Twist

Diamond Border

Feathered Twist

Tulips

Diamond Cable

Cable

Braided Cable

Pumpkin Seed

Corners

Copy these designs to the size
you require.

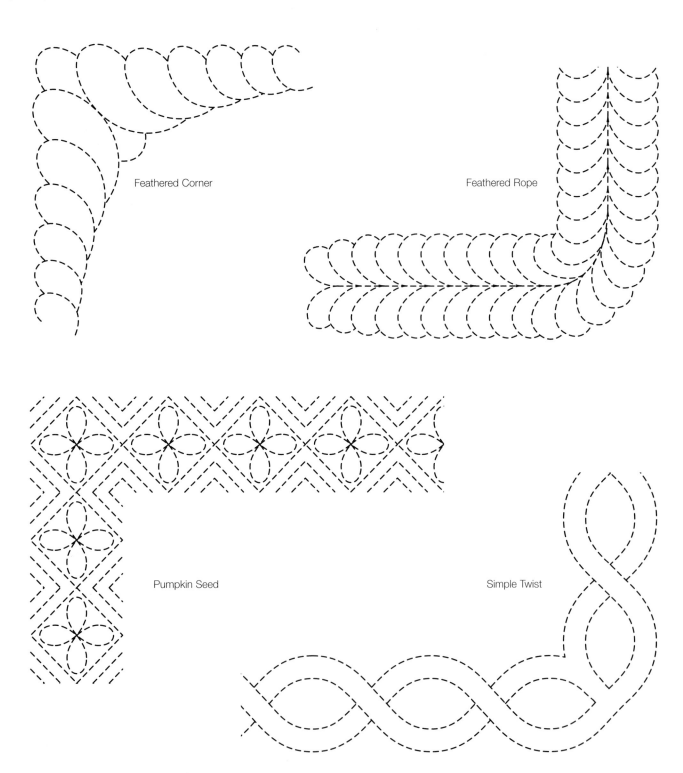

Feathered Corner

Feathered Rope

Pumpkin Seed

Simple Twist

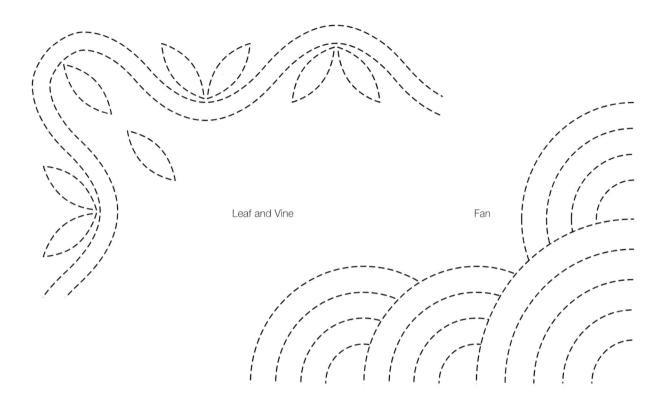

Leaf and Vine

Fan

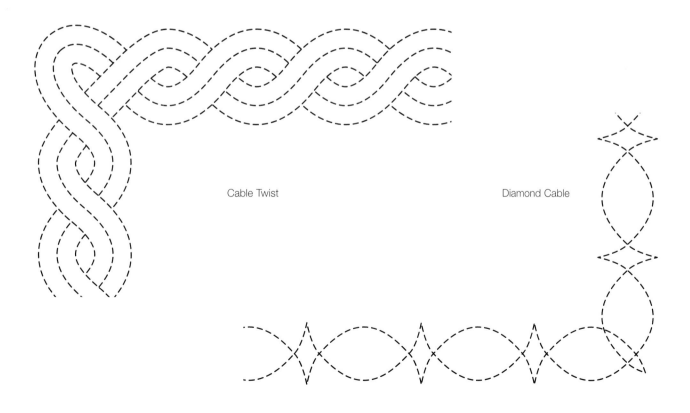

Cable Twist

Diamond Cable

Motifs

Copy these designs to the size
you require.

Clamshell

Exploding Star

Feathered Cross

Feathered Heart

Feathered Ring

Leaf

Tulip Ring

Square Swirl

Lover's Knot

pieced quilts

Pieced, or patchwork, quilts are generally made up of many small pieced blocks. A quilt may feature lots of the same block, or different blocks combined in an almost limitless range of ways. Many traditional block designs are based on straight seams, but a few have curved seams. Some blocks can give the illusion of curved seams by the way they are set.

marking and cutting

Accuracy is crucial when cutting out shapes for patchwork, particularly when making a series of identical blocks. Templates and paper patterns will help make the process of cutting many shapes much easier. The time-honoured method is to hand-cut with scissors; rotary cutting will make the process much faster – it allows you to cut through several layers in one go to create many identical shapes.

Making templates

Templates can be made in paper, card or template plastic. If you only want use a template a couple of times, paper or card will be quite adequate.

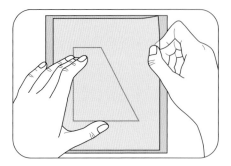

1 To cut a quantity of irregular shapes, first make a template. Draw around the shape on tracing paper, then either transfer the line to a piece of card or glue the tracing paper to the card.

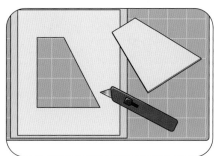

2 Cut out the shape, following the line very carefully. If you are not cutting many shapes, you can use this cardboard template. For cutting a large number of shapes, it is safer to use a template made of special template plastic.

Cutting skills

Always use a craft knife and a metal ruler to cut cardboard and template plastic – plastic rulers are easily damaged.

Make sure the blade is really sharp or you may get rough edges on the template.

If you are cutting several templates, change the blade as soon as it becomes harder to cut – this is a sign that the blade is becoming blunt.

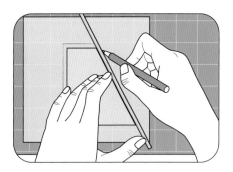

3 Draw around the shape to transfer it to a piece of template plastic. If you are making a window template, add a 5mm (¼in) border on all sides for the seam allowance. You can either measure this by hand or use a quilter's quarter.

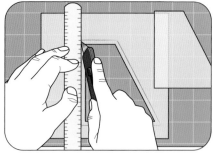

4 Cut out the inner window. Then cut around the seam allowance line. The inner window is for support papers or for marking the stitching line. The outside of the template is for cutting fabric patches accurately.

Window templates

To cut the papers for English paper piecing (see page 90), window templates are ideal.

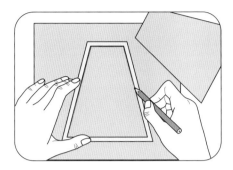

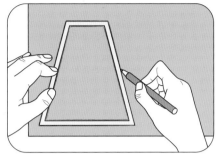

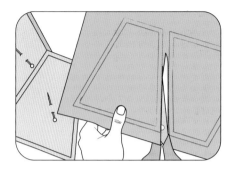

1 The inside window of the template is the line to use to mark the backing paper. Cut one paper for each fabric piece.

2 Use the outside edge of the template to cut the fabric pieces. If possible, align the template with the straight grain and don't drag the marker along the fabric, as this may stretch the fabric out of shape.

3 Cut out each fabric piece and each paper piece. Pin a paper piece to the wrong side of each fabric piece.

Paper patterns

If the shape has curved lines or is complex, a paper pattern may be easier to use.

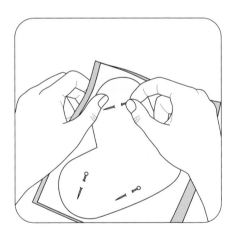

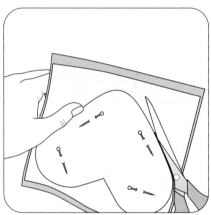

1 Trace the shape on to paper, then pin the paper to the fabric; it will be easier to cut along the marked line if you don't cut out the paper shape before pinning. Cut along the marked line, through paper and fabric.

2 You can probably cut several pieces at the same time, as long as the shape is not very complex or the fabric very thick. Use sharp fabric scissors, even though you are also cutting through paper – but use thin, lightweight paper if possible.

rotary cutting

When working with a rotary cutter, take great care to follow safety guidelines. There are many different brands of cutter, so find the one that best suits you as then you will be more comfortable using it. Rotary-cut strips can be stitched together in sequence and then cut across into pieced strips, which can be assembled in a different way.

Using a rotary cutter

To avoid cutting by mistake into the section of fabric you actually want to use, cover it with the rotary ruler and cut away the waste.

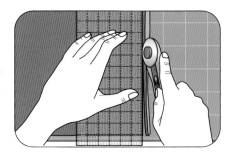

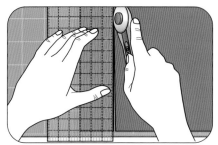

1 Fold the fabric along the straight grain and fit it on to the mat. Align the folded edge along one of the mat lines, then use the rotary ruler to straighten the raw edge.

2 Turn the piece of fabric around and measure the width of the piece you want to cut. Cover the measured piece with the rotary ruler. Cut carefully along the grain.

Cutting pieced strips

After you have made up pieced units, you may need to cut them into smaller units to stitch together in a different orientation to create the block design.

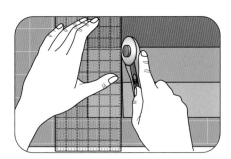

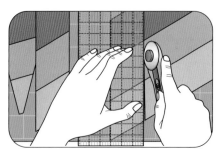

1 Press seams to one side. Lay the pieced fabric right side up, trim the edge and then measure and place one of the ruler's gridlines along the trimmed edge. Cut pieced strips as required.

2 If you want to cut the pieced strips at an angle, measure the angle and trim off the edge. Align the ruler on the trimmed edge and cut the pieced strips in the same way as in step 1.

Rotary safety

A rotary cutter has a very sharp blade, so it comes with a safety guard. Make sure you put the guard back on the blade as soon as you finish cutting. Always cut away from yourself, and replace dull or damaged blades as soon as you notice them. Use a self-healing cutting mat to protect the worksurface and extend the life of the cutting blades.

Mats and rulers

Mats come in many sizes and are generally marked in a grid, which is useful for aligning pieces but should not be used as a measure.

Rotary rulers are available in many sizes and shapes, including ones for complex shapes such as triangles, stars and fans. Usually made of transparent plastic, they are marked in a grid, using metric or imperial measurements.

hand piecing

Piecing by hand is often much quicker and easier than working on a machine – particularly if you are working with very small pieces, curved seams, or seams that are cut on the bias. Many quilters find handstitching more relaxing and meditative than working on a machine, and you can also carry parts of your project about with you to work on whenever you have a spare moment.

Single straight seams

Stitching a perfectly straight seam may require a bit of practice. Starting and stopping on the seam line is the key to accurate piecing at corners. Small pieces can be joined together with a small, neat running stitch or backstitch.

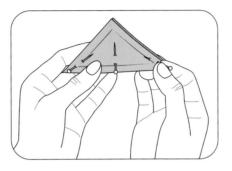

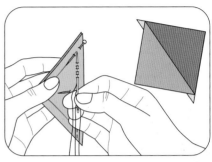

1 Lay the two pieces with right sides together, matching raw edges and corners. Pin the two pieces firmly in place.

2 Sew along the seam line, making sure that you start and finish exactly in the corner so there will be no gap at these points. Press the seam towards the darker fabric.

Joining seamed pieces

When you want to join a pair of seamed units, it is better to stitch outwards from the seam in the centre, so it will stay aligned across both units.

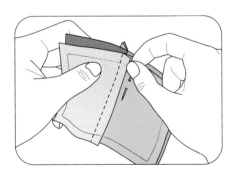

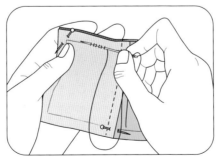

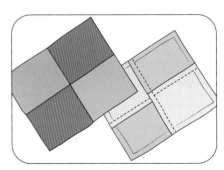

1 Join two pairs of pieces together, as described above. Pin the two units together, right sides facing, matching the seams exactly.

2 Stitch the units together, working one side from the centre outwards along the seam line, then sewing the other side in the same way.

3 Press the seams flat on the wrong side. On the right side (seen left) the four sides should line up perfectly in the middle.

English paper piecing

This traditional method uses paper templates, which remain inside the fabric pieces until they are all stitched together.

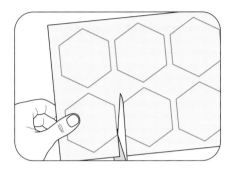

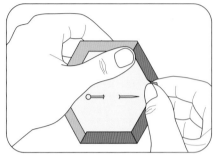

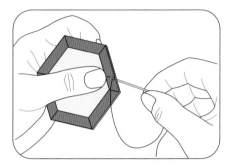

1 Make a plastic window template, as described on page 87. Use the inside window to mark the shape on paper – you will need one paper template for each piece. Iron the fabric, then use the outer edge of the template to mark the fabric shapes. Cut out the paper and fabric shapes.

2 Centre a paper template on the wrong side of one of the fabric pieces, making sure the seam allowance is the same all the way round, then pin in place. Fold the edges of the fabric over the paper, making sure the corners are neatly tucked in. Tack (baste) around the shape to attach the fabric to the paper. Repeat with the other pieces.

3 Place two pieces with right sides together, aligning the edges and corners. Whipstitch along each edge to hold the two pieces together, being very careful not to stitch through the paper template. Keep adding pieces in the same way to make up the design.

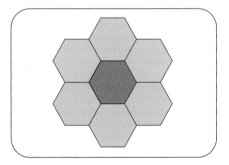

4 Leave the paper templates in place until all the pieces of a unit have been joined. As you make up each unit, press it flat. Join up the units in the same way to make the quilt top, removing the paper patterns before you add wadding (batting) and backing.

Portable projects

If you want a project that is easy to work on in different locations, English paper piecing is ideal. Once you have made all the paper templates and cut the fabric, you can carry a selection of the pieces around, along with a needle and thread, and stitch whenever you have a few spare minutes.

Make sure all the fabrics used are of an equal weight and of the same composition.

When tacking (basting) the fabric to the paper template, leave the knotted end of the thread on the right side, so the tacking stitches are easy to remove later.

machine piecing

As soon as sewing machines became more generally available in the early 1800s, quiltmakers began to use them to speed up the making process. New techniques were quickly developed to make better use of the machine and to further cut down the time required on repetitive tasks. A simple sewing machine is all that is required for most quiltmaking projects – but there are also machines that are specifically designed to meet the requirements of quilters.

Strips

A straight seam and an accurate seam allowance are both essential if you want to achieve perfectly aligned strips.

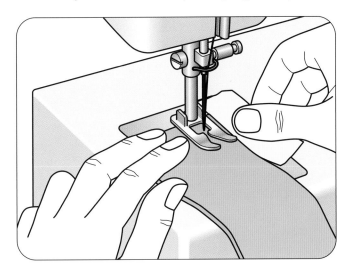

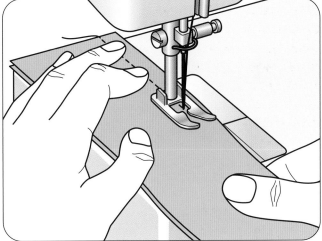

1 A special foot that measures an exact 5mm (¼in) seam allowance is available for most machines, but marking the needle plate with a strip of masking tape is just as effective. Check the measurement on a scrap piece of fabric before you begin sewing a new project and replace the tape if it becomes worn or grubby.

2 Cut a good selection of strips to work with. Take two and place them with right sides together, lining up the raw edges. Stitch the two pieces together, taking care to keep the seam exactly straight and 5mm (¼in) from the raw edges.

Sewing strips

There is generally no need to pin or tack (baste) strips together before you machine-stitch them, but make sure the raw edges stay aligned and that the seam is perfectly straight.

Chain piecing

You can speed up the process of making a block by chain-piecing as much as possible.

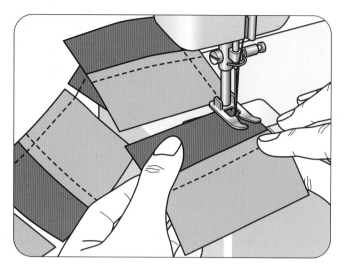

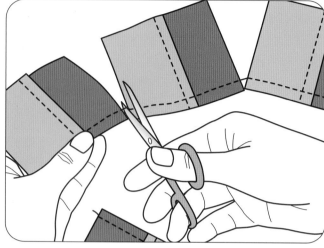

1 Cut a good selection of each of the various pieces you will be using and place them in separate piles near your machine. Feed one unit after another through the machine, stitching continuously without pausing to raise the presser foot or cut the thread between units.

2 You will end up with a chain of units, held together by a short length of thread. Cut the units apart when you have finished stitching.

Curved seams

When working on curved seams, be very careful not to stretch the fabric out of shape, or the finished unit will not lie flat when pressed.

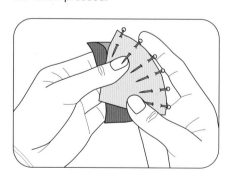

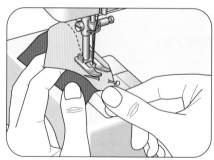

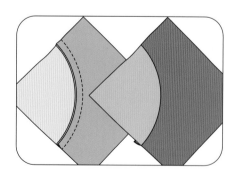

1 Working on the wrong side, mark the stitching line on one piece. Align the two pieces to be stitched together with right sides facing. Pin at right angles to the stitching line.

2 Place the unit under the needle and lower the needle at the end of the marked stitching line. Lower the presser foot and stitch along the line, removing pins as you go.

3 Clip the curve if necessary, then press the seam towards the concave edge.

Joining pieced units

The biggest problem, when joining many pieced units, is getting all the seams to line up correctly. Make sure you join pieces together in the correct order, and keep checking their alignment as you work.

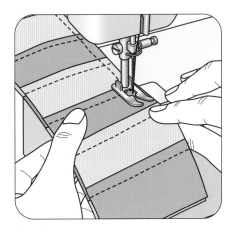

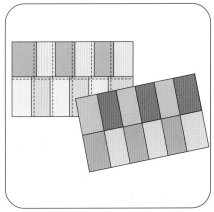

1 Make up a selection of pieced units and press the seams to one side. Place two units with right sides together, aligning raw edges and matching seams. Stitch the units together.

2 Press the seams to one side on the reverse (above left). On the right side (above right), the seam lines between the pieces should run in a perfectly straight line, with perfectly square corners.

Joining plain and pieced units

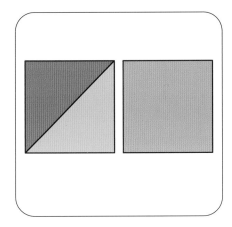

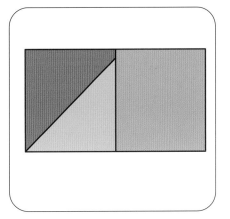

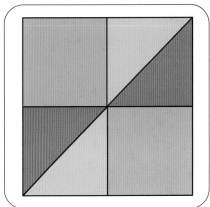

1 Some designs call for a pieced and a plain unit to be joined. Make up the pieced unit to the same size as the plain unit.

2 Place the pieced unit and the plain unit with right sides together and stitch. On the right side, the diagonal seam on the pieced unit should fall exactly 5mm (¼in) below the edge of the block.

3 When the paired units are stitched to the next pair, all of the corners should meet exactly in the centre. To achieve this, completely accurate measuring and stitching of seams is absolutely essential.

Ripping seams

You may need to unpick a seam, because some construction methods involve several seams that are manipulated in some way and then opened up again, or stitched and then cut apart. Using a special seam ripper is the best way to open a seam neatly – but be careful not to slit the fabric as the blade is very sharp.

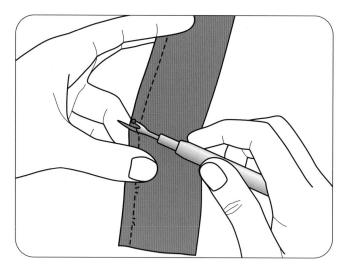

1 Hold a section of the seam taut and slide the point of the seam ripper into a stitch on the wrong side. Break the stitch thread with the ripper blade. Repeat every few stitches.

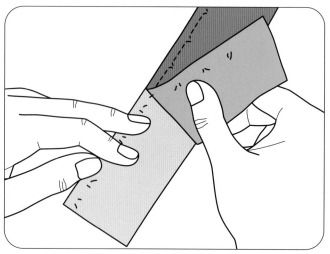

2 Lay the unit on a worksurface and gently lift up the top piece, pulling it away from the bottom piece and separating the stitches.

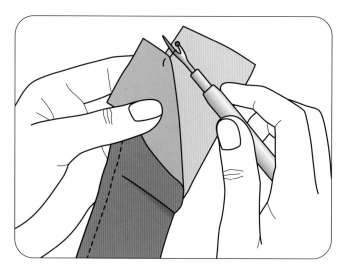

3 Alternatively, hold the seam open with the right sides of the fabric towards you. Slide the point of the seam ripper into the seam and break a thread. Pull the seam apart carefully.

Tacking (basting) techniques

When thread-tacking, use a bright thread in a contrasting colour to the fabric, so that the stitches can be seen easily when you come to remove them.

Make the tacking stitches large, but not absolutely gigantic or they will not hold the layers correctly in alignment with each other.

Triangle squares

Triangle squares are the basis for many traditional block designs. Here is a quick way to make several units at once.

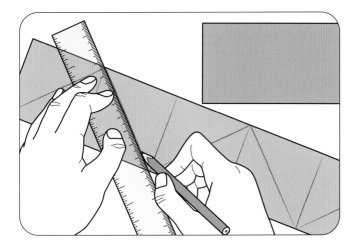

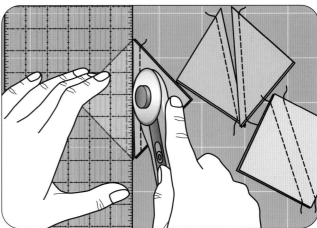

1 Cut strips of fabric in two different colours. On the wrong side of the lighter colour, mark lines at intervals to divide the strip into squares. Draw a diagonal line across the first square in one direction, then across the next square in the other direction. Repeat down the strip. Lay the marked lighter strip on top of the second unmarked darker colour strip with wrong sides facing.

2 Stitch 5mm (¼in) away down one side of the diagonal line, then continue along the diagonal line in the next square. Continue until the end, then turn around and work back, stitching along the opposite side of each diagonal line. This stay stitching will help to stop the edge on the bias from stretching out of shape. Cut the squares apart, then cut carefully down the diagonal line, between the double lines of stitching.

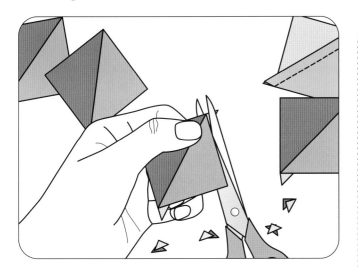

3 Press the seams to the side in the darker colour and trim off the triangles at each end of the seam to square up the block.

Variations for making triangle squares

A variation on the method shown here for making triangle squares is to individually mark the fabric strips, then stitch and cut each as in step 2 to give you triangles of fabric in each colour.

Place two contrasting triangles together with raw edges on the diagonal aligned and corners matching. Stitch the triangles together carefully, being careful not to stretch the fabric. Then press seams and trim seam ends as in step 3.

Alternatively, to make two triangle units at a time, see steps 1 and 2 on page 128.

Foundation piecing

In this technique, pieces are stitched in order on to a foundation (or backing) fabric. It is ideal for irregular shapes and edges cut on the bias, as the foundation fabric will stabilize them. If your design is unsymmetrical, remember that the pattern on the final block will be a mirror image of the original drawn pattern when finished. this is because you stitch the fabric pieces to the reverse of the foundation fabric so you can see the stitching lines to follow.

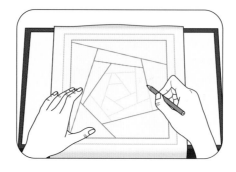

1 Draw the pattern of the block on the foundation fabric, which can be a non-woven stabilizer (see page 249) or a suitable fabric. Number the shapes in the order that they have to be stitched, working from the centre outwards.

2 Trace the pattern of the block on to tracing paper and cut this into the individual pieces. Use these as templates to cut the pieces of fabric. Remember to add a 5mm (¼in) seam allowance all around the edge of each.

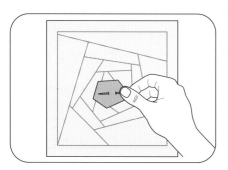

3 Place the foundation fabric on the worksurface, with the unmarked side facing up. Place the first piece of fabric on top, in its relevant position, and pin in place. Check on the reverse to make sure the fabric piece covers the stitching line all round.

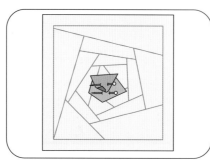

4 Place the second piece of fabric on top of the first piece (right sides together) with edges aligned so that when it flips over, it will be in its correct position in the design. Pin in place.

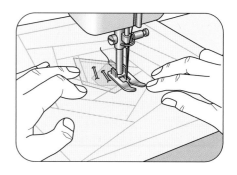

5 Working with the marked side of the foundation fabric facing you, stitch the marked line between the first two shapes. Turn over, flip the second piece of fabric into its correct position and press.

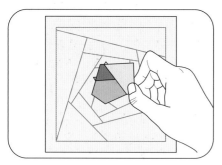

6 Place the third piece of fabric on top of the other two (right sides together) with edges aligned, so that when it flips over it will be in its correct position in the design. Pin in place, then sew.

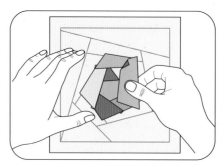

7 Continue to sew on the pieces, keeping carefully to the marked order on the foundation fabric.

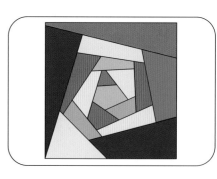

8 When the block is complete, press and trim the edges to square it up as necessary.

Quilt-as-you-go

This is a technique in which the blocks have wadding (batting) added as they are stitched, so after they are joined together, the final quilt just needs backing and binding. The technique can also be used to make a small quilt.

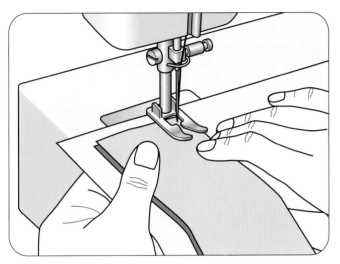

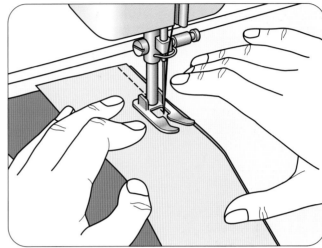

1 Cut the wadding (batting) approximately 5cm (2in) larger all around than the size of the finished block or quilt. Cut all the fabric strips you will need to complete the block. Take the first two strips of fabric and place them with right sides together and edges matching. Align the left-hand edge of the strips with the left-hand edge of the wadding. Stitch 5mm (¼in) from the right-hand edge of the strips, through all three layers. Fold over the top strip so it is right side up.

2 Take the third strip of fabric and place it on top of the second strip (right sides together), aligning the right-hand raw edge. Stitch 5mm (¼in) from the right-hand edge of the second and third strips, through all three layers. Fold over the third strip so it is right side up.

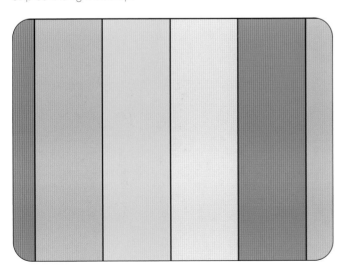

3 Carry on working across the piece of wadding (batting) in this way until it is completely covered with fabric. Trim to square up the edges as required.

Machine stitching

When machine-stitching strips of fabric, there is often no need to pin or tack (baste) them together first, although stitching totally straight lines does require some practice. Cut the strips accurately, keep raw edges aligned and use the 5mm (¼in) seam foot on the machine or the markings on the needle plate to keep seam allowances consistent.

strips

Strips are perhaps the simplest shapes that can be pieced together, but despite this there is a very wide range of interesting designs that can be achieved with them. Perhaps the most well-known strips-based block is Log Cabin; it is such an ancient design that no one really knows where it originated.

Rail Fence

Traditional Rail Fence needs at least three different fabrics, which are first strip-pieced and then cut down into striped squares. The striped squares are then rotated and alternated to create a zigzag pattern across the block. The block can be made up as a Four-Patch or a Nine-Patch. Blocks can be set to create secondary patterns across the quilt.

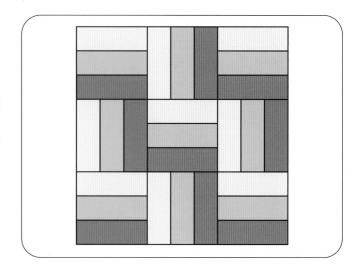

Making a Rail Fence block

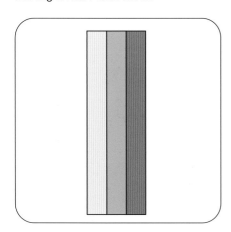 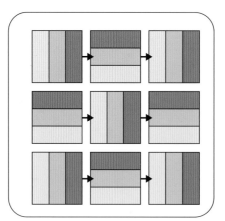 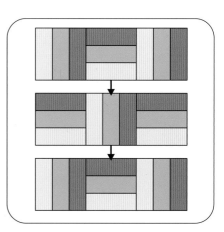

1 Cut strips in fabrics A, B and C, all of an equal width. Stitch them together along the long edge, using a 5mm (¼in) seam. Press the seams to one side. Cut the pieced strips into several equal sized squares.

2 Alternate the striped squares horizontally and vertically. Stitch them together into three rows, as indicated above. Press the seams in alternate directions.

3 Join the three rows to form a block. For a professional-looking result, be very careful that seams match perfectly across the rows. Press the seams in opposite directions where possible, which will help the block lie flat.

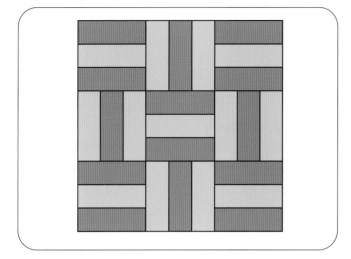

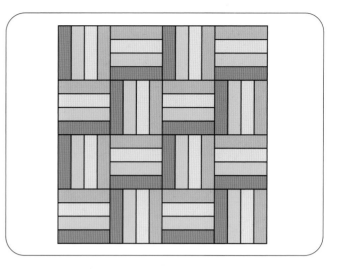

Basketweave

This block is made up of only two different fabrics, placed alternately. When the pieced squares are alternated and joined in exactly the same way as in the standard Rail Fence, the result is a weave pattern.

Four-Fabric Rail Fence

If you use four different fabrics, you get a very similar effect to the standard Rail Fence block, but the zigzag pattern will be spaced wider apart.

Brick

As its name may suggest, Brick consists of rectangles arranged in offset rows like the bricks in a wall. If you use the strip-piecing method, the bricks will be arranged symmetrically unless you unpick some seams to switch things around. If you cut and piece the rectangles individually, you can achieve a completely random effect.

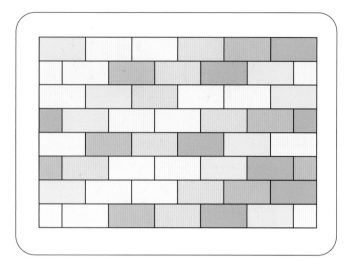

Making a Brick block

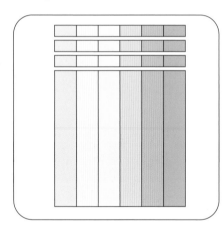

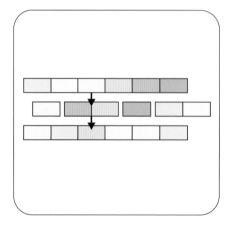

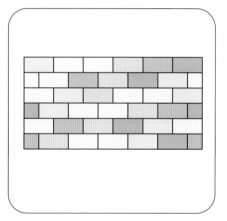

1 Cut many strips of different fabrics to an equal width. Stitch them together along the long edge, using a 5mm (¼in) seam allowance. Press seams to one side, then cut the pieced strips into rows; the height of each row should be half the width of the original strips.

2 Place the rows next to one another, offsetting the seams so they fall in the centre of the 'brick' in the row above. To achieve a random effect, you will have to unpick some seams between 'bricks' and switch them around until you get an interesting effect.

3 Restitch the seams. Stitch the rows together, making sure the seams stay aligned. Trim the overhangs at the edges to get a block with straight edges.

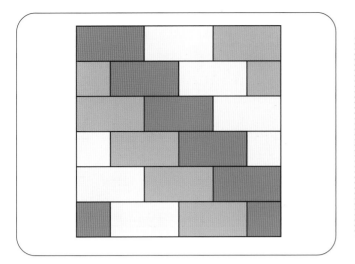

Stitching by hand

Small pieces can be joined together with running stitch or backstitch. If you use running stitch, try to keep stitches small and even.

Keep to the seam line – don't stitch into the seam allowance, because you will end up with different sized blocks. You also may need to trim seams later to eliminate bulk.

London Stairs

If you do not unpick and rearrange some of the 'bricks' before you sew the rows together, you will get a repeating steps pattern that is known as London Stairs.

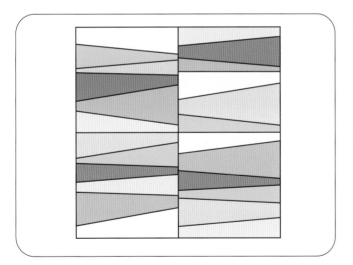

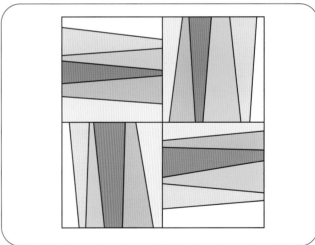

String piecing 1

There are often odd-shaped strips of fabric left over after the rotary cutting of fabric, and string piecing is a great way to use these up. Sew the strips together along their long edges to make a pieced fabric. Press the seams to one side, then cut square blocks from the pieced fabric, which can be arranged in various ways – including this Four-Patch design.

String piecing 2

If you rotate the square string-pieced blocks, the effect achieved is a random version of Rail Fence.

Log Cabin

This is probably one of the most commonly made pieced patterns of all time. It is simple enough to be suitable for a beginner, but its endless possible variations mean that it is also a great favourite with more expert quilters. The central square is traditionally made in a bright fabric, usually red, and represents the hearth, around which 'logs' are stitched.

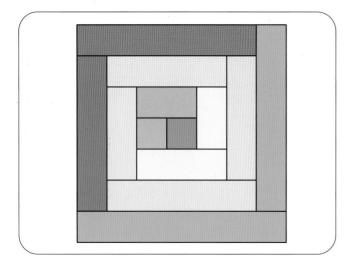

Making a Log Cabin basic block

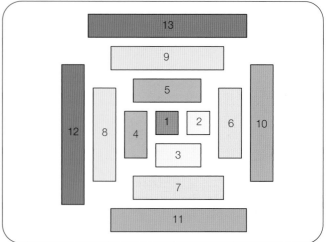

1 Cut strips of a selection of light and dark fabrics, all of an equal width. The central square is cut the same width as the strips. Place the central square, then cut another square the same size in light fabric, which will be strip 2. Strip 3 (light) and strip 4 (dark) are both twice the depth of strip 2; strip 5 (dark) and strip 6 (light) are three times the depth. Continue around in this way in a clockwise direction, so all the light strips are on one side of the block and all the dark strips on the other. Use 5mm (¼in) seams throughout, and press the seams in the same direction.

Log Cabin basic block setting patterns

One of the reasons that Log Cabin is so popular is that the basic block can be set in so many different ways, which often creates unusual and beautiful secondary patterns.

A few of the more traditional setting patterns for this block are shown here and on the following pages, but the design possibilities are almost endless!

pieced quilts

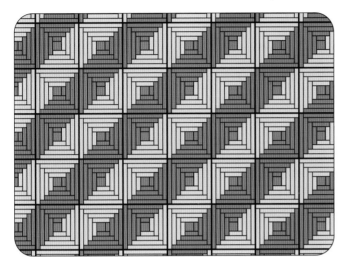

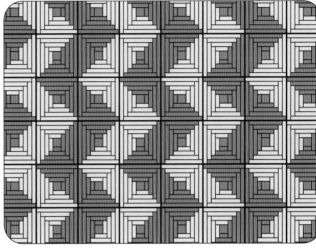

Straight Furrow

This setting creates strong diagonal stripes running across the quilt, reminiscent of the shadows and highlights created by light slanting across a ploughed field.

Streak of Lightning

Zigzag lines look like streaks of lightning. If the zigzags change direction halfway across, the pattern is known as Zigzags and Diamonds, while if they run across the quilt it creates a design called Rippling Waters.

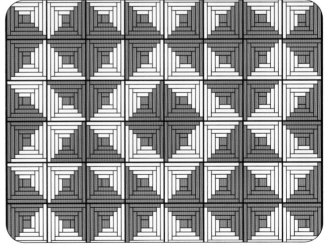

Steps

There are many different steps patterns – this one is probably the simplest and creates a strong chevron design.

Diamond Star

A combination of zigzags with a central diamond creates the Diamond Star pattern.

Sunshine and Shadow

Also known as Light and Dark, the effect of this simple pattern can be changed simply by altering which row of blocks comes first. Decide on the border by choosing whether dark or light half-blocks come at the edges; light ones will create a light border all around, dark ones a dark border.

Light and Dark Diamonds

This pattern can be read in many ways, but basically it shows alternating light and dark diamonds.

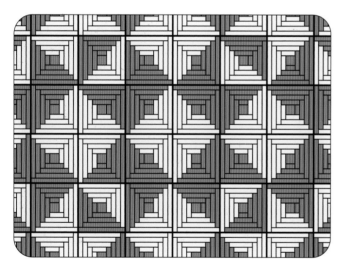

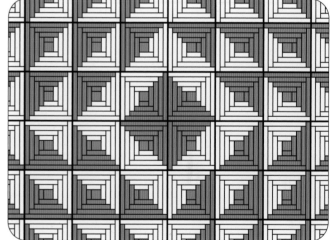

Log Cabin Star

Here a central cross of complete diamonds is surrounded by more fragmented shapes.

Scintillating Diamond

The shape of the central diamond is echoed towards the edges of the quilt, like ripples spreading outwards.

Barn Raising

Concentric diamond-shaped rows create the classic Barn Raising pattern. Note that the central diamond is dark.

Hole in the Barn Door

This is basically the same design as Barn Raising, but since the central diamond is light, it is known as Hole in the Barn Door.

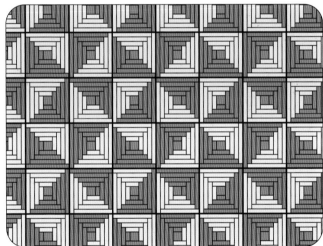

Maltese Barn Raising

A variation of the traditional Barn Raising pattern, in which the strong shape of the diagonal lines is broken by adding a dark edge all around the basic block.

Pinwheel

If the blocks are set with light and dark sides alternating, a rotating pinwheel effect is created. There are many variations that can be created around this theme.

Log Cabin Courthouse Steps

The variation known as Courthouse Steps has the lights and darks arranged opposite each other. The centre can have three identical squares, or a different central square flanked by two the same.

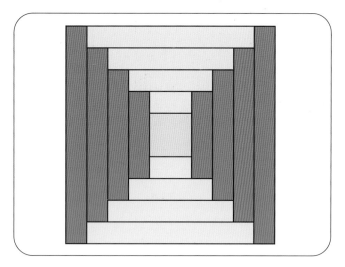

Making a Courthouse Steps block

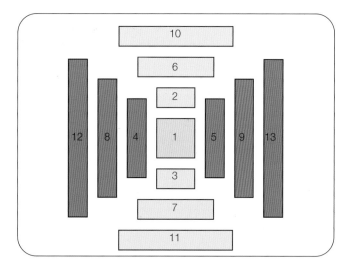

1 Cut strips of a selection of light and dark fabrics, all of an equal width. The central square is cut the same width as the strips. Place the central square, then cut another two squares the same size in light fabric, which will be strips 2 and 3 (light) above and below the central square. Strips 4 and 5 (dark) are both three times the depth of the central square and go on either side. Strips 6 and 7 (light) are also three times the depth of the central square and go above and below. Continue in this way, so the lights are above and below the central square and the darks are on either side. Use 5mm (¼in) seams throughout.

Courthouse Steps setting patterns

The Courthouse Steps block is very linear, so it lends itself to being set in columns. It also combines very well with the basic Log Cabin block – see pages 113–14 for some examples of this.

Variation 1

Here the blocks are set with the light strips arranged vertically and horizontally in alternate vertical columns.

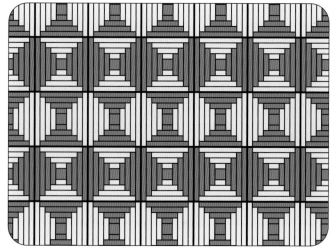

Variation 2

Here the blocks are set with the light strips arranged vertically and horizontally in alternate horizontal columns.

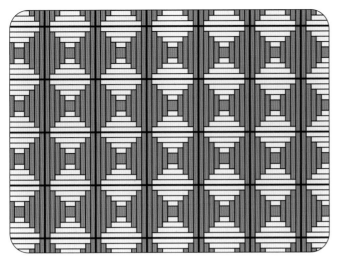

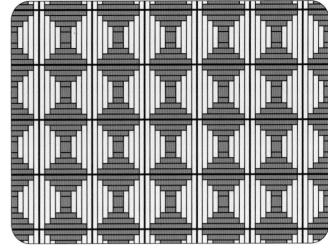

Variation 3

Making the blocks with a centre square in the same colour as strips 4 and 5, and setting them running in the same direction, gives a chequerboard effect.

Variation 4

This is similar to Variation 3, but the centre square here is the same colour as strips 2 and 3, which creates a more linear feel.

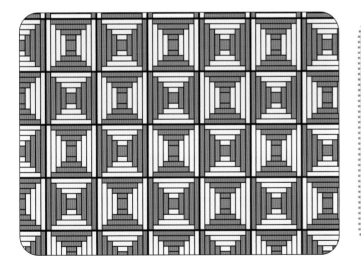

Pressing blocks

To help square up a skewed block, you can carefully steam-press it; by the same token a damp block will stretch out of shape more easily, so take care when using steam.

In general, press seam allowances towards the darkest fabric to prevent them showing through on the right side.

Variation 5

Here the blocks are alternately vertical and horizontal, which creates interesting secondary patterns.

Log Cabin Pineapple

Also known as Windmill Blades, this pattern starts with the central square, which can also be set on point. The 'logs' may begin as triangles, and then lengthen into strips with 45° angled ends. The placement of the colours can completely change the effect achieved, as shown in the two different examples below.

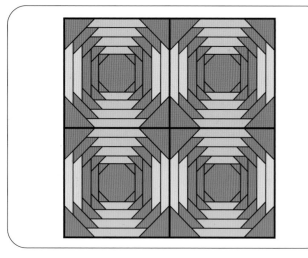

Pineapple basic block

Here the horizontal 'logs' are all the same colour, but the vertical 'logs' are in two colours, breaking up the lines of the pattern that will be achieved when the blocks are set. See the Octagon Pineapple for an example of what the pattern might look like if both diagonal and horizontal 'logs' are made in the same colour.

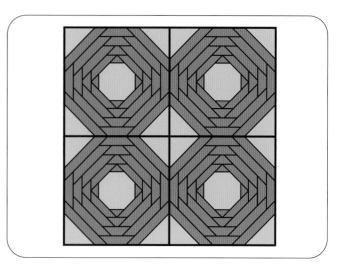

Octagon Pineapple block

Using only two colours, as here, destroys the linear effect and creates a repeating octagonal pattern.

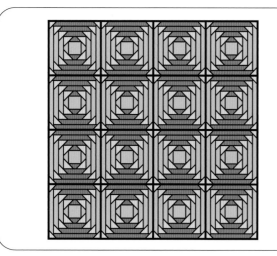

Flying Geese Pineapple block 1

Adding Flying Geese triangles to the Pineapple basic block adds another layer of complexity to the design, creating a chequerboard effect outlined by a line of contrasting colour.

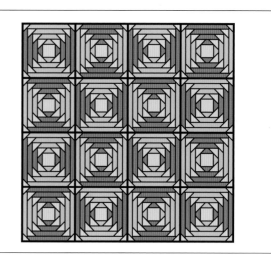

Flying Geese Pineapple block 2

In this example, the blocks are made in exactly the same way as in Flying Geese Pineapple block 1, except the central square is in the same colour as the Flying Geese triangles and the blocks are set with light and dark alternating to highlight the diagonal trellis.

Other Log Cabin block designs

There are many other Log Cabin block designs, some of which can be used on their own; others are usually combined with other blocks to add an extra effect to the setting pattern.

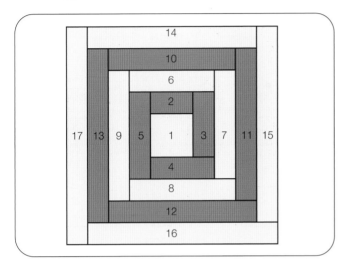

Cabin in the Cotton

This is constructed in the same way as the basic Log Cabin block, but the light and dark 'logs' radiate out from the centre in concentric squares.

Thick and Thin

Also known as Off-Centre Log Cabin, here the starting square is placed off centre and the strips are wide on one side and narrow on the other. These blocks can be set in all the standard patterns, but the effect achieved is very different.

Chimneys and Cornerstones

In this variation of Log Cabin, a small square is added to every alternate strip before it is attached, creating a diagonal line of squares across the block.

Other Log Cabin block shapes

When making a Log Cabin block, you do not have to start with a square. Using another geometric shape can give very interesting and unusual results, but the range of setting patterns that can be utilized can become a little more limited.

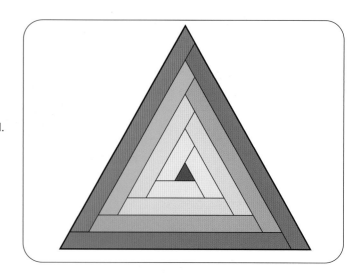

Equilateral Triangle

A difficult block to construct, as at least two of the edges will be cut on the bias. Since the triangle has an uneven number of sides, 'logs' must be added in sequence – either clockwise or anticlockwise.

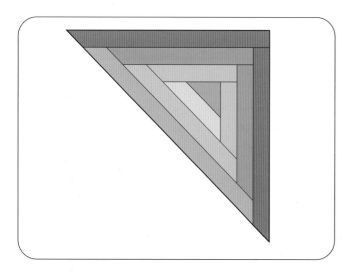

Right-Angled Triangle

With this triangle, two edges can be cut on the straight grain, which makes the shape more stable. Two of these blocks can be combined to make a square.

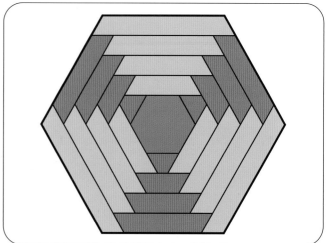

Hexagon

Another challenging block to work, as only two sides can possibly lie on the straight grain. However, the even number of sides means you can work around in sequence, or from side to side. Hexagonal blocks can be set alone, or with equilateral triangles or diamonds as spacer blocks.

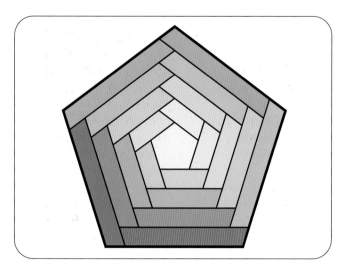

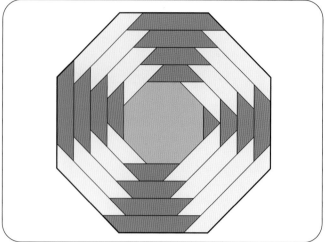

Pentagon

A very difficult block to set, since the pentagon does not combine that well with other geometric shapes, but it can be used to make unusual contemporary patterns. Again the uneven number of sides means that the 'logs' can only be added in sequence.

Octagon

The even number of sides on an octagon means you can work around in sequence, or from side to side. Octagons work well set alone, but can also be combined with squares set on point.

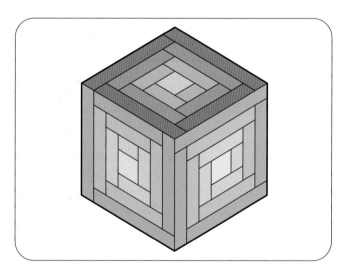

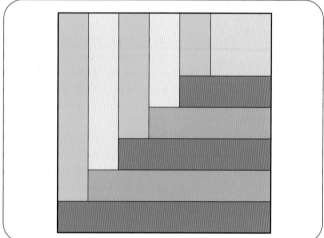

Diamond

Diamond Log Cabin blocks can be used together to make any setting pattern that uses diamonds. 'Logs' can be added in sequence, or on opposite sides.

Chevron

Also known as Half-Log Cabin, here the starting square is placed in one corner and the 'logs' are only added on two sides. The light can be on one side and the dark on the other, as shown here, or they can be in alternate rows.

Log Cabin combination setting patterns

Using more than one Log Cabin block design in a setting pattern adds even more possible variations.

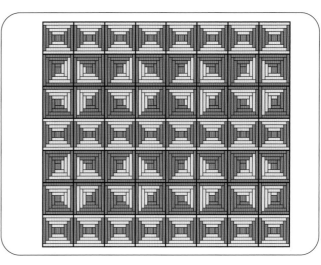

Justice
Courthouse Steps and Log Cabin basic block.

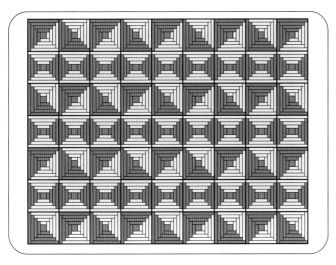

Totem Poles
Courthouse Steps and Log Cabin basic block.

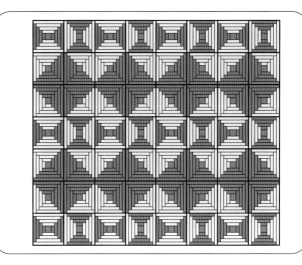

Bow Ties
Courthouse Steps and Log Cabin basic block.

Pressing rules

When you press seam allowances open it does decrease the strength of the piece; however, it will make it smoother, especially when the quilting stitches run parallel to the sewing stitches.

If you are using fabrics of different weights, turn the seam allowances towards the one that is lightest in weight to make the work smoother and more uniform.

Sometimes pressing rules contradict one another – trial and error or experience will tell you which rule to follow in a given situation.

Mexican Cross
Cabin in the Cotton and Log Cabin basic block, plus one-colour blocks.

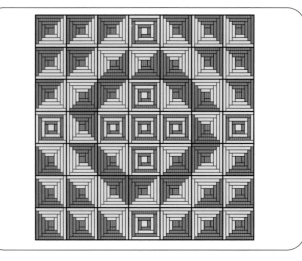

Space Flight
Cabin in the Cotton and Log Cabin basic block.

Square in a Square in a Square
Cabin in the Cotton and Log Cabin basic block.

Little and Large Diamonds
Courthouse Steps and Log Cabin basic block.

Cabin in the Cotton

The Cabin in the Cotton block (see page 109) is usually used in combination with other block patterns and is an excellent block to use to create some kind of balance in the overall quilt design.

Roman Stripe

Roman Stripe is a good block for beginners – it looks quite complex and you can make some great patterns with it, but it has no tricky points or angles to stitch. It is often found in Amish quilts – usually with a black or dark blue triangle and plain, brightly coloured stripes. Roman Stripe has many variations, some of which are shown here.

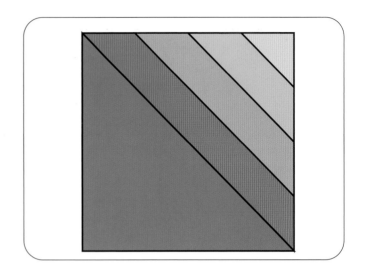

Making a Roman Stripe block

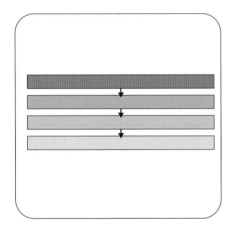

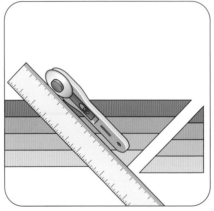

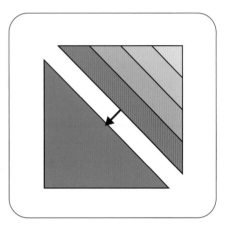

1 Cut strips of fabrics A, B, C and D to be used as the stripes, all of an equal width. Stitch them together along a long edge, using a 5mm (¼in) seam. Press all the seams in one direction.

2 Place the pieced strip (right side up) on a cutting mat. Measure and cut one end off at a 45° angle. Swing the ruler around and cut another 45° angle, creating a right-angled triangle. Cut a triangle the same size as this pieced triangle from a piece of plain fabric E.

3 Join the longest edge of the pieced triangle to the longest edge of the plain one. Remember that the edge of the plain one will be cut on the bias, so handle it with great care as you are stitching the seam.

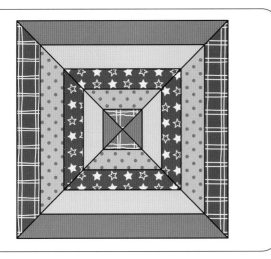

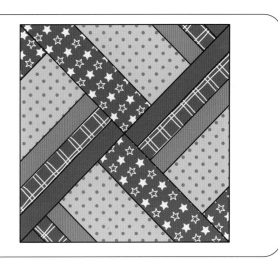

Mitred Triangle block

This block is made from two different pieced strips, which are cut into triangles as in the basic Roman Stripe block, but then pieced together without a plain triangle. It is trickier to make, as the stripes must be carefully matched and mitred at the seams to get the right effect.

Pinwheel Triangles

For this block, again start by joining strips of fabric as for Roman Stripe, but then cut the pieced strip into two squares. Cut each square across diagonally to create four right-angled triangles, then piece the triangles together alternately with the right angle in the centre.

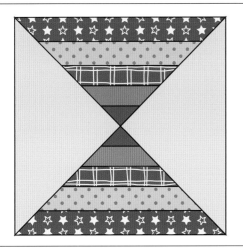

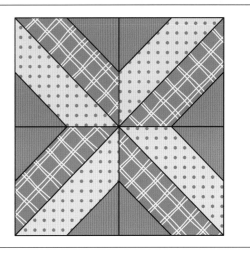

Triangle block

The elements of this block are the same as in the basic Roman Stripe, but you need two striped triangles and two plain. This block can be set to create alternate striped and plain squares, or with alternate blocks rotated to make a pattern of triangles.

King's Cross

This block is more complex than it looks, as it is made of eight triangles, each pieced in two fabrics. In each case the apex of the triangle is in the same fabric, but there are two different fabrics for the stripe. Two different triangles are stitched together along their longest edge to make a square, then the squares are put together like a Four-Patch block (see pages 124–25).

Seminole

Traditional Seminole work dates from the early twentieth century, originally made by the women of the Seminole tribe of Native Americans based in Florida. Its key features are plain, bright colours pieced together into stripes, which are then cut and rotated to make a range of geometric patterns. Seminole designs were originally used on skirts and bags rather than quilts, and even today they are rarely used over an entire quilt – but the technique is often used to make beautiful and complex-looking pieced borders.

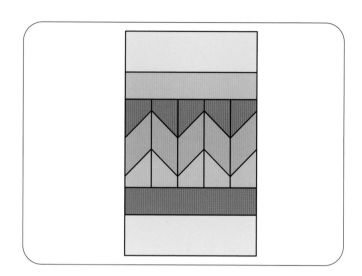

Making a Seminole block

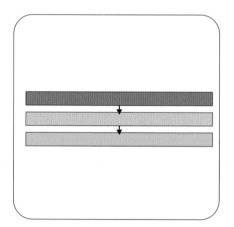

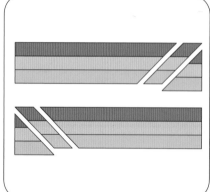

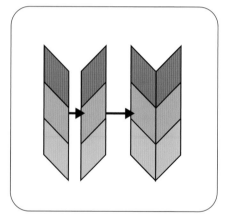

1 Cut strips of three brightly coloured fabrics, A, B and C, all of an equal width. Stitch the strips together along the longest edges, using a 5mm (¼in) seam. Press the seams in one direction. Make a second pieced strip with the fabrics in exactly the same order.

2 Cut the end of the first pieced strip at a 45° angle at the right-hand end, then cut at the same angle at intervals along the length to create several equal lengths. Cut the second strip at a 45° angle at the opposite end, then cut at the same angle at intervals along the length to create several equal lengths.

3 Take one length from each strip, pair them up with right sides together and with colours matching, and then stitch together along the longest edge. Repeat with all the lengths, then stitch the pairs together to create a row with a chevron pattern.

Seminole work

Since the pieces of fabric used are quite small and are cut apart at an angle, Seminole work is usually made in plain bright colours, although very small print designs are sometimes used.

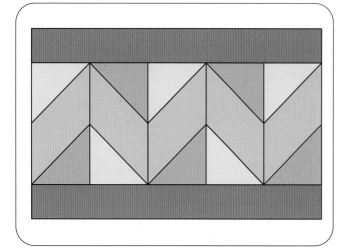

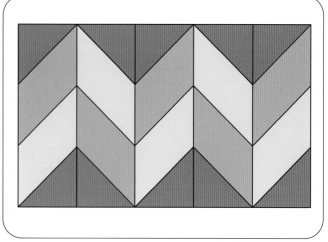

Single Chevron

Although it looks quite different, this design has been created exactly the same way as in the steps opposite, but the two lengths are rotated alternately so the darker colour is first at the bottom and then at the top. This makes the central zigzag much more prominent.

Double Chevron

This block uses four fabrics, with the same one used both top and bottom. When the lengths are rotated alternately this time, the central diagonal lines create a chequerboard design.

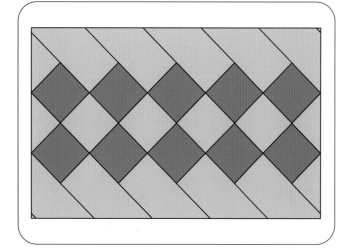

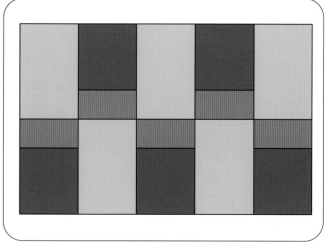

Diamonds

To make this design, cut two wide strips in the main fabric, then three narrow strips, one in the main fabric and two in the contrast fabric. Piece the strips together so the two wide strips are at the ends and the three narrow ones alternate in the middle. Square off one end of the pieced strip, then slice off lengths that are each the same width as one of the inner stripes. Piece these lengths together, staggering the central squares, then turn so the squares are on point and trim across all the edges to square up the block.

Steps

This simple, but effective pattern is made by piecing three strips of fabric of different widths. Slice the pieced strip into lengths, then alternate the lengths to create the stepped pattern and stitch together again.

Nine-Patch

There are perhaps more patterns based on Nine-Patch than on any other block, because it offers a wide variety of possible combinations. It can either be strip-pieced – as shown here – or made from individual squares as shown for Four-Patch on pages 124–25. The way the colours are placed can change the look entirely, and it is an ideal block to make to use up odd scraps of fabric.

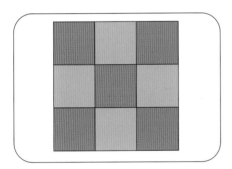

Making a Nine-Patch block

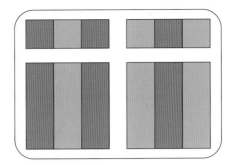

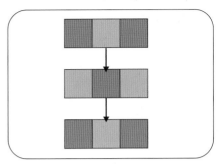

1 Cut three strips each of fabrics A and B, making each strip one-third of the finished block width plus 1cm (½in) for seam allowances. Take two strips of A and one of B and piece together alternately. Piece together the remaining three strips; you should now have two pieced strips, one ABA and the other BAB. Stitch the sets of three strips together along the long edge, using a 5mm (¼in) seam. Press seams to one side. Cut both of the finished pieced strips into rows, with each row one-third of the finished block width plus 1cm (½in) for seam allowances.

2 Take two rows from the first pieced strip and one from the second, and lay them in alternate order. Stitch the rows together with a 5mm (¼in) seam.

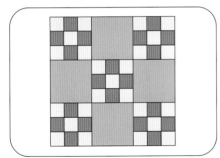

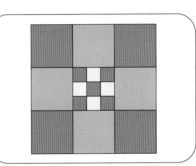

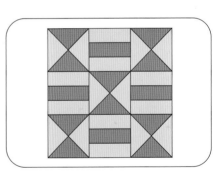

Double Nine-Patch

This Nine-Patch within a Nine-Patch is made of five small Nine-Patch blocks joined together in a large Nine-Patch block, with plain squares in between. When several of these blocks are set together, the small squares create a diagonal grid across the quilt. See also Irish Chain on pages 122–23.

Double Nine-Patch Variation

A simpler version of the block above: this one has a single small Nine-Patch block at the centre of a larger Nine-Patch. This creates a diminishing perspective effect, in which the larger cross is echoed in the smaller one.

Chain and Hourglass

In this more complex Nine-Patch, five of the squares are small Triangle blocks as seen on page 156, while the other four are single squares from Rail Fence, as seen on pages 98–99. When viewed horizontally, the pattern looks like rows of offset chains; when viewed vertically you can see offset hourglasses.

Irish Chain

Despite its name, this pattern almost certainly did not originate in Ireland, but it has been very popular in Britain and America since the eighteenth century. It has many variations including Double Irish Chain, which is illustrated opposite. It is constructed from two different blocks, one pieced and the other much plainer.

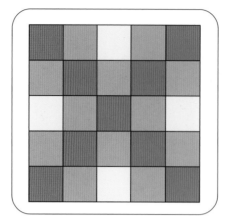

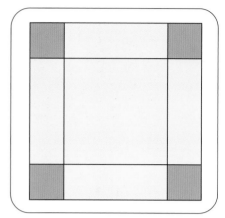

Making Double Irish Chain blocks

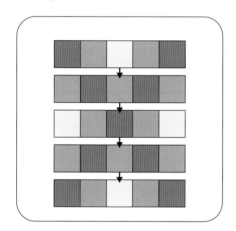

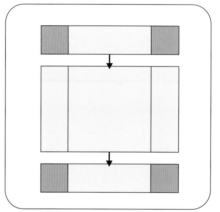

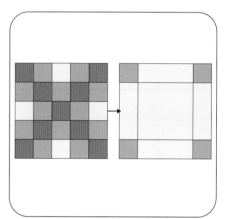

1 Cut strips of fabrics A, B and C, each one-fifth the width of the finished block plus 1cm (½in) for seam allowances. Join the strips together with 5mm (¼in) seams, working in three different orders: ABCBA, BABAB and CBABC. Cut each pieced strip into rows one-fifth the width of the finished block plus 1cm (½in) for seam allowances. Stitch five rows together in the order shown, with 5mm (¼in) seams.

2 Cut a centre square from fabric C that is three-fifths the width of the finished block plus 1cm (½in) for seam allowances. Cut four strips from fabric C, each one-fifth the width of the finished block plus 1cm (½in) for seam allowances, and a length equal to three-fifths the width of the finished block plus 1cm (½in) for seam allowances. Cut four squares from fabric B, one-fifth the width of the finished block plus 1cm (½in) for seam allowances. Join these pieces into rows as shown, using a 5mm (¼in) seam, and then into a block.

3 Join the pairs of blocks together using a 5mm (¼in) seam, matching seams carefully across the join.

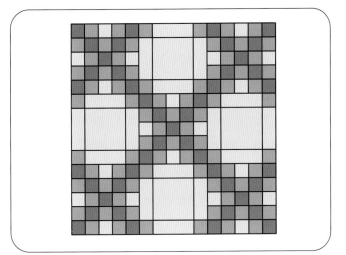

Double Irish Chain

When the blocks shown in the steps are joined together in a traditional Double Irish Chain pattern, a diagonal grid of chains begins to develop across the quilt.

Single Irish Chain

Here the second block is a plain square with no piecing, and the pieced block is only made in two colours. The plain block is ideal for quilting.

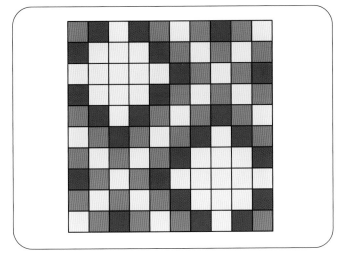

Triple Irish Chain

An even more intricate version, in which the second block is pieced in three colours. The chains are much more complex, but the pieced second block is harder to quilt.

Planning an Irish Chain quilt

When making an Irish Chain quilt, remember that you are using two different blocks to make up the pattern, so you will need to plan the quilt using an odd number of blocks both across and down to make sure the design is centred on the quilt. The four corner blocks must be the same pattern, and there should be one block at the centre.

squares and triangles

Squares are the basis for some of the oldest patchwork patterns and are as simple to work as strips, since again you are only working with straight seams. If you cut a square in half diagonally you get a right-angled triangle, and many traditional patterns are based on these two shapes, either used alone or combined.

Four-Patch

The Four-Patch design is very straightforward and easy to make, but it can be made to look very different depending on the placement of the fabrics and the way the blocks are pieced together. The squares can be combined as shown here, or using the strip-piecing method illustrated for the Nine-Patch block on page 121.

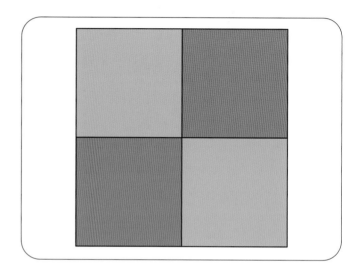

Making a Four-Patch block

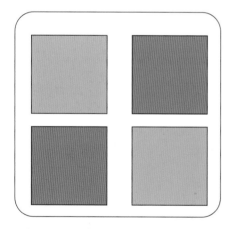 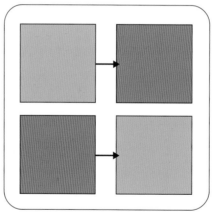 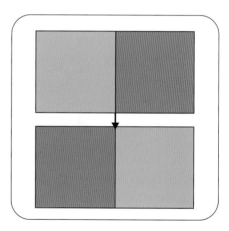

1 Cut two equal sized squares in each of fabrics A and B.

2 Use a 5mm (¼in) seam and join each A square to a B square.

3 Matching the centre seam carefully, join the two pairs together, with A next to B.

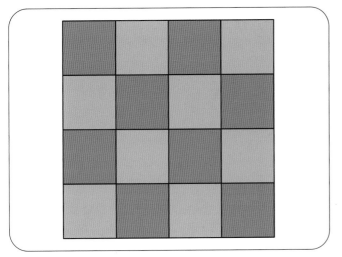

Double Four-Patch

Also known as Sixteen-Patch, this block is created by joining four Four-Patch blocks. If you use two contrasting colours the effect created will be a chequerboard, as here, but if the colours tone the result will be more like a Mosaic pattern (see pages 146–51).

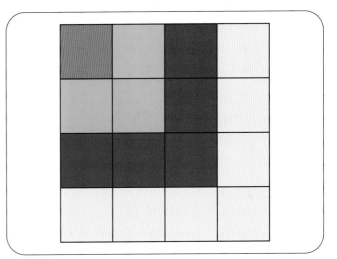

Double Four-Patch Variation

This block uses four different fabrics, but contains only two different Four-Patch designs. The top left and bottom right are the same layout – each has a square in one fabric combined with three others in a different fabric. The other two Four-Patch blocks are identical – just rotated. The block can be set in several ways: in lines, creating a series of chevrons; in rotation to make concentric squares; or on point to look like an abstract flower. If you add plain squares, the possibilities multiply further.

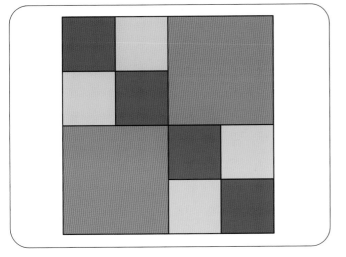

Four-Patch and Squares

This simple, but effective block is made from two Four-Patch squares joined with two plain squares. The use of plain squares in the design creates a perfect space for quilting motifs.

Working with Four-Patch

Four-Patch may look quite simple, but a large number of much more intricate designs are based upon it. The individual squares can be made up using combinations of other shapes, as in Broken Dishes and its variations (see pages 128–29) and Drunkard's Path patterns (see pages 162–63).

Friendship Star

Although at first glance this block looks quite complex, in fact it is a simple variation on the standard Nine-Patch. It is made of squares and right-angled triangles, so it is easy to cut the shapes. Depending on how the fabrics are placed within the design, the result can look quite different.

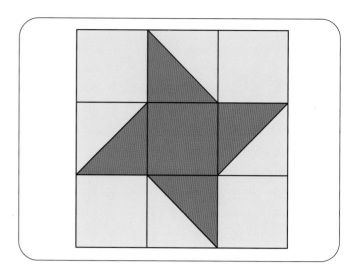

Making a Friendship Star block

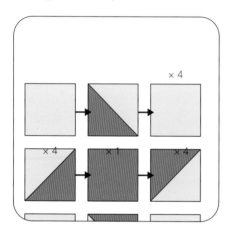

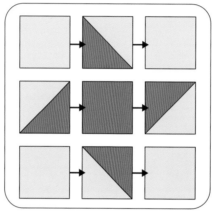

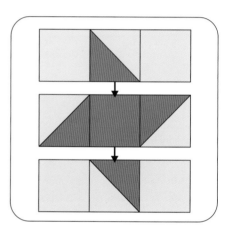

1 Cut two squares of fabric A and two of B, and cut them in half diagonally to get four right-angled triangles in each fabric. Take one A triangle and one B triangle and join them along the diagonal, using a 5mm (¼in) seam. Repeat with the other triangles to make four triangle squares. Use one completed unit as a template to cut four plain squares the same size from fabric A and one from fabric B.

2 Arrange the squares as shown above. Stitch the top row of three together, using a 5mm (¼in) seam, then stitch the middle and bottom rows in the same way. Press seams to one side.

3 Match the seams across the rows and then stitch the three rows together, again using a 5mm (¼in) seam.

Triangle squares

For a quick method of making triangle squares, see the technique in steps 1 and 2 on page 128.

When using shapes with points, completely accurate measuring and stitching is absolutely essential. See page 93 for instructions on joining plain and pieced units.

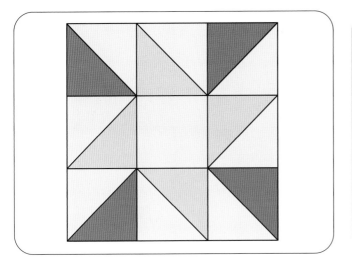

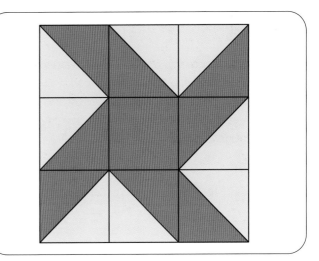

Nine-Patch Star

This block is made in the same way as shown in the steps opposite, but the four corner squares are pieced using a contrasting third fabric, which gives a lively rotating effect.

Box or Formal Garden

Formal gardens were once divided up with low box hedges, which perhaps explains how this block got its alternative names. It is made in exactly the same way as the Nine-Patch Star, but using only two fabrics instead of three.

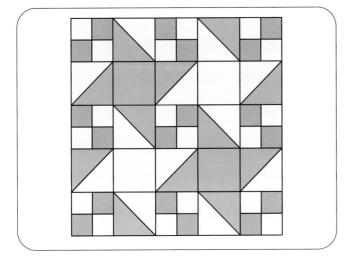

Milky Way

Although this design may look like a series of simple Friendship Star blocks just pieced together, in fact it is much more complex. The stars share their corner blocks, which are pieced as Four-Patch blocks and run in alternate directions. You could make a series of Friendship Star blocks with Four-Patch corners and then join them with strips made of a triangle block + plain block + triangle block + centre star block, repeating this sequence as required.

Alternatively, you could make up lots of Four-Patch and triangle squares and then assemble the whole quilt in rows, adding the plain squares and centre star squares as required for the design.

Broken Dishes

This block is based on a simple Four-Patch. Traditionally, four of the units shown here are joined together to make one big block and then this block is set alternately with a plain one the same size. If several tones of the same two colours are used, a gloriously fragmented effect can be achieved.

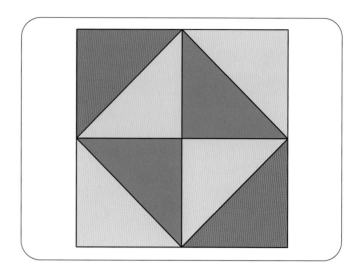

Making a Broken Dishes block

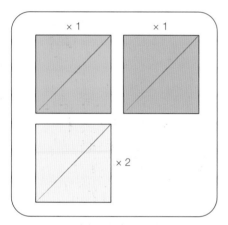

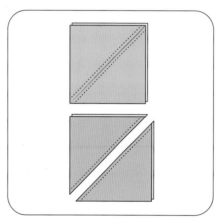

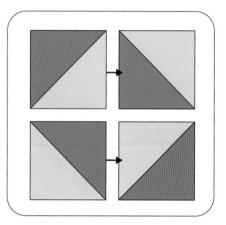

1 For each block cut one square each of fabrics A and B, and two squares of fabric C. Mark a diagonal line on the wrong side of all the blocks, being careful not to stretch the fabric out of shape on the bias.

2 With right sides together, place a square of A on top of one square of C, and a square of B on top of the other square of C, matching the diagonal lines. Stitch 5mm (¼in) away from the line down one side, then turn and come back 5mm (¼in) away down the other side. Cut along the diagonal line between the two lines of stitching, then press the triangle squares flat with the seams to one side.

3 Take two of the triangle squares, one with fabric A and one with fabric B, and join them together as shown. Repeat with the other two triangle squares. Matching seams, join the two pairs together into a block.

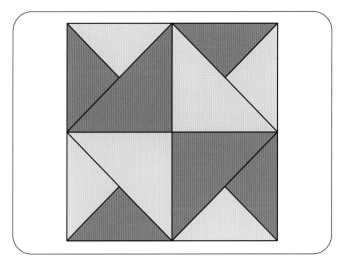

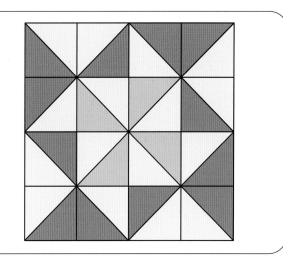

Southern Belle

This lively design has a centre made in exactly the same way as a basic Broken Dishes block. However, the outer triangles are further divided into smaller right-angled triangles, which gives the block a sense of rotating movement.

Peace and Plenty

This design is a variation of Broken Dishes and is made of a series of triangle squares in exactly the same way. The central block uses slightly different fabrics, which have been set in a Pinwheel (see pages 130–31).

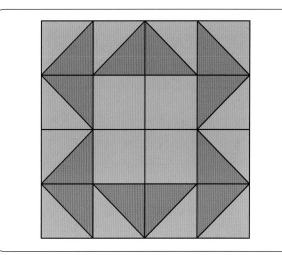

Fancy Stripe

This is a very simple block to piece because it is made up of sixteen identical triangle squares – the square design is created entirely by the way the squares are combined. If set as a square, the corner triangles will combine to make further small squares. Alternatively, it can be set on point, as illustrated here, combined with spacer triangles.

Buzzard's Roost

The centre of this block is made of four plain squares, but apart from this it uses triangle squares. When set in rows, the dark triangles at the sides will combine to make squares set on point.

Pinwheel

The triangles in this Four-Patch block are set so they rotate around the centre, creating a block called Pinwheel, Windmill, or Flutter Blades. The design is always full of movement and vitality and can be set in several different ways. There are also many possible variations on the basic block, which makes it popular with quilters.

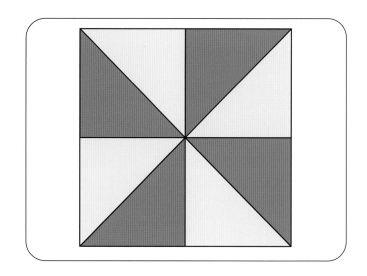

Making a Pinwheel block

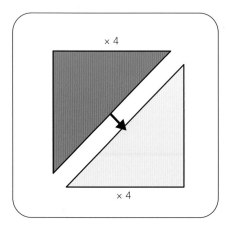

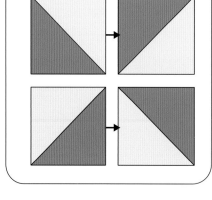

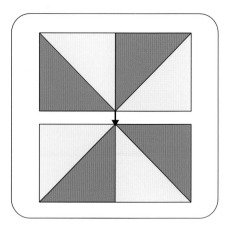

1 Cut two squares from fabric A and two from fabric B. Cut each in half along the diagonal to make four right-angled triangles in each fabric. Take one triangle of A and one of B and join along the diagonal, using a 5mm (¼in) seam. Press the seam to one side. Repeat with the other triangles.

2 Arrange the triangle squares so that the triangles rotate. Stitch the top two squares together, then stitch the bottom two together.

3 Match the seams carefully in the centre, and pin. Stitch the two rows together, stitching over the pin.

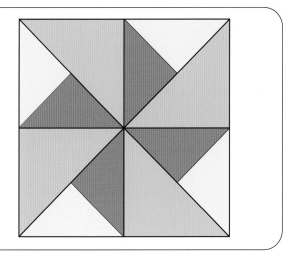

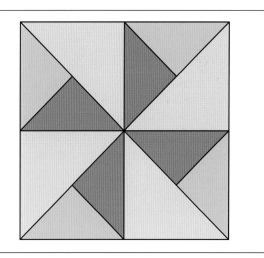

Double Pinwheel

The Double Pinwheel uses three fabrics and creates a spiral within a spiral. Each alternate blade is pieced from two triangles – here the dark fabric used for the inner blade is quite dominant, but if the larger blade were in the deeper colour, the block would look quite different. There is a variation on this block called Turnstile: in this the large blades and the outer triangles are in the same colour.

Broken Pinwheel

This block – a variation of Double Pinwheel – is made with the outer triangles and small blades alternating dark and light. The easiest way to make these is to make two triangle squares with the two colours, and then cut each on the diagonal at right angles to the seam.

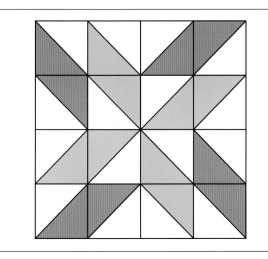

Creating Pinwheel blocks

The orientation of the triangles is critical when making the Pinwheel block and its variations. Lay out the pieces before beginning to stitch, and check the block as you work to make sure that the 'blades' are all rotating in the correct direction.

Trailing Star

Although it looks quite different, this block is yet another variation of the Pinwheel, made entirely of triangle squares. The outer blades add even more movement to the design.

Shoofly

The Shoofly block is a Nine-Patch variation made from squares and triangle squares, so it is a very easy block to piece. The plain squares are broken down further in some variations and it is also very effective set on point. It is a particularly popular block with Amish quiltmakers.

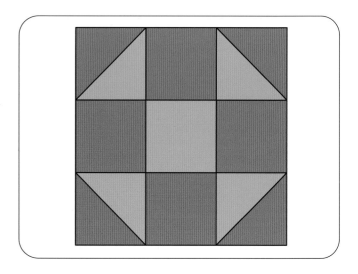

Making a Shoofly block

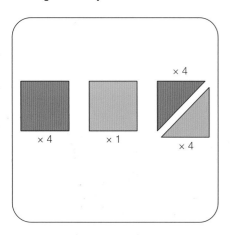

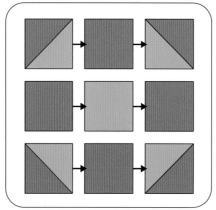

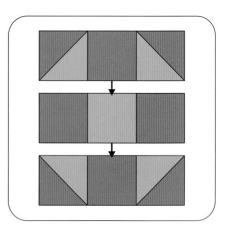

1 Cut two squares from fabric A and two from fabric B. Cut each in half along the diagonal to make four right-angled triangles in each fabric. Take one triangle of A and one of B and join along the diagonal, using a 5mm (¼in) seam. Press the seam to one side. Repeat with the other triangles. Using one completed triangle square as a template, cut four squares the same size from fabric A and one from fabric B.

2 Place the nine squares in three rows, with the triangle squares in the corners and the square of fabric B in the centre. Join the squares into three rows using a 5mm (¼in) seam. Press all the seams to one side.

3 Matching the seams carefully, join the three rows into a block.

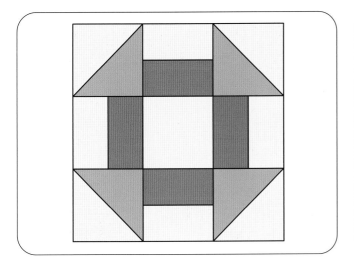

Churn Dash

This simple variation of Shoofly has the central squares on each side pieced from two equal-width strips of different fabrics.

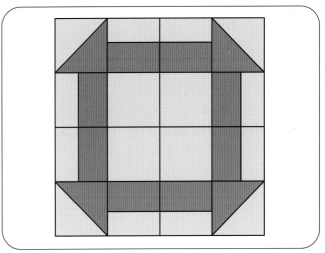

Hole in the Barn Door

A variation of Churn Dash, in which the central square is twice the size of the corner ones and the side units are elongated into rectangles. The central square offers an excellent area for a quilting motif.

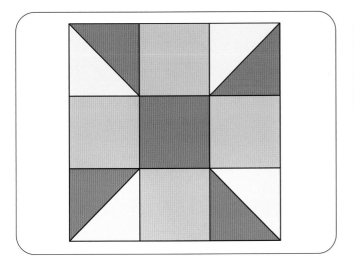

Calico Puzzle

Although this design looks quite different, it is constructed in exactly the same way as the Shoofly block, except that the corner triangle squares are rotated so the diagonal seam runs towards the centre.

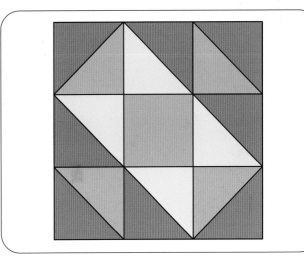

Box Kite

Here a third fabric is used to create triangle squares on each side, with diagonally opposite units mirroring each other to create the shape of a kite.

Maple Leaf

The shape of the maple leaf is very easy to create using triangles and there are many variations on this design. Although this shape may look quite complex to cut and stitch, in fact it is a simple Nine-Patch block constructed only of squares and triangles.

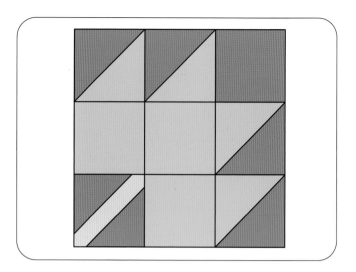

Making a Maple Leaf block

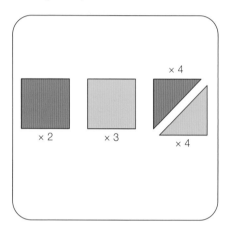

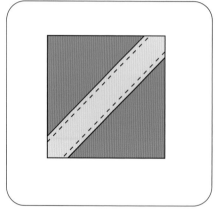

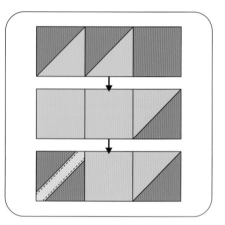

1 Cut two squares from fabric A and two from fabric B. Cut each in half along the diagonal to make four right-angled triangles in each fabric. Take one triangle of A and one of B and join along the diagonal, using a 5mm (¼in) seam. Press the seam to one side. Repeat with the other triangles. Using one finished triangle square as a template, cut two squares the same size from fabric A and three from fabric B.

2 Cut a narrow strip of fabric C, turn under the edges and stitch it diagonally across one of the squares of fabric A.

3 Place the nine squares in three rows as shown. Join the rows of squares using a 5mm (¼in) seam. Press the seams to one side. Matching the seams carefully, join the three rows into a block.

Maple Leaf design

If you set Maple Leaf blocks in different directions across a quilt, it will create an wonderful impression of windblown leaves.

The stem of the maple leaf can be made with a length of narrow ribbon instead of as shown in step 2 (you do not have to turn under the edges). You could also sew it using an embroidery stitch.

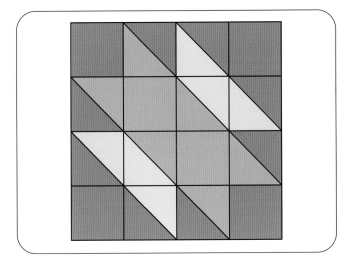

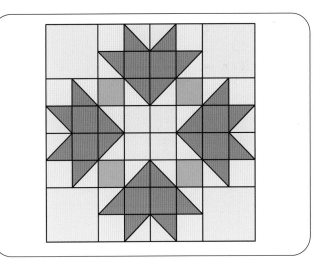

Anvil

This block contains sixteen squares: a mixture of plain squares and triangle squares, using three different fabrics. It can either be assembled in four rows of four, or as four Four-Patch blocks that are then stitched together.

Crow's Foot

This is quite a large basic block, but all the units are either plain squares or triangle squares, so it is easy to make. The corner squares can either be plain, as shown here, or pieced as Four-Patch blocks like the central square.

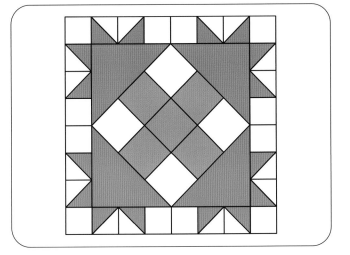

Lilies

Although the shape of the flowers looks similar to the Maple Leaf block, it is easier to make this block in a different way. First make a Nine-Patch block for the centre, turned on point, then add corner triangles to make it into a square. The outer units are alternate pairs of plain squares and triangle squares, with a single plain square in each corner. They are made up in rows and added around the outside of the block like a border.

Snail's Trail

One of the interesting features of this block is the visual effect of curving lines that is created purely by using larger and larger triangles spiralling out around the centre. It is most effective made in two highly contrasting fabrics, although some interesting variations occur when other colours are added.

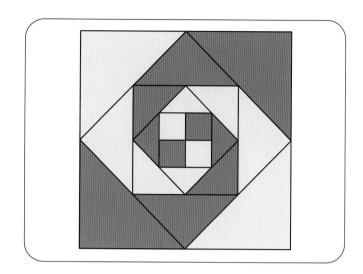

Making a Snail's Trail block

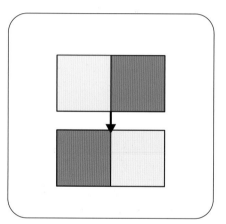

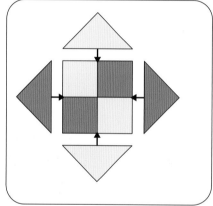

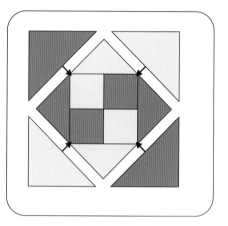

1 Cut two small squares from fabric A and two from fabric B. Stitch two different squares together, then stitch the units to one another to create a small Four-Patch block.

2 Cut a square of fabric A and of fabric B so the diagonal of each square is the length of the side of the Four-Patch block, plus 5mm (¼in) seam allowance. Cut the squares diagonally to make two right-angled triangles from each square. Add a triangle of fabric A at the top and bottom of the Four-Patch block. Add triangles of fabric B on each side.

3 Cut another square of fabric A and of fabric B so the diagonal of each square is the length of the side of the block made so far, plus 5mm (¼in) seam allowance. Cut the squares diagonally to make two right-angled triangles from each square. Add the next row of triangles, keeping both A and B triangles opposite each other. Carry on in this way, making the triangles bigger each time to match the sides of the block – the final block has four different sized triangles, with two of each size in each colour.

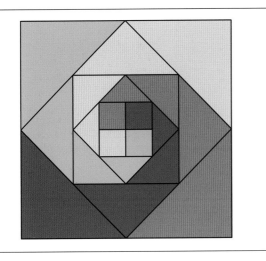

Monkey Wrench

This design uses four different colours, but is created in exactly the same way as Snail's Trail. When blocks like this are set, unusual secondary patterns can be created across the quilt.

Rough Sea

Although this pattern is constructed using the same principles as Snail's Trail, it uses a wider variety of shapes. The central square in each block is pieced from four triangles instead of four squares, and the next row of surrounding triangles is the same size. After that come alternate parallelograms and squares, finishing with triangles in each corner.

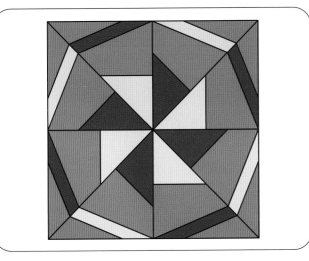

Wheel of Fortune

Although this block is not constructed in the same way as Snail's Trail, it shows another way in which straight-sided shapes can be used to suggest curves. It is made as a Four-Patch block (see pages 124–25) and uses four different shapes: two triangles, a trapezium and a narrow strip.

Working with Snail's Trail

The Snail's Trail block is great for beginners – although it may look as if it has very complex curves, it is only made up of squares and triangles so it is fairly simple to stitch.

A series of Snail's Trail blocks in just three colours set in a row would give a wonderful impression of breaking waves.

Jacob's Ladder

This is an ideal block for using up scraps of fabric, as the pieces required are small. Broken down into its component parts, the basic block is a Nine-Patch with each alternate square either a Four-Patch or a triangle square.

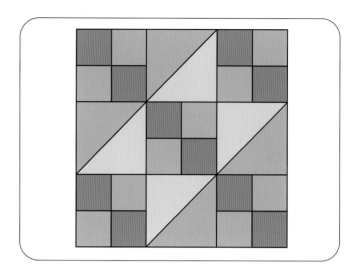

Making a Jacob's Ladder block

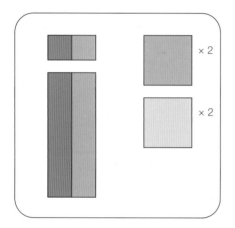

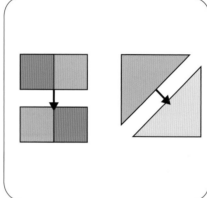

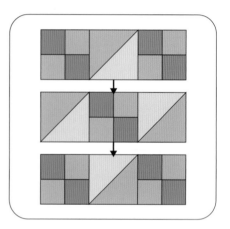

1 Cut equal-width strips of fabrics A and B. Stitch them together along their length using a 5mm (¼in) seam. Press the seam to one side. Cut the strip into ten two-patch units. Cut two squares from fabric B and two from fabric C. Cut each in half along the diagonal to make four right-angled triangles in each fabric.

2 Join pairs of two-patch units together to make five Four-Patch blocks. Take one triangle of A and one of B and join along the diagonal, using a 5mm (¼in) seam. Press the seam to one side. Repeat to make another three triangle squares.

3 Place the nine pieced squares in three rows, as indicated. Stitch the squares together into rows, and then stitch the rows into a square – matching seams and using 5mm (¼in) seams. Press seams to one side.

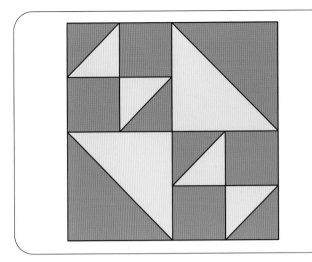

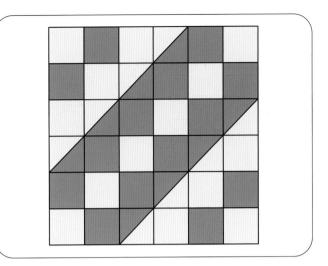

Crosses and Losses

This Double Four-Patch is made up of small squares and two different sizes of triangle square. The unusual name probably has biblical connections – many traditional patterns have names that reflect the importance of religion in the daily lives of the early colonists in North America.

Railroad

Although at first glance this block may look complicated, it is simply made of lots of plain squares with just eight triangle squares running diagonally across it in two parallel rows to create the railroad track effect.

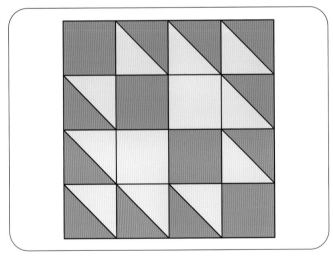

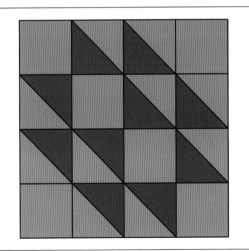

Double Cross

A Double Four-Patch block made of squares and triangle squares. Here, two opposite corner squares are triangle squares, but in a similar variation all four corner squares are plain squares.

Hovering Hawks

This block perhaps gets its name because the double triangles resemble the outstretched wings of a hovering bird. Most of the units are triangle squares, except for the four corner squares and the two in the centre.

Pine Tree

Motifs from nature, such as trees, flowers and leaves, have always been very popular with quilters. Tree motifs are perhaps some of the easiest to make in patchwork, as triangles can be put to use to suggest branches very effectively. The trunk can either be indicated by a square, or made in appliqué as in the Maple Leaf on pages 134–35.

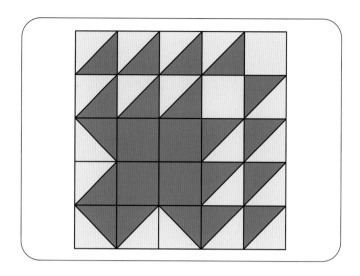

Making a Pine Tree block

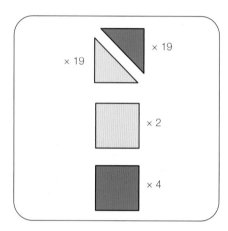

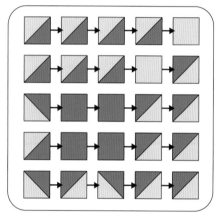

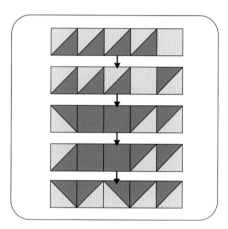

1 Cut ten squares from fabric A and ten from fabric B. Cut each in half along the diagonal to make twenty right-angled triangles in each fabric. You need nineteen for this block, so put one of each aside. Take one triangle of A and one of B and join along the diagonal, using a 5mm (¼in) seam. Press the seam to one side. Repeat with the other triangles. Using a finished triangle square as a template, cut two squares the same size from fabric A and four from fabric B.

2 Arrange the twenty-five squares in five rows of five, as indicated above. Stitch each row of five squares together into a strip, using a 5mm (¼in) seam. Press the seams in opposite directions on each row.

3 Matching the seam lines and points carefully, join the five rows together into a block.

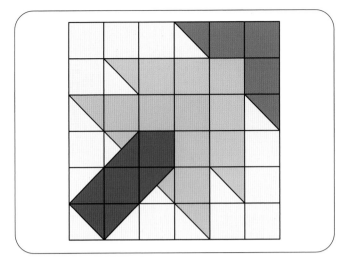

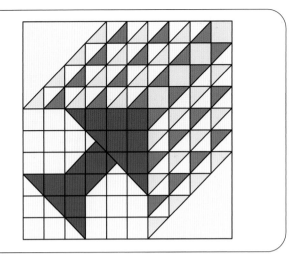

Tall Pine Tree

This pine tree is made using exactly the same principles as the basic Pine Tree block, using squares and triangles. Here, each layer of branches is in a different fabric, but they could all be made in a single fabric.

Tree of Paradise

This massive motif would work very well as the central motif in a simple quilt. It is made of squares and triangles as before, but with two larger triangles in opposite corners. The easiest way to make this design is to make the triangle squares first, then piece as much as possible in rows.

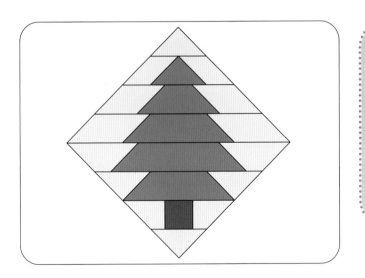

Setting tree blocks

To get the best tree effect, all these blocks should be set on point. If you set them square, the effect can still be very pleasing, but the design may look much more like an abstract pattern than a forest of trees.

Evergreen

This variation is not made of squares and triangles, but uses strips that are pieced and then cut down into a square. It must be set on point, either with lots of the same blocks to create a forest of trees, or with spacer triangles to make it into a square block.

Bow Tie

This is one block that really looks like its name and although it looks complex, it is made as a simple Four-Patch block. It looks most dramatic made only in two colours, as long as they contrast well, but effective designs can also be made with the bow tie part in different colours.

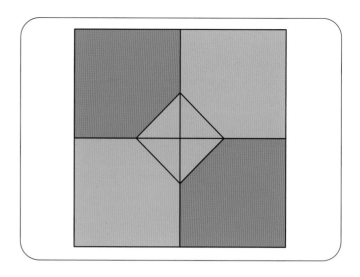

Making a Bow Tie block

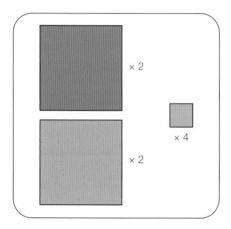

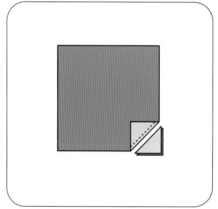

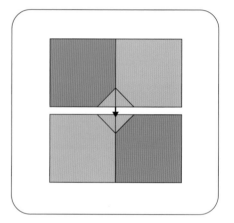

1 Cut two squares from fabric A and from fabric B, and four much smaller squares from fabric B. On the wrong side of the small squares, draw a diagonal line from one corner to the opposite corner.

2 Place one of the small squares over the corner of one of the large squares (right sides together). Stitch along the diagonal line marked in step 1. Trim off the corner close to the stitching, leaving a 5mm (¼in) seam allowance. Press the seam towards the centre. Repeat for the other three sets of squares.

3 Place the units so that the corner triangles are all in the centre, with the squares of fabric A diagonally opposite one another. Join as for a Four-Patch block (see pages 124–25), making sure that seams align and the points stay sharp.

Spare triangles

This method means you will trim off lots of small triangle pieces in step 2. Don't throw these away – you can use them to make a miniature quilt.

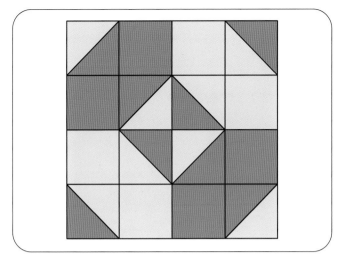

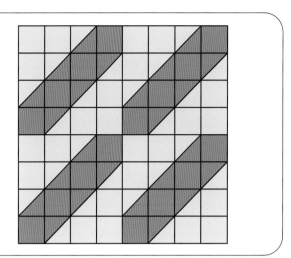

Robbing Peter to Pay Paul

This block name is used for several designs – it indicates that the shapes used are mirrored in contrasting colours for a positive/negative effect, rather than describing any particular pattern. The design shown here mirrors along both diagonals and is made of squares and triangles.

Indian Hatchet

This design, with its strong diagonal feel, is made of four Double Four-Patch blocks, each constructed of a series of squares and triangle squares.

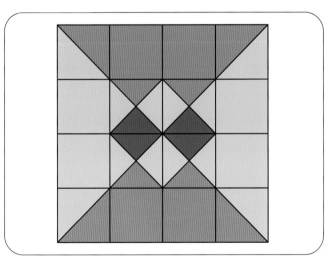

Granny's Choice

Although this looks very similar to a basic Bow Tie, this design is more complex and is constructed in a different way. The central Four-Patch has four squares pieced from quarter-triangles and set so the centre forms a square set on point. Around this is a border made up of plain squares and triangle squares.

Sawtooth

The jagged teeth of the Sawtooth block add a look of great complexity to any quilt design, but it is simply made from triangles and squares. In the example shown here, it is constructed as a Nine-Patch block, but the teeth can also be used to edge other shapes.

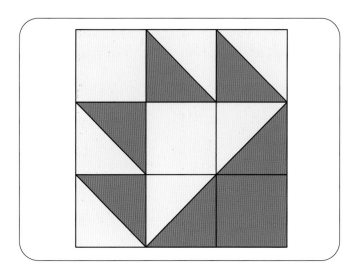

Making a Sawtooth block

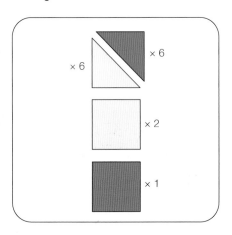

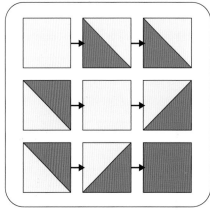

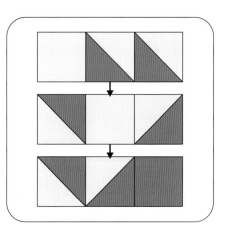

1 Cut three squares from fabric A and three from fabric B. Cut each in half along the diagonal to make six right-angled triangles in each fabric. Take one triangle of A and one of B and join along the diagonal, using a 5mm (¼in) seam. Press the seam to one side. Repeat with the other triangles. Using a finished triangle square as a template, cut two squares the same size from fabric A and one from fabric B.

2 Arrange the nine squares in three rows of three, as indicated above. Stitch each row of three squares together into a strip, using a 5mm (¼in) seam. Press the seams in opposite directions on each row.

3 Matching the seam lines and points carefully, join the three rows together into a block.

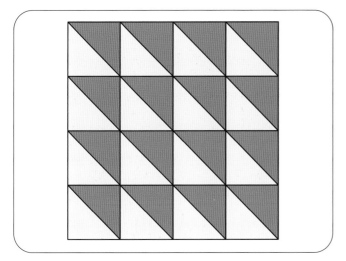

Sawtooth Rows

This design couldn't be simpler – it's just four identical rows of triangle squares. It would be an ideal design for using up scraps.

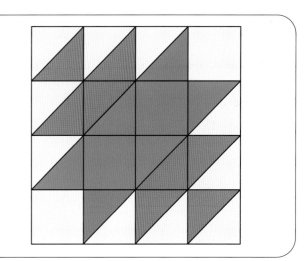

Mrs Taft's Choice

Helen 'Nellie' Taft was the wife of the twenty-seventh president of the United States, but it is unclear how this block came to be named after her. It is simply a Double Four-Patch (see page 125) made in three different fabrics.

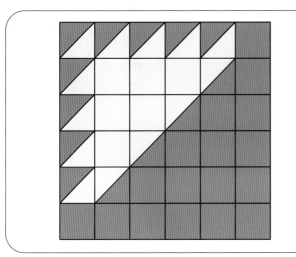

Sawtooth Four-Patch

This block can be constructed as a Four-Patch in which each Four-Patch block is a Nine-Patch, or could be assembled in strips. It would also be very effective set on point.

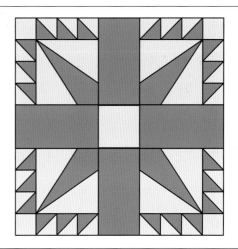

Old Star

The rather intricate design of this block means it would probably look best set with plain sashing. It could be constructed in several ways, but the simplest method is probably as a Nine-Patch with the sawtooth border added on.

mosaics

Ancient Roman and Greek mosaics were made in small pieces of stone, ceramic or glass, but the technique of combining small pieces to make something bigger is ideal for patchwork. Although mosaics can be used to create a pictorial scene, here we feature them as regular and repetitive patterns.

Grandmother's Flower Garden

The hexagon is one of the basic geometric shapes, and hexagons can easily be joined together without the need for spacer blocks – except perhaps at the outermost edges. The simplest method of working this shape is to use the English paper-piecing method (see page 90).

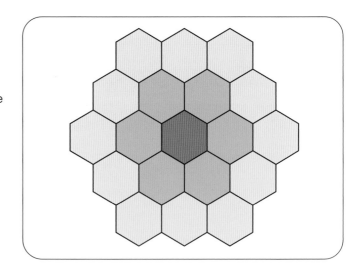

Making a Grandmother's Flower Garden block

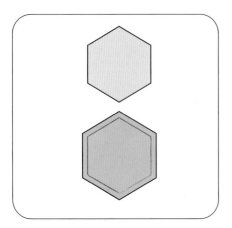

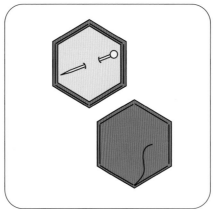

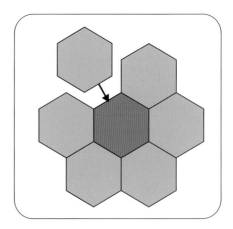

1 Use the hexagon template on page 172. Cut nineteen hexagons from paper, using the inner line of the hexagon. Using the outer line of the template, cut one hexagon in fabric A, six in fabric B and twelve in fabric C. Mark a 5mm (¼in) seam allowance on the wrong side of all the fabric pieces.

2 Pin a paper hexagon to the wrong side of each fabric hexagon. Fold the seam allowance marked on the fabric over the edge of the paper shape all around and press, then tack (baste) the fabric in position.

3 With the hexagon in fabric A at the centre, add a hexagon in fabric B to each side, whipstitching the seam. When all the hexagons are in place, whipstitch the seam between adjoining B hexagons. Repeat with the outer row of C hexagons.

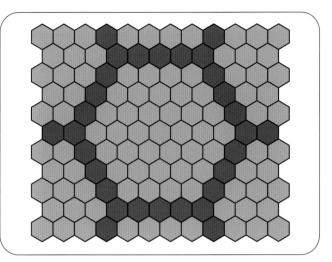

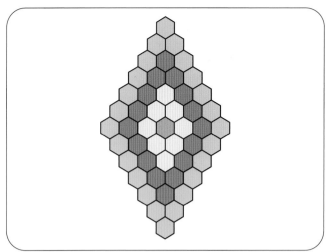

Hexagon Tile

In this design, the centre hexagon and the next three rows are the same colour, but the fourth row is a contrast colour, creating a trellis of hexagons across the quilt. A variation would be to work a Grandmother's Flower Garden block in the centre of each large outline hexagon.

Diamond

By changing the placement of different fabrics, the hexagon-shaped Grandmother's Flower Garden block can easily be extended into a diamond.

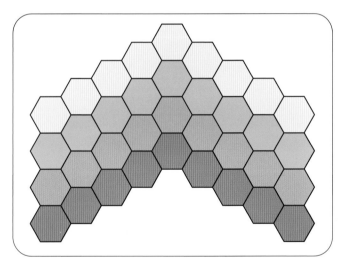

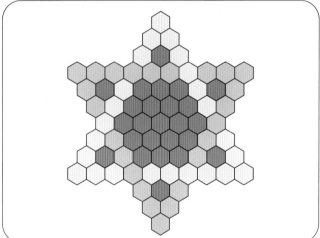

Ocean Wave

This name can be used for several designs, but here the rise and fall of waves is suggested by rows of different coloured hexagons that run upwards in rows to a peak, and then run back downwards again.

Hexagon Star

Here hexagons in three different fabrics are used to create a secondary pattern – an interlocking six-pointed star.

Postage Stamp

Traditionally, the Postage Stamp design is created from scraps, with the colours and patterns placed randomly. The technique shown here is for strip-piecing a random design. However, the tiny squares can also be arranged to create repeating patterns, as shown in the variations.

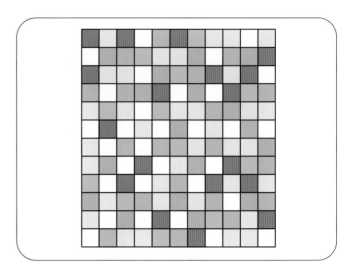

Making a Postage Stamp block

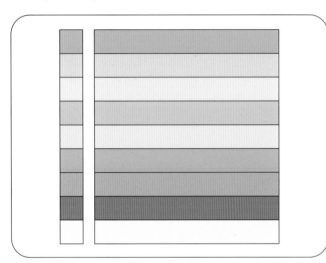

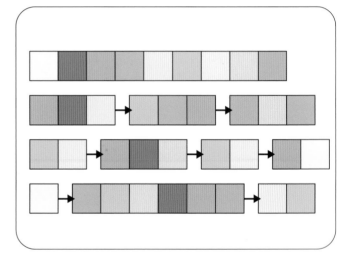

1 Cut narrow strips of nine different fabrics, all of an equal width. Stitch the strips together along their width, with a 5mm (¼in) seam allowance. Press all the seams to one side. Cut a length from one end of the pieced strips to get a row of equal sized squares. Repeat until you have nine rows of squares.

2 Lay the rows of squares next to one another. Cut some of the rows apart and rotate some sections until you have achieved a pleasing random effect. Stitch the cut rows back together again, then stitch the rows together, matching seams carefully, to create a block.

Making Postage Stamp designs

This design was very popular during the Great Depression in America in the 1930s, when the recycling of fabric scraps was a necessity.

You can make Postage Stamp by cutting lots of separate squares, stitching them in rows and then stitching all the rows together, but accurate cutting and seaming will be even more essential.

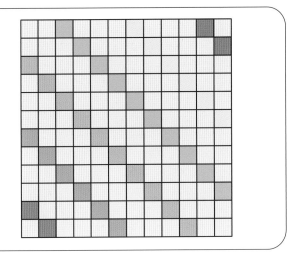

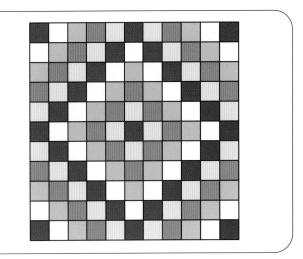

Kite Tails

This design can either be created using the strip-piecing method illustrated for the basic Postage Stamp block, or by joining the squares into rows and the rows into blocks. The kite tails would look even more effective – and reminiscent of their name – if they were against a pale blue background.

Trip Around the World

In this pattern, the lines of different fabrics radiate out from the centre. A variation of this pattern is Sunshine and Shadow, in which the tones vary from light to dark and back again. Both of these patterns are regularly used by Amish quiltmakers.

Tumbling Blocks

This pattern gives a strongly three-dimensional effect when made in dark, medium and light fabrics. It is also known as Baby Blocks and, like Grandmother's Flower Garden, is usually constructed using the English paper-piecing method (see page 90).

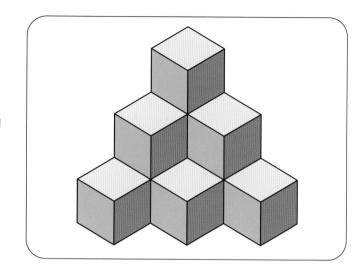

Making Tumbling Blocks

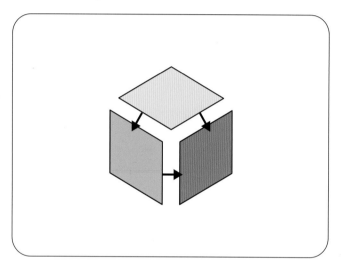

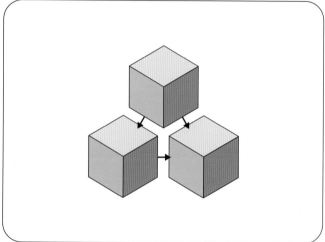

1 Use the diamond template on page 172. Cut three diamonds from paper for each unit, using the inner line of the diamond. Using the outer line of the template, cut one diamond in fabric A, one in fabric B and one in fabric C. Mark a 5mm (¼in) seam allowance on the wrong side of all the fabric pieces. Pin a paper diamond to the wrong side of each fabric piece. Fold the seam allowance marked on the fabric over the edge of the paper shape all around and press, then tack (baste) in position. Whipstitch the three diamonds together to make one unit.

2 Make as many units as required, then join the units together as indicated, whipstitching the seams.

Working with bias seams

The diamond shapes used for this design mean that there are lots of seams to stitch on the bias. The paper templates will hold the fabric stable – do not remove them until the quilt top is complete and ready for wadding (batting) and backing.

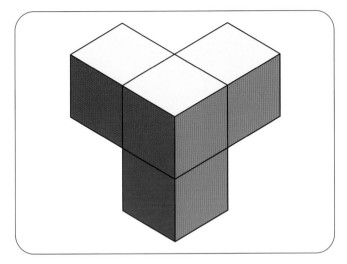

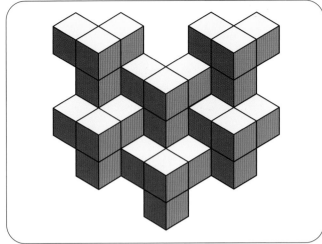

Inner City Block

In this variation of Tumbling Block, there are two extra diamonds added at both sides and the bottom to make a Y-shape. To keep the three-dimensional look, the extra diamonds should be in the same fabrics as the adjacent diamonds – or at least the same tone and colour.

Inner City Block pattern

This is the pattern that is achieved when blocks of Inner City Block are stitched together – making it obvious how the block got its name. It can be used pictorially but is also tremendously effective just as an abstract design.

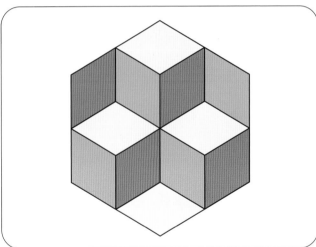

Block Puzzle

Here, three Tumbling Blocks are joined together with corner diamonds to create a hexagon. The pattern could also be viewed as a central six-pointed star with spacer diamonds around the edge – an effect that would be more pronounced if the spacer diamonds were all in a different colour.

stars

Star patterns come in many different types and sizes. The simplest designs have only four or six points, while some can have thirty-two or even more. Since all the seams are straight, many star patterns can be pieced by machine – although joining the points at the centre is always fiddly.

Four-Pointed Star

There are many types of Four-Pointed Star – just a few are shown here. The simplest way to keep the points neat and the bias seams straight is to use the English paper-piecing method (see page 90).

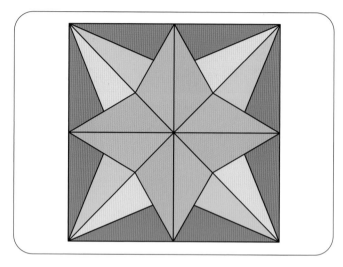

Making a Four-Pointed Star block

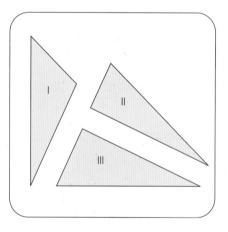
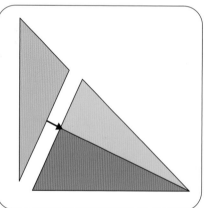
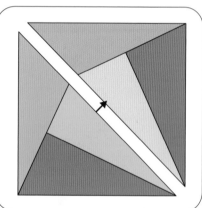

1 Cut eight triangles from paper in each of shapes I, II and III. Using the outer line of template I, cut four triangles in fabric A and four in fabric B. Using the outer line of template II, cut four triangles in fabric C and four in fabric D. Using the outer line of template III, cut eight triangles in fabric E. Mark a 5mm (¼in) seam allowance on the wrong side of all the fabric pieces. Pin a matching paper triangle to the wrong side of each fabric piece.

2 Fold the seam allowance marked on the fabric over the edge of the paper shape all around and press, then tack (baste) in position. Join four triangles in fabric E to triangles in fabric C. Join the remaining four triangles in E to the triangles in fabric D. Add a triangle in fabric A to the end of each E/C unit and a triangle in fabric B to the end of each D/E unit. Check the picture of the block regularly to make sure you are adding the colours in the right place.

3 Take two different units and join them together to make a square block. Repeat with the other units so you have four identical square blocks. Finally, join the squares as for a Four-Patch block (see pages 124–25), being very careful to keep the points sharp at the centre.

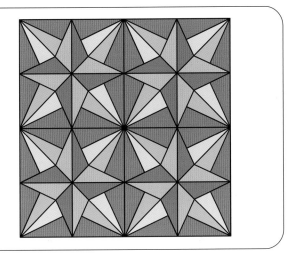

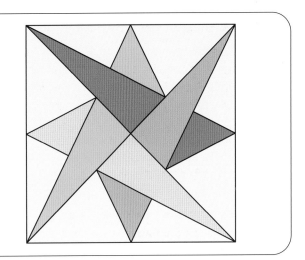

Blazing Star

This illustration shows the effect of several Blazing Star blocks combined directly. As often happens, a secondary pattern emerges – here an almost circular shape can be seen in the centre of the pattern. The use of different colours can make this effect more prominent.

Laced Star

The long, slanting diagonal points give this Four-Pointed Star the look of a Pinwheel, but it is constructed using the same principles as a basic Blazing Star block. There are four triangles needed – two for the background and two for the points, with both these last two cut in the same fabric for the two pieces of each point.

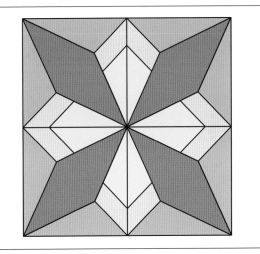

North Star

This variation of Blazing Star uses triangles and diamonds, but again is made in basically the same way. The small centre triangles could be made in the same fabric as the long points, giving a cross effect, or in the same fabric as the large points, making the central star more prominent.

Barbara Bannister Star

Named after a well-known American quilter, this block is constructed in the same way as Blazing Star but has four shapes: outer triangle, diamond point, inner triangle and a trapezoid strip that creates the square on point. Changing the colour values creates very different effects, emphasizing the square or the star.

Eight-Pointed Star

In its simplest form, the Eight-Pointed Star is made from diamonds in two alternating colours, with triangles and squares to fill in around the edges. Even on this version there are eight seams meeting in the middle, so it can be tricky to keep the points sharp and the seams aligned.

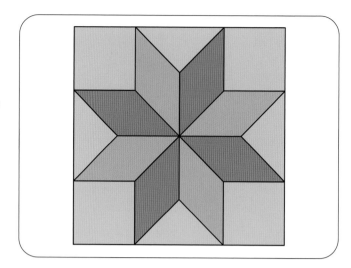

Making an Eight-Pointed Star block

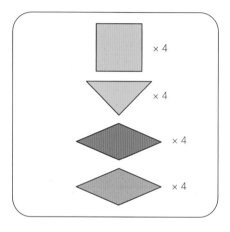

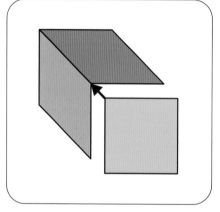

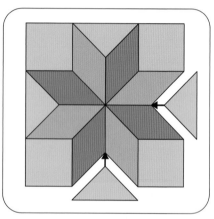

1 Use the diamond and right-angled triangle templates on page 172, and make up a square template to fit in the angle of two diamonds as shown. Draw an inner line 5mm (¼in) in from the edge all around the square template. Cut eight diamonds, four triangles and four squares from paper, using the inner line. Using the outer line of the template, cut four squares in fabric A, four triangles in fabric A, four diamonds in fabric B and four in fabric C. Mark a 5mm (¼in) seam allowance on the wrong side of all the fabric pieces. Pin a matching paper shape to the wrong side of each fabric piece. Fold the seam allowance marked on the fabric over the edge of the paper shape all around and press, then tack (baste) in position.

2 Using a 5mm (¼in) seam, stitch two diamonds in different colours together along one edge. Repeat with the other six diamonds, so you have four pairs of diamonds. Add a square in the angle made by two diamonds, sewing from the centre point outwards each time. Repeat with the other three pairs of diamonds. Stitch two pairs together, then stitch the two units together into the star.

3 Add the triangles on the sides, using a 5mm (¼in) seam and stitching from the inner point outwards each time. Press the seams open.

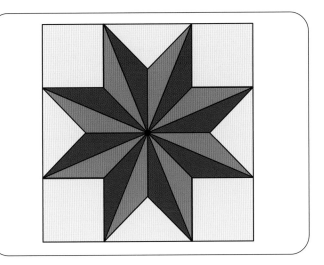

LeMoyne Star

It is believed that this design was named after Pierre and Jean-Baptiste LeMoyne, who were early residents of New Orleans. Further north it is known as Lemon Star, which is almost certainly a corruption of LeMoyne. It is made in the same way as the basic Eight-Pointed Star block, but each diamond is pieced from two triangles – creating even more seams at the centre.

Virginia Star

This is a simple version of the intricate Lone Star, also known as Star of Bethlehem, which features concentric bands of diamonds radiating out from a central eight-pointed star, but retaining the eight-point shape.

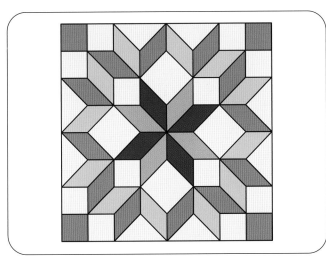

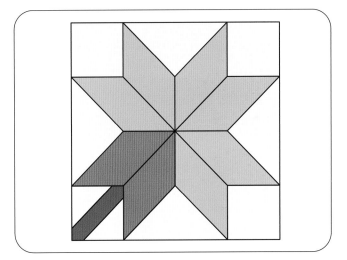

Broken Star

This pattern, which is also known as Carpenter's Wheel, is made quite three-dimensional by the use of a third colour in the outer ring. The squares around the central eight-pointed star create a second star shape.

Lily

It is simple to make the star look like something else – here an added appliquéd stem and different colours used in two segments create the shape of a stylized flower.

Ohio Star

The Ohio Star block is a popular pattern that is quick to piece and has many variations. It is constructed using only two shapes: a square and a quarter-triangle. The finished block looks quite intricate on its own, so it is generally set simply with plain spacer blocks, or just in rows with plain sashing.

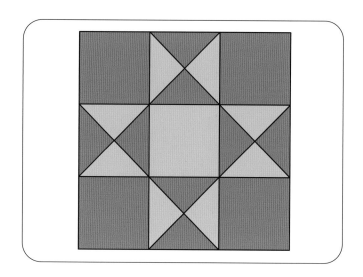

Making an Ohio Star block

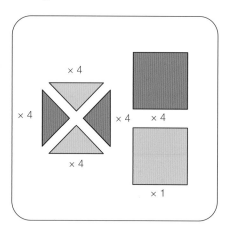

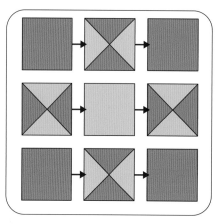

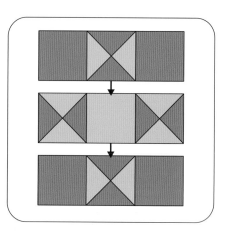

1 Cut two squares in each of fabrics A and B. Cut each square across on both diagonals to make four right-angled triangles, making a total of eight right-angled triangles in each fabric. Take two triangles in each colour and piece into a new square as indicated. Repeat with the other triangles. Press the finished squares and use one as a template to cut four squares the same size in fabric A and one in fabric B.

2 Arrange the squares in rows, with the top and bottom line running A–pieced square–A and the middle row running pieced square–B–pieced square. Join the squares together, using 5mm (¼in) seams. Press seams to one side.

3 Join the rows together, matching both vertical and diagonal seams carefully. Press seams to one side.

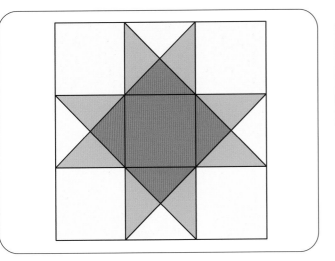

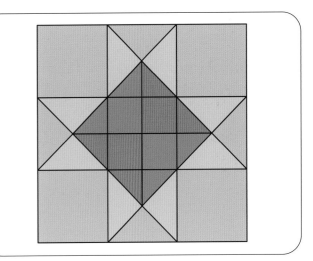

Variable Star

This block is constructed in the same way as the basic Ohio Star block, but uses three fabrics instead of two. Since the square in the centre and its surrounding triangles are in the same fabric, they read as a square set on point.

Country Farm

The use of four fabrics gives yet another effect. The corner squares and outer triangles are in one fabric, the points of the star in a second, while the central square and inner triangles are pieced from the third and fourth fabrics. The central square is a simple Four-Patch block. Make all the pieced units first, then combine them as for the basic Ohio Star block.

Stitching quarter-triangles

If your quarter-triangles do not come out as a perfect crossed square – despite accurate cutting and stitching – try cutting them a little bit bigger, then stitch and trim to size.

Card Basket

This block again has four fabrics, but used in a different way. The corner squares are made up of triangles in two fabrics, the points of the star and the central square set on point are in a third fabric, and the fourth fabric is used for the small triangles around the central square and the inner triangles, which creates a diamond.

curves

Designs based on curves are often intricate and may be difficult to stitch by machine, unless the curves are very gentle. Despite this, they are popular because beautiful designs with swirling shapes, full of vitality, can be created. Many patterns are also ideal for using up odd shaped scraps of fabric.

Clamshell

This is a very traditional pattern, but it is rather complicated to construct. The easiest method is to use English paper piecing (see page 90), but even then the long, thin point of the clamshell is fiddly to work.

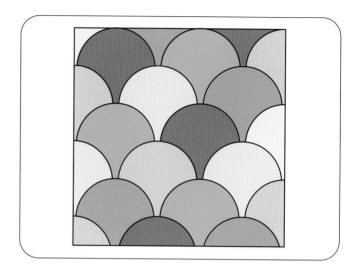

Making a Clamshell block

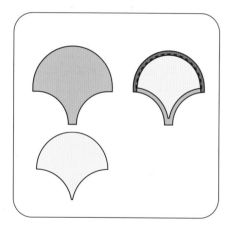

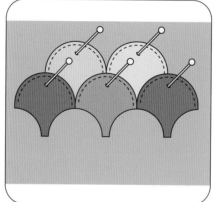

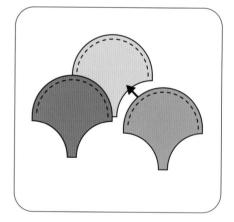

1 Use the clamshell template on page 173 to cut several clamshells from paper. Make a second template, adding an extra 5mm (¼in) seam allowance all around, and use this to cut a selection of clamshells in various fabrics. Mark a 5mm (¼in) seam allowance on the wrong side of all fabric pieces. Pin a paper shape to the wrong side of each fabric piece. Fold the fabric's seam allowance over the edges of the paper. Press, then tack (baste) in position. Mark the centre top on each clamshell.

2 Use a spare paper clamshell template to draw a row of curves across the bottom of a piece of thick card or a pinboard. Pin a row of fabric patches in position along the scalloped line. Add a second row staggered above the first, adjusting the position of colours until you are totally happy with the design.

3 Make sure the edge of the first patch in the second row aligns with the marked centre top point on the first patch in the bottom row. Slipstitch the two patches together, starting at the centre top point and stitching along the seam line of the lower curve of the bottom patch. Add the next patch in the bottom row in the same way.

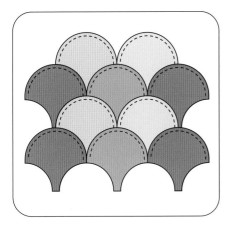

4 Keep repeating this sequence, adding alternate patches from the top and bottom rows. When you have stitched all the patches on the pinboard, pin another two rows in place and then start again.

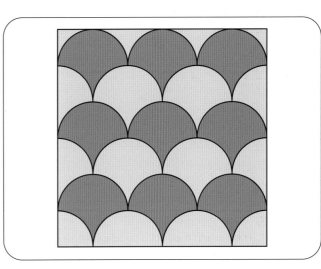

Shells
Here the basic Clamshell is worked in rows of two alternating colours. The rows could also run diagonally, giving a slightly less curvy effect.

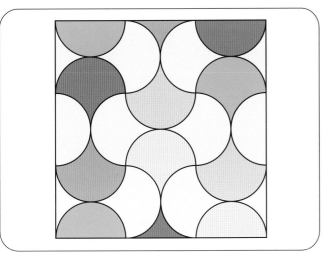

Shell patchwork
The double curves of the clamshell shape fit into one another, so if the patches are rotated so that the points face one another, two further clamshells can be used to fill in the gaps on each side. This creates an interesting curvy mosaic.

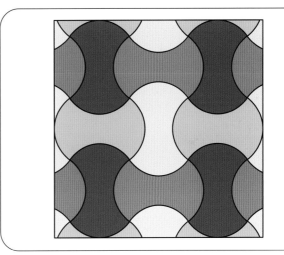

Double Axehead
This is similar in concept to the Shell patchwork, but is based on a double unit in which the curve at the top of the clamshell is not so long, and at the centre the points are wider to form a waist. If you use the same round shape to make both curves, the shapes will fit into one another as shown here.

Fan

This fan design has many variations. The fan itself can have many more blades, and four Fan blocks together create the well-known design called Dresden Plate. Rotating the Fan blocks can create interesting secondary patterns.

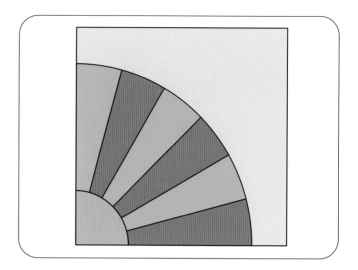

Making a Fan block

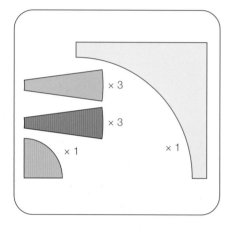

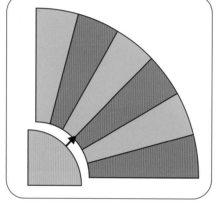

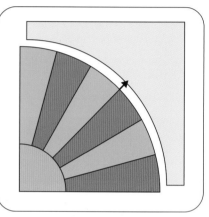

1 Use the Fan templates on page 174. Using template I, cut three blades in fabric A and three blades in fabric B. Using template II, cut one corner piece in fabric C. Using template III, cut one background piece in fabric D.

2 Using a 5mm (¼in) seam, stitch one blade A to one blade B. Repeat with the other two pairs, then stitch the pairs together into the fan. Press the seams open, or to one side. Add the corner piece, being very careful not to stretch the curved seam as you stitch.

3 Add the background piece, again being very careful not to stretch the curved seam as you stitch. You can handsew or machine-sew this, but it must lie perfectly flat. Clip the curved seam if necessary.

Working the Fan block

The corner piece can also be made as an appliqué to cover the pointed ends of the blades running right down into the corner.

The blades should alternate in colour to get the best result from the Fan design, but you can use many more than two colours if you wish – it is a great way to use up scraps.

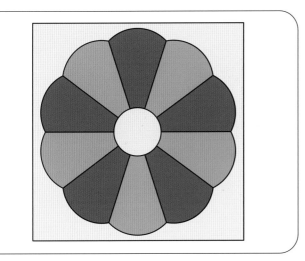

Simple Dresden Plate

This is a very simple Dresden Plate, but is still attractive. The large segments and limited number of colours make it quite easy to stitch – if you make the central circle as an appliqué you don't have to worry about the central points meeting perfectly.

Dresden Plate

This more traditional version of Dresden Plate uses three fabrics for the plate design, and two shapes: rounded and pointed. The design was perhaps most popular in the 1920s and 1930s.

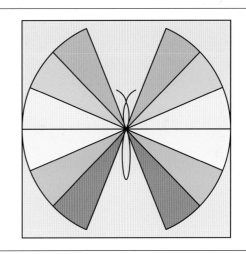

Snake in the Hollow

This design is made with blocks containing double fans in opposite corners. When the blocks are set next to one another, a secondary design of sinuous curves appears.

Butterfly

The fans can also be used to make representational forms, such as this butterfly. The fans themselves could either be pieced or made as appliqué.

Drunkard's Path

Drunkard's Path patterns use a square with a quarter-circle in a contrasting colour across one corner. This square can be set in many ways to create an endless series of variations. The staggered look of the design is supposed to recall a drunkard staggering home; blue and white versions of the design dating from the nineteenth century are thought to have been made in support of the temperance movement.

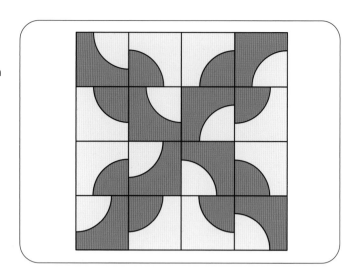

Making a Drunkard's Path block

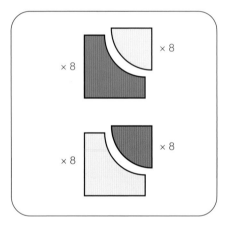

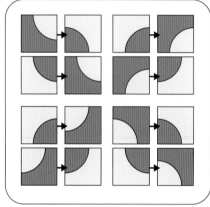

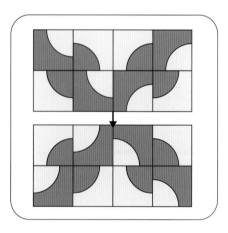

1 Using the templates on page 173, cut eight pieces of each shape in fabric A and eight in fabric B. Join the small pieces in fabric A to the large pieces in fabric B and vice versa, so you have sixteen squares, each with a contrast section across one corner. Clip curves in the seam allowance and press all the seams flat.

2 Lay out the sixteen squares as shown. Join the pairs together first to make eight pairs of squares, following the diagram above closely. Join the pairs together to create four pieced blocks.

3 Join the four squares together, matching seams across joins carefully, following the instructions for a Four-Patch block on pages 124–25.

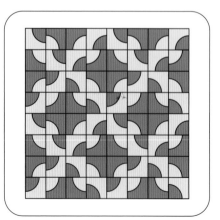

4 When you combine several Drunkard's Path blocks without sashing, complex patterns and sinuous curves begin to develop.

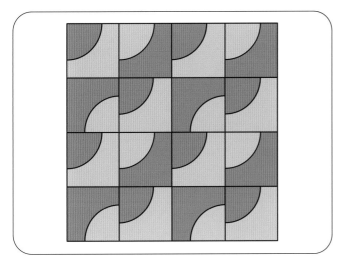

Falling Timbers

This design uses exactly the same elements and techniques as the basic Drunkard's Path block, but the squares are orientated to run in diagonal lines. When it is worked in greens and browns, the diagonal lines suggest fallen tree trunks on the forest floor: hence the block's name. If the darks and lights were reversed and the squares turned so the continuous staggered lines ran vertically, the design would be known as Vine of Friendship.

Dove

This is another variation using exactly the same components as Drunkard's Path, but with the squares arranged to make a central jagged shape. When more of the same blocks are added around this one, the corner pieces will combine into the same central shape but rotated by 90°.

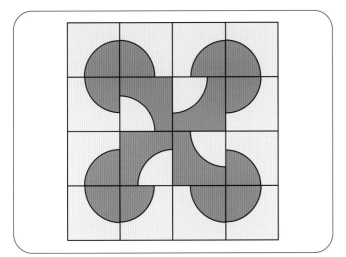

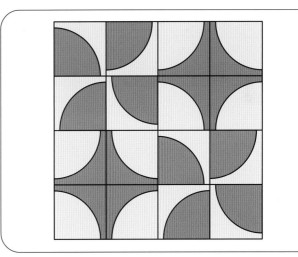

Wonder of the World I

Although made using the same principles, this design does not use identical elements to Drunkard's Path; instead of equal numbers there are only four dark squares with light corners, and twelve light ones with dark corners.

Wonder of the World II

In this variation, the eight light/ dark squares are arranged to make two windmills placed in opposite corners of the Double Four-Patch block. In the opposite corners, the eight dark/ light squares make crosses.

Josephine's Knot

It is possible that this block is named after the Josephine's Knot used in macramé and in Celtic jewellery, but it is not clear who the original Josephine was. The block is made of three shapes, with the ribbons and curved segments creating the look of a knot in the centre.

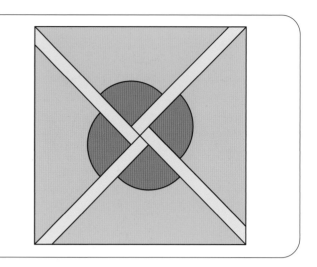

Making a Josephine's Knot block

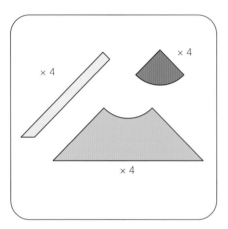

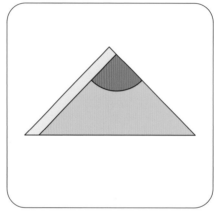

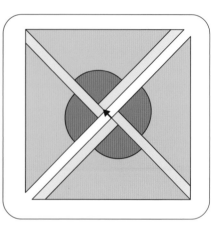

1 Use the templates on page 174. Cut four pieces of the triangle base in fabric A, cut four pieces of the strip in fabric B, and cut four pieces of the cone in fabric C.

2 Using a 5mm (¼in) seam, join the cone to the base triangle along the curved seam. Handle the curve carefully to avoid stretching it as you work. Add the strip to the left-hand side of the unit. Repeat this step to make another three identical units.

3 Stitch the four pieced units together in pairs, as indicated. Stitch the two halves together, matching the central seam exactly.

Stitching curved (bias) seams

When machine-stitching a bias seam, work with great care so that you do not stretch the fabric as you pull it through the sewing machine.

It is often a good idea to cut notches on matching curved edges, so you have fixed points to work with.

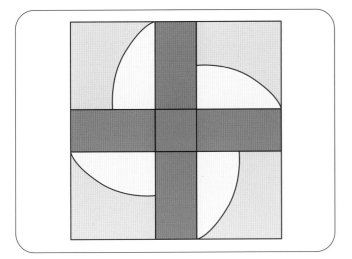

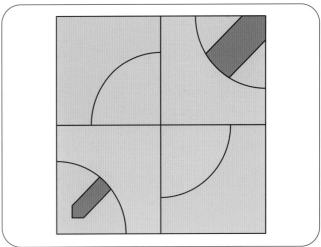

Nocturne

Although based on similar shapes to a Josephine's Knot block, this design is pieced in the same way as a Nine-Patch block (see page 121).

Turtle

This charming turtle is made of similar units to Josephine's Knot, but the strips are added as appliqué to represent the head and tail of the turtle. If you join several blocks, add sashing to retain the look of a turtle in each.

Wedding Ring

The block, which is also known as Double Wedding Ring, is a favourite with experienced quilters for showcasing their skill. It was developed early in the twentieth century, but its greatest popularity occurred during the Great Depression, because the design is ideal for using up lots of scraps.

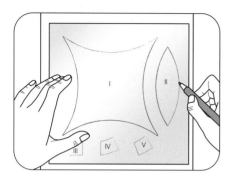

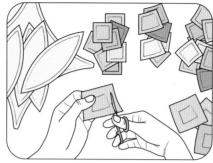

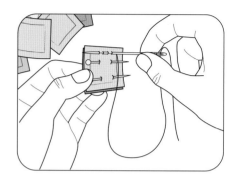

1 Copy the templates on page 176 on to plastic and make separate templates for each part of the design, adding a 5mm (¼in) seam allowance to each all round. For each block, cut one central square (piece I) in a plain fabric, and four of piece II in the same colour.

2 From a selection of patterned fabric scraps, use the templates to cut eight of piece III, sixteen of piece IV and thirty-two of piece V. Keep the shapes in separate piles so you don't get them mixed up.

3 Mark the seam line on the back of each patterned fabric piece. Place two of the piece V shapes with right sides together and pin. Join the pieces together with running stitch along the seam line.

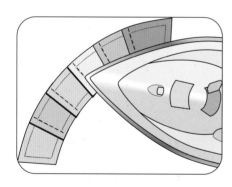

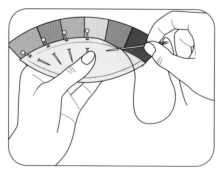

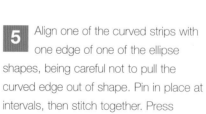

4 Add another two of piece V in the same way to make a strip, then add one piece IV to each end of the strip. Repeat to make eight curved strips. Press alll the seams to one side.

5 Align one of the curved strips with one edge of one of the ellipse shapes, being careful not to pull the curved edge out of shape. Pin in place at intervals, then stitch together. Press the seam to one side.

6 Repeat step 4 with the other three ellipse shapes. Take one of the four remaining curved strips and add one piece III to each end. Repeat with the other four curved strips.

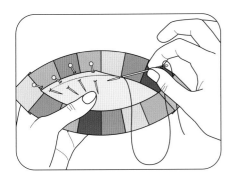 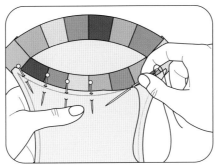 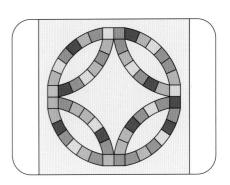

7 Pin and then stitch one of the longer curved strips made in step 5 to the other side of one of the ellipse shapes, lining up the seams on the curved strips on each side. Be careful when working with the curved seam.

8 Press all the long seams on the ellipse unit to one side. Pin one of the completed ellipse units to one side of the central square. The seam between pieces III and IV needs to fall exactly at the finished point of the square, so the circular seam will line up all round.

9 Repeat with the other three ellipse units on the other three sides of the central square.

10 The wedding rings need to intersect on a full quilt top: each block that surrounds the central Wedding Ring block needs to be made with three ellipse blocks.

Making a Wedding Ring quilt

For a simpler way of making the quilt top, make the block as a square with the four arcs meeting in the middle as a curved 'X'. This means the central square will be pieced in two halves, but when the top is quilted, this will almost certainly not show.

The American quiltmaker, Eleanor Burns, has developed a much simpler way of achieving the look of a Double Wedding Ring quilt by using fusible interfacing to create the rings and then appliquéing them to the background fabric. The finished product looks very authentic.

representational

Quilters have always represented the everyday items around them in their quilting work; this is generally done in appliqué, but there are several representational blocks that can be made in patchwork with Basket and Schoolhouse being the most common.

Basket

The Basket block is generally made up of triangles, but lots of different designs can be made with these and it is a particularly popular motif. The design is ideal for using up scraps – although the basket itself will look better made in one fabric, the contents could be made in an assortment of many different scraps.

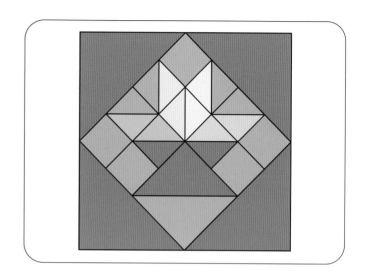

Making a Basket block

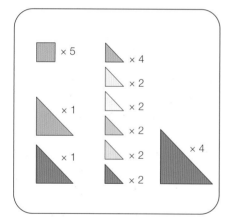

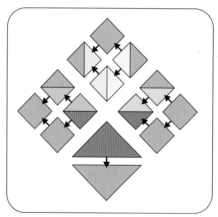

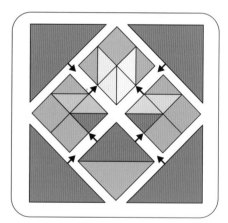

1 Cut two squares from fabric A and one each of fabrics B, C, D, E and F. Cut each in half along the diagonal to make four triangles in A and two in each of the other fabrics. Join pairs of triangles as follows: AB, AC, AD, AE, BC, EF and DF. Using a finished triangle square as a template, cut five matching squares from fabric A. Cut a medium triangle in fabrics A and F. Cut two large squares in fabric F; cut each in half along the diagonal to make four large triangles.

2 Join the twelve squares and triangle squares to make three Four-Patch units, as shown. Join the two large triangles to make a large triangle block.

3 Join the four Four-Patch units using a 5mm (¼in) seam, matching seams and points carefully. Add the large right-angled triangles to each side of the basket to make the finished block square. Press seams to one side.

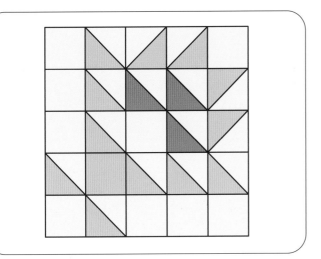

Fruit Basket

The block, made up of twenty-five squares, just contains squares and triangles. First make fifteen triangle squares and ten squares the same size, then assemble all the squares in rows.

Cake Stand

Another Basket variation, this Cake Stand block has a handle made of triangle squares with a plain square at the top. This block has been sashed, but to set it on point you will need to add spacer squares or triangles.

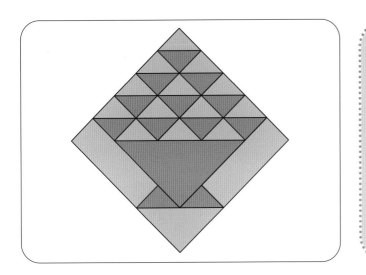

Basket blocks

The Basket design is particularly popular and there are many versions. The basket is usually made of triangles, but you can also use parallelograms. Multi-fabric diamonds above the base would give the effect of a mass of flowers in the basket. Try out different ideas and effects – you can always combine different blocks into a sampler quilt.

Basket of Flowers

This machine-pieced Basket of Flowers is made in a slightly different way, because the 'bowl' is a large triangle with two small triangles as its base. First make up three triangle squares and assemble into a chevron for the centre, then add three triangles across the base of the chevron to make it into a triangle. Add the large triangle to the bottom edge for the bowl, making a triangle square. The remaining elements of the block are assembled as strips and added around the edge, with a plain triangle to complete the square at the bottom.

Schoolhouse

The Schoolhouse block, a traditional design that is also known as Little Red Schoolhouse, has always been popular and has many variations depicting churches, barns and different public buildings. The shapes are quite intricate and need to fit together perfectly, so templates are a must.

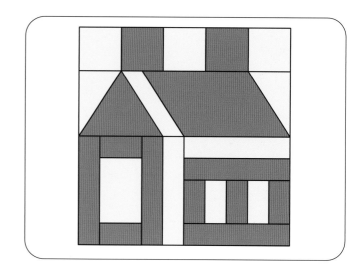

Making a Schoolhouse block

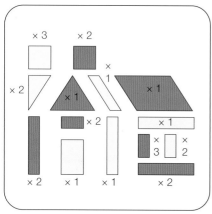

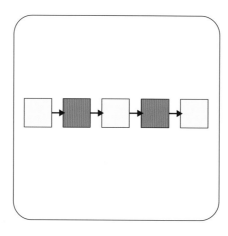

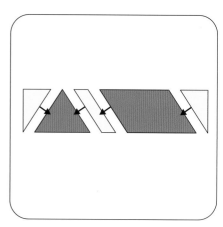

1 Use the templates on page 175. From fabric A, cut two pieces each of templates I, IV, V and VI; one each of templates II and III; and three of template VII. From fabric B, cut one each of templates IV, VI, VIIII and X; two each of templates VII and IX; and three of template I. You should have thirteen pieces of A and eleven of B: twenty-four pieces in total.

2 Use 5mm (¼in) seams throughout. Join pieces I, X and XI into a strip in the order BABAB as shown.

3 Next join pieces II, III, IX and XII into a strip in the order BABAB as shown above.

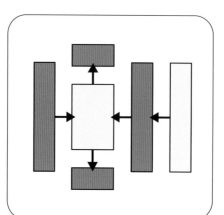

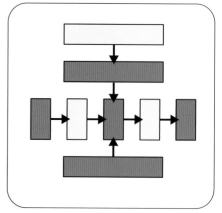

4 Join pieces V and VIII into a strip in the order ABA as shown. Then add one strip IV in A on each side and then another one in B to the right.

5 Join the four VII pieces into a strip in the order ABABA. Add the VI strips in A top and bottom, then the B strip at the very top.

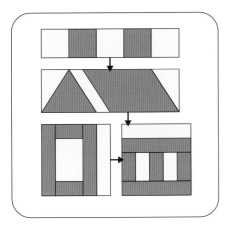

6 Join the four pieced strips together as indicated, carefully matching all seam lines from the first chimney down the corner of the building.

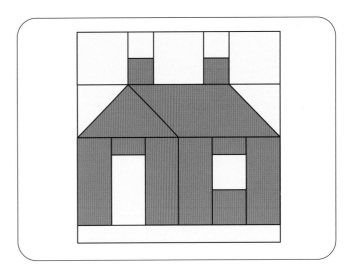

Schoolhouse Variation
This simplified variation of the Schoolhouse block is designed to be made up quickly, using rotary cutting and machine piecing.

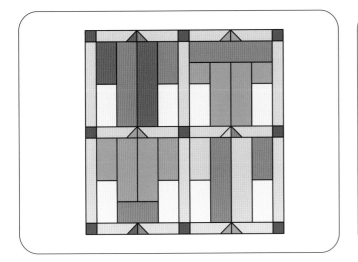

Kimono
The same principles can be used to make a variety of simplified shapes. Here, strips and triangles have been used to make a kimono block, which is put together with striped sashing and red corner blocks.

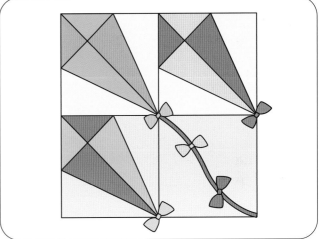

Kite
This charming kite is pieced from six triangles, and is set with alternate blocks that have an appliquéd tail adorned with ribbon bows.

templates

Diamonds

Copy the template to the size you need, adding a 5mm (¼in) seam allowance all around.

Hexagons

Copy the template to the size you need, adding a 5mm (¼in) seam allowance all around.

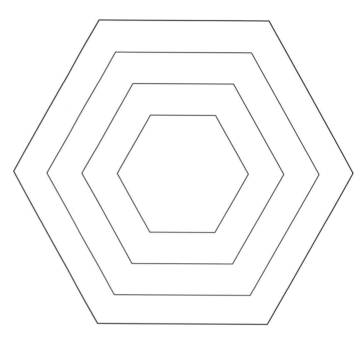

Pentagons

Copy the template to the size you need, adding a 5mm (¼in) seam allowance all around.

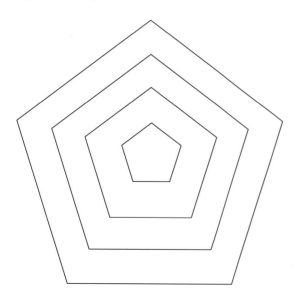

Triangles

Copy the template to the size you need, adding a 5mm (¼in) seam allowance all around.

Right-Angled Triangles

Equilateral Triangles

Drunkard's Path

Reduce or enlarge the templates to the size you need, adding a 5mm (¼in) seam allowance all around.

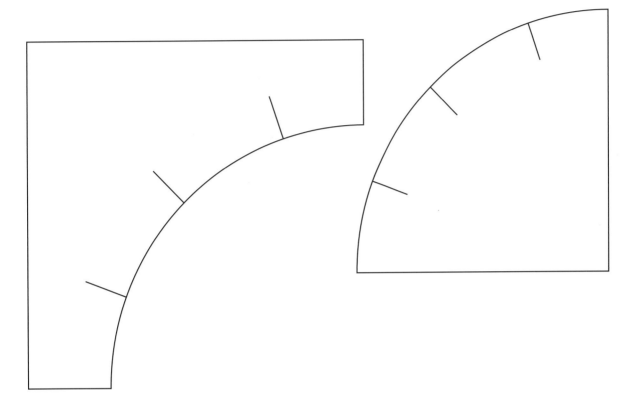

Clamshell

This template is for the paper piece (see page 158). Reduce or enlarge it to the size you need. For the fabric piece, add a 5mm (¼in) seam allowance all around.

Fan

Reduce or enlarge the templates to the size you need,
adding a 5mm (¼in) seam allowance all around.

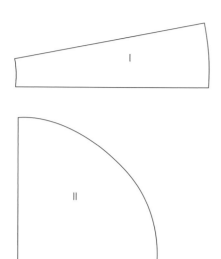

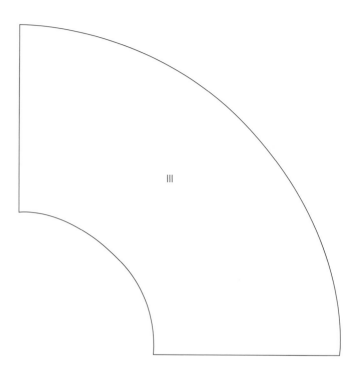

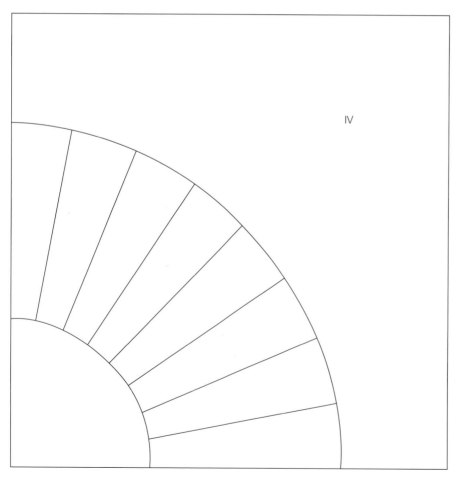

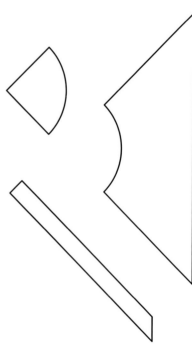

Josephine's Knot

Reduce or enlarge the templates to the
size you need, adding a 5mm (¼in)
seam allowance all around.

Four-Pointed Star

Reduce or enlarge the templates to the size you need, adding a 5mm (¼in) seam allowance all around.

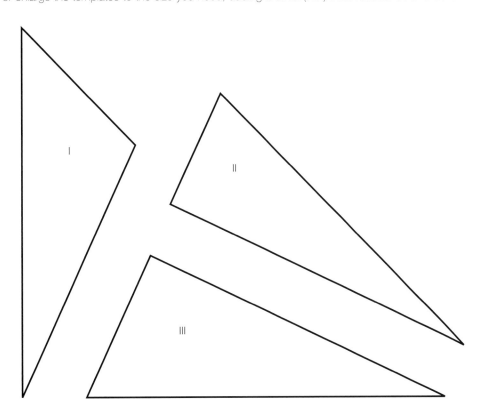

Schoolhouse

Reduce or enlarge the templates to the size you need, adding a 5mm (¼in) seam allowance all around.

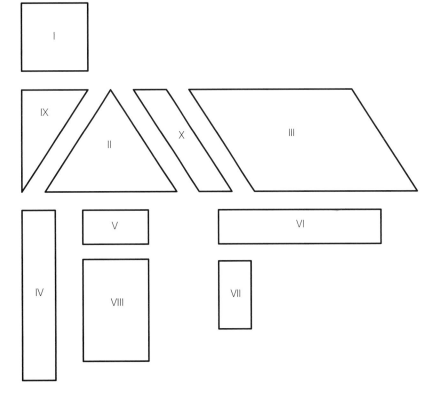

Wedding Ring

Enlarge or reduce these templates to the size you need for your project, adding a 5mm (¼in) seam allowance all around.

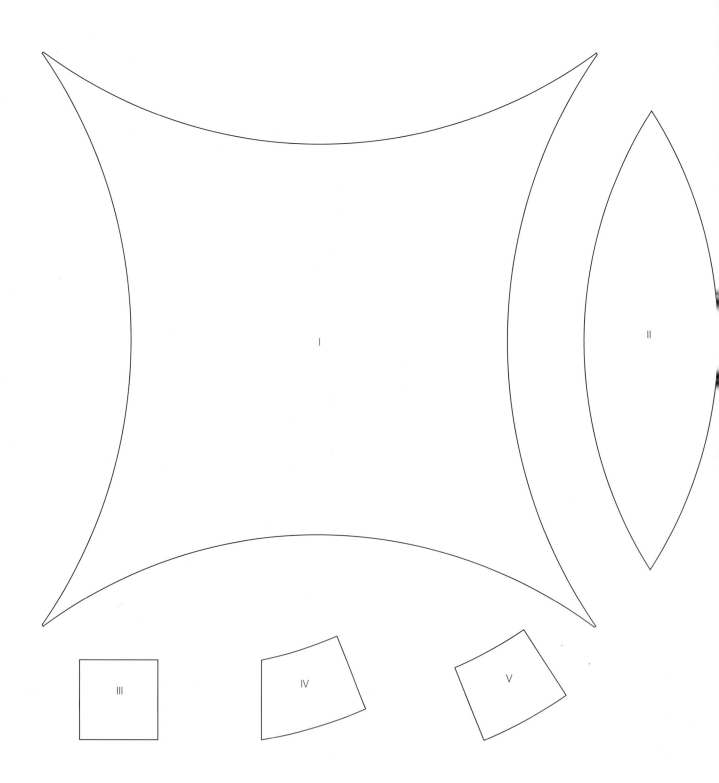

appliquéd quilts

Appliqué is the decorative technique of applying cut-out fabric pieces or motifs to a background fabric, and it has been used to decorate all kinds of textiles for centuries. It has often been used by quilters, and in many different ways – sometimes just to add extra detail to only one area of a quilt, at other times to create the entire design.

techniques

The basic technique of appliqué is very simple, but modern tools and equipment have led to more sophisticated variations. In most cases, the fabric used and the effect that is aimed for will dictate which appliqué technique is best for the job. The stitching that is used to attach the piece to the background fabric can be merely functional or decorative as well.

Hand appliqué

The traditional way to work appliqué is to stitch by hand, and this method is still best if you are working with small or very irregular shapes. Handstitching is always very satisfying, and many quilters prefer it to machine-stitching.

Folk art appliqué

Also known as cut and sew, this is the most basic form of appliqué, which works well with felt or when you are using a fabric backed with iron-on interfacing to stop it fraying.

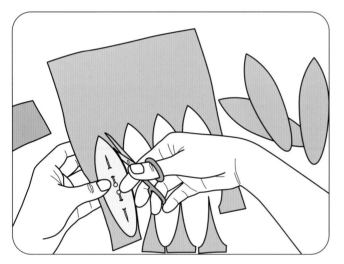

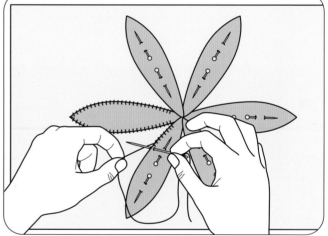

1 Draw the motif directly on the fabric, or make a template of the shapes and draw around them. Cut out all the shapes with sharp scissors.

2 Use a suitable embroidery stitch (see pages 210–17 for a selection of embroidery stitch techniques) to stitch the motif to the background fabric.

Folk art motifs

Motifs used in folk art work are generally much less complex than in most other types of appliqué. They are often based on everyday objects, but in a stylized form. Both plants and animal forms may be featured, but the shapes are simplified so they have a charming, naive quality. Hearts are also popular, but usually only on quilts intended for a newly married couple.

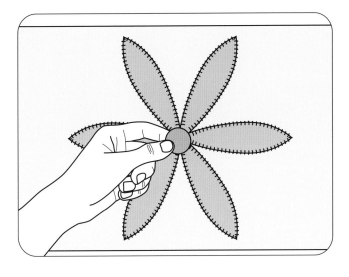 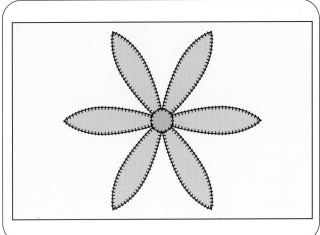

3 Here the petals meet in the centre, but there is a ragged gap at their ends. This can be covered with a small circle of fabric, in a different colour, to represent the centre of the flower.

4 The motif can easily be further embellished by adding more embroidery, sequins or beads, but actually it usually looks fine if it is left fairly plain.

Turned edge 1

In turned-edge appliqué, the edge of the motif is turned under with the very tip of the needle as you work.

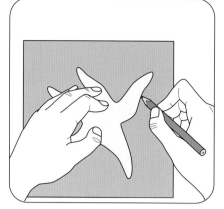

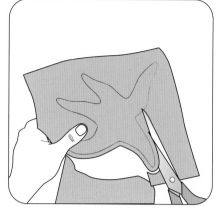

1 Make a template for the motif (see page 86). Place the template on the right side of the fabric and draw a line around it.

2 Cut out the motif with scissors, leaving a border approximately 5mm (¼in) wide all around the outside of the marked line.

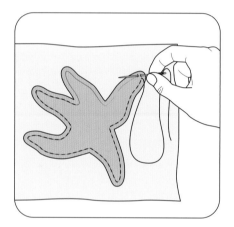

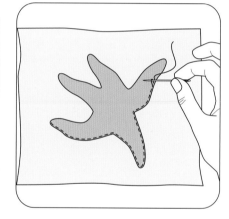

3 Place the motif, right side up, on the right side of the background fabric. Tack (baste) it in position, stitching approximately 5mm (¼in) inside the marked line.

4 Use the point of the needle to turn under a short section of the motif's edge, until the raw edge meets the tacking (basting) line. Slipstitch the folded edge to the background fabric, then turn under the next section. Continue in this way until the motif is stitched all the way round.

5 Remove the tacking (basting) stitches and gently press the motif from the wrong side. On the right side, the edges of the motif will be smooth.

Turned edge 2

An alternative method of starting a turned-edge appliqué motif is to begin by working from the reverse.

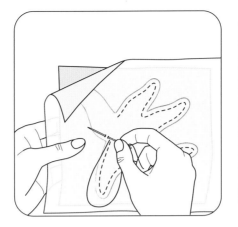

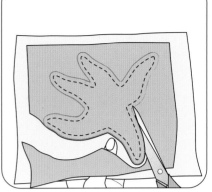

1 Using the template, draw the motif on the reverse of the backing fabric, then turn the backing fabric right side up. Cut a piece of appliqué fabric and pin it in place, right side up, on the right side of the backing fabric, completely covering the motif. Turn the backing fabric over and, working from the wrong side in a contrasting thread, tack (baste) the appliqué fabric to the backing fabric 3mm (⅛in) in from the edge of the motif.

2 Turn the backing fabric right side up again. Cut out the appliqué shape around 5mm (¼in) out from the line of tacking (basting) stitches, being careful not to cut through the backing fabric. Complete the motif by following steps 4–5 for Turned Edge 1.

Working appliqué by hand

If you cannot to find a thread that exactly matches the fabric used for the motif, the rule of thumb is to choose one a shade lighter if you are appliquéing to a light background, but use a shade darker if you are appliquéing to a dark background.

Keep the stitches as small and neat as possible – they should barely show, unless you are working folk art appliqué with a decorative embroidery stitch.

If the edge of an appliqué piece will be covered by another piece that is going to be added later, there is no need to turn the edge under.

Peaks and valleys

Many appliqué motifs will have one or more sharp, convex points and may also have concave dips. These are often hard to work neatly, and this is the way to deal with them.

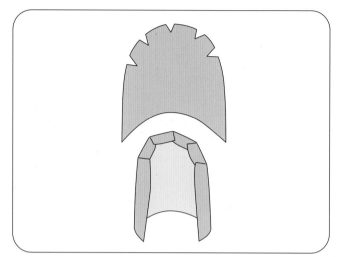

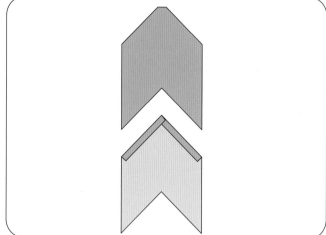

1 When working points, you will need to carefully remove excess fabric to achieve a smooth line. Cut small notches in the seam allowance of convex curves, so the excess fabric will fold over and overlap, producing less bulk.

2 Carefully snip off the top of sharp peaks down to the seam allowance line, so when the seam allowance is folded over, you will achieve a sharp point.

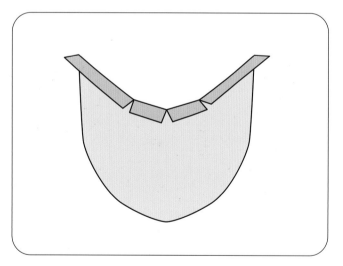

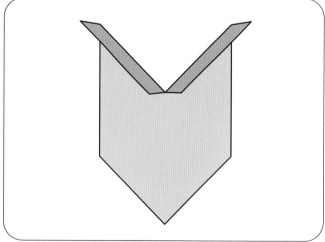

3 Shallow, rounded concave shapes should be notched as required while you are stitching – don't cut the notches in advance or it will be difficult to achieve a smooth curve.

4 Concave points should be snipped down to the seam allowance to enable this to fold back neatly on each side. Again, only make the cut as you near the point when stitching.

Freezer paper

Freezer paper was designed to store food, but quiltmakers quickly discovered that it was ideal as an aid for appliqué.

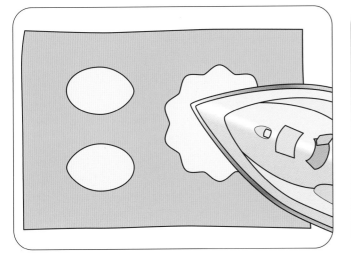

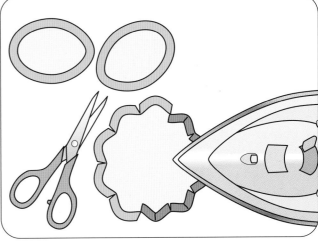

1 Make a template (see page 86) for each shape, place each template on the paper side of the freezer paper, draw around it and then cut out the shapes. Place the appliqué fabric, wrong side up, with the freezer paper shapes (sticky side down) on top. Iron the paper in place, then cut out the shapes, leaving a 5mm (¼in) seam allowance all around.

2 Snip into any concave edges or inner corners. Press the seam allowance to the wrong side, over the edge of the freezer paper. If you prefer, you can tack (baste) the seam allowance over the paper.

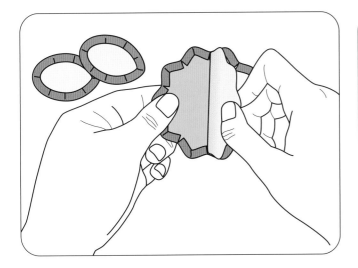

3 Peel the freezer paper away from the appliqué piece. If you have tacked (basted) the seam allowance down, leave the paper in place until the motif has been stitched to the background fabric.

4 Either tack (baste) or pin each motif to the background fabric, placing the motifs in order so they overlap each other as in the design. If the paper template is still in place, it can be extracted after the tacking has been removed.

 5 Slipstitch around the edge of each motif, using matching thread and working small stitches. Remove any tacking (basting) stitches and paper templates before completing the edge stitching.

6 Press the finished motif carefully from the reverse side. You could also machine-stitch the pieces of the motif in place, using a blind stitch and invisible (monofilament) thread.

Working freezer paper appliqué

When you are using the freezer paper technique, remember that the appliqué shape will be very hot immediately after ironing, so be careful not to burn your fingers.

If you are working with a light coloured background, you may be able to place the pattern underneath and use it as a guide for placing all the different elements. With backgrounds made of darker fabrics, it may be possible to use a lightbox beneath the pattern so it will show through enough on the fabric.

Fused appliqué

Fusible webbing has made appliqué much quicker and easier, and is particularly good for working with complicated shapes.

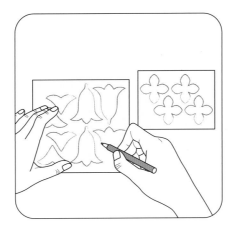

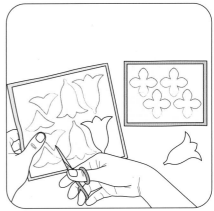

1 Trace all the appliqué shapes on to the paper backing of the fusible webbing – the shapes can be quite close together to save on materials.

2 Cut off the area of fusible webbing with the motifs, and iron it on to the reverse side of the fabric you will be using for the appliqué.

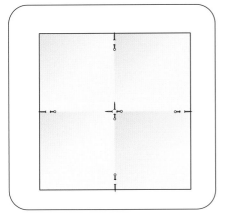

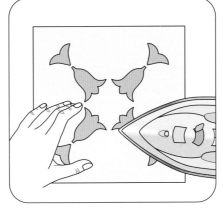

3 On the background fabric, mark the centre point of where the motif will be positioned, or place the pattern underneath to act as a guide, as explained on page 68.

4 Peel the backing paper off the appliqué motifs and carefully place the first pieces on the background fabric. Iron into position.

5 Add the remaining pieces and iron into place. You can hand-embroider or even satin stitch by machine around the edges if you wish.

Working in reverse

Remember that if you are working on the back of the fabric, the motif will be reversed when it is right side up. This may not be a problem with most shapes, but it certainly will be if you are using letters or numbers as part of the design.

When tracing the shapes on to the backing of the fusible webbing, group pieces in the same colour and cut them out in one block to iron to the fabric. This means you only have to cut carefully around each shape once.

Reverse appliqué

In reverse appliqué, layers of fabric are added behind the background fabric, which is then cut to reveal the colours lying beneath.

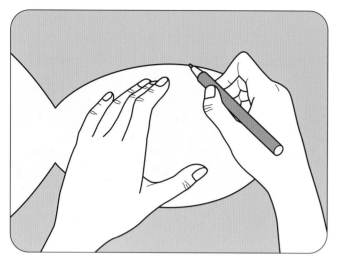

1 Layer the different fabrics in the correct order under the background fabric and behind the motif you will be working on. Tack (baste) the layers together and then mark the main outline of the motif on the background fabric (the top layer).

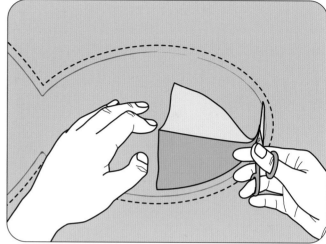

2 Tack (baste) through all layers 5mm (¼in) outside the outline of the motif. Cut out the motif through one layer of fabric only, working 5mm (¼in) inside the marked outline, to reveal the next layer. Don't cut into any of the other layers.

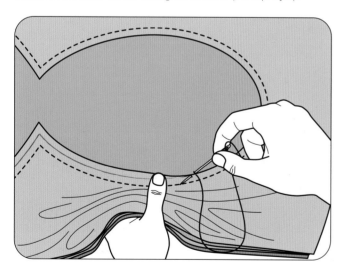

3 Turn under the edges all around the motif, so the raw edge butts up to the line of tacking (basting) stitches. Slipstitch the folded edge in place, trying to stitch only into the second layer if possible.

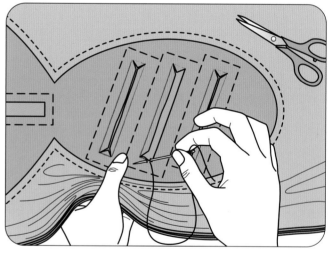

4 Mark the outline of the next coloured shape within the motif on the second layer. Proceed as for steps 2 and 3, this time only cutting into the second layer to reveal the third layer.

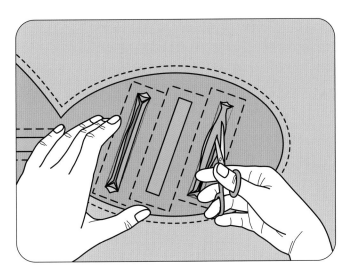

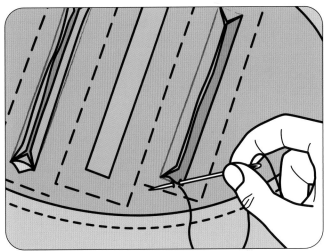

5 Mark the outline of the next coloured shape within the motif on the second layer. Proceed as for step 2, this time cutting into both the second and third layers to reveal the fourth layer.

6 Turn under the raw edges all around the shape as before. Slipstitch the folded edges in place.

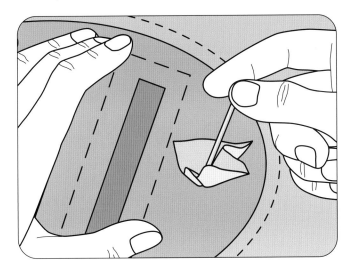

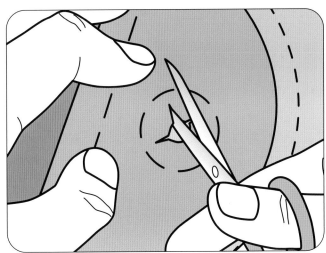

7 This example features the eye of a fish. Since the eye is small, it does not have a complete layer of fabric. Instead, cut a small slit in the eye area and insert a small scrap of fabric to cover the eye area behind the background.

8 Mark the eye shape and clip the seam allowance. Slipstitch the raw edge under as before. Remove all the tacking (basting) stitches and press the motif from behind to finish.

Inlay appliqué

This is also sometimes known as channel appliqué and is a variation of reverse appliqué (see pages 188–89).

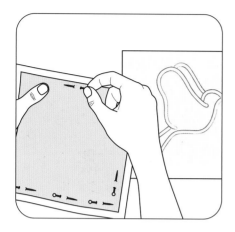

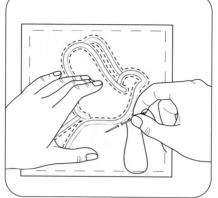

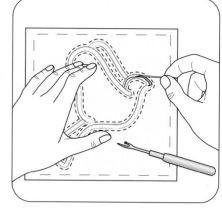

1 Mark the outlines of the motif on the background fabric. Cut a piece of contrast fabric large enough to cover the entire motif and tack (baste) this behind the background fabric, with the right sides of both layers facing upwards.

2 Tack (baste) along both sides of the marked lines of the motif, working 5mm (¼in) away from the line each time. For easy removal at the end, tack in a contrasting thread, leaving any knots on the face of the fabric.

3 Use sharp-pointed scissors or a seam ripper to slit along the lines of the motif. As you cut each section, use a needle to turn under the raw edges to butt up to the line of tacking (basting) on each side. Slipstitch the folded edge in place.

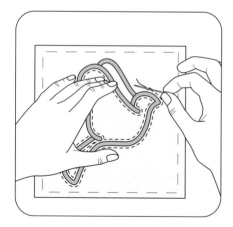

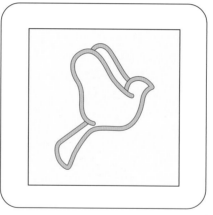

4 When you have cut and stitched all the lines of the motif, remove the tacking (basting) stitches. If the fabrics you are using are bulky, cut away the excess contrast fabric near the stitching lines.

5 Carefully press the finished motif from the wrong side.

Inlay appliqué

Simple designs are very effective, but if you want to add more complex details, you can use several layers of fabric as in reverse appliqué.

Since you will be cutting away the marked lines of the motif, you don't need to worry about what type of marker to use to draw the outlines.

As with most other forms of appliqué, you can easily add further embellishments to the outlined shapes.

Shadow appliqué

Also known as shadow quilting, this is a technique in which a thin layer of translucent fabric, such as organza, is stitched over all or part of an appliqué motif for a more muted effect.

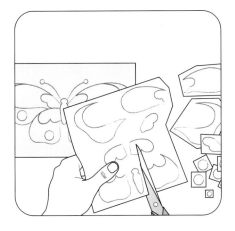

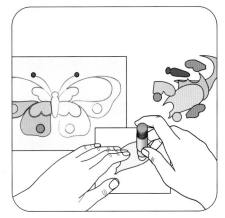

1 Trace the motif on to the background fabric and go over the lines with a fine marker. Trace each separate part of the motif on to the paper side of freezer paper, grouping pieces of the same colour together. Cut the freezer paper into sections, with each section having a group of shapes that will be in the same colour.

2 Lay a piece of appliqué fabric wrong side up, and place the appropriate section of freezer paper on top (sticky side down). Iron the paper in position with a hot iron. Cut out each shape carefully just inside the outline – there should be a narrow band of background fabric showing between the pieces.

3 Peel the freezer paper off each shape and set the pieces of fabric in position over the motif on the background fabric. Stick down all the appliqué pieces with a little fabric glue.

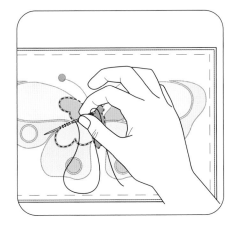

4 Lay a piece of organza over the motif and tack (baste) in position around the edges. Outline the motif and between each section of the design by working lines of running stitch in a fine contrasting thread.

5 Add any further detailing required using the same contrasting thread.

Fabrics

Use strong colours for the original appliqué: pastels may disappear entirely when over-laid with the translucent fabric.

For the overlay you can use any type of translucent fabric, such as net, voile, tulle or gauze.

appliquéd quilts

Machine appliqué 1

To work machine appliqué, you will need a machine with a good zigzag stitch that can be worked closely, like satin stitch. Many machines also have other decorative stitches that can be used for appliqué.

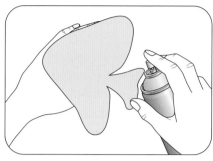

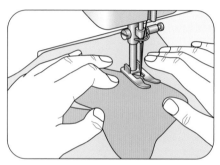

1 Place a piece of appliqué fabric right side up. Draw around a template of an appropriate piece of the motif, making sure the template is the correct way up.

2 Cut out the piece of appliqué and spray the wrong side of it with a light coating of temporary adhesive spray.

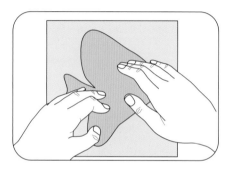

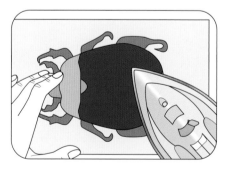

3 Lay the appliqué piece in the correct position on the background fabric and smooth into place.

4 Set the sewing machine to a close zigzag stitch and stitch carefully around the outline of the appliqué piece.

Machine appliqué 2

You can also use fusible webbing to attach the appliqué pieces before machine-stitching them.

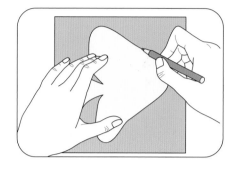

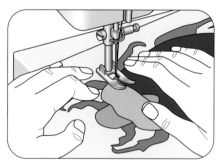

1 Work steps 1–4 as shown in fused appliqué on page 187. Add all the pieces to the background without any spaces between them.

2 Set the sewing machine to a close zigzag stitch and stitch around all the outlines of the appliquéd design.

Bias strip appliqué

In this technique, also known as stained-glass appliqué, the different colours are outlined in a bias binding to give the effect of a piece of stained glass. You can use narrow purchased bias binding, or make your own (see page 63).

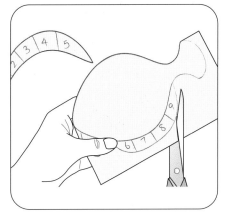

1 Trace all the appliqué shapes on to the paper backing of the fusible webbing – you don't need to follow the spacing on the final pattern: the shapes can be put quite close together to save on materials.

2 Cut off an area of fusible webbing with a group of appliqué shapes, and iron it on to the reverse side of an appropriate colour of appliqué fabric. Cut out all the shapes.

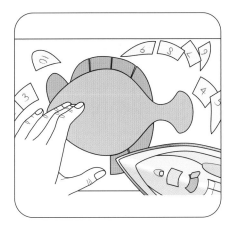

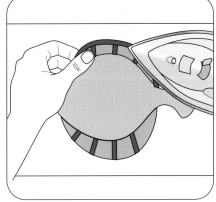

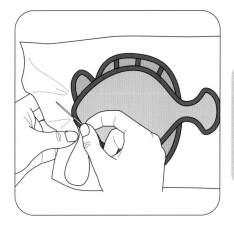

3 Peel the backing paper off the appliqué motifs and carefully place the first pieces on the background fabric. Iron into position, then add the other shapes to complete the design.

4 Start applying the bias strips, working in order so that raw edges are covered by the following strip if possible. Tack (baste) each strip, then machine-stitch into place.

5 Add the last strip. The final raw end should not fray as it is cut on the bias, but if you prefer, you can turn it under. Hold in place with a few stitches.

Working bias strip appliqué

There is an iron-on bias tape, 5mm (¼in) wide, called Quick Bias. It is quick and easy to use for bias strip appliqué – just iron it in place and machine-stitch to secure.

Although this technique is usually worked in black bias binding, if you make your own binding, you can use any colour you choose.

Oak Leaf and Reel

The Oak Leaf and Reel is one of the most traditional appliqué designs, typically made in red and green fabric on a white or cream background. There are many minor variations on the design, but there is always a central reel, with four oak leaves radiating out. The pattern first appeared in the mid-nineteenth century; it was popular on America's east coast.

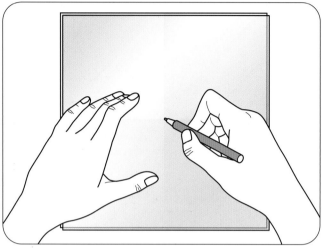

1 Cut a plain background square, fold it horizontally and vertically to find the centre point, then open it out again. Cut a piece of clear plastic film the same size and lay it over the background. Make a small dot in the centre with a marker.

2 Trace the template on page 204 on to the piece of plastic film, using a permanent marker. Copy the templates for the four oak leaves, the centre of the reel and the four reel sections on to the paper side of freezer paper and cut them all out.

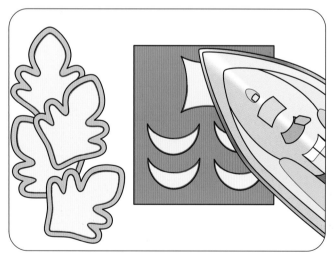

3 Iron the freezer paper shapes to the right side of the appropriate red or green fabric. Cut out all the shapes, remembering to allow slightly extra all around as a seam allowance to be turned under as you work.

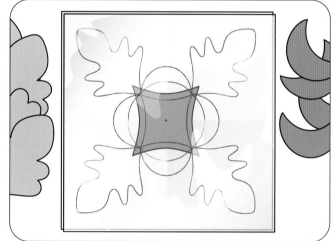

4 Use the clear plastic film to position the centre of the reel in the middle of the background square.

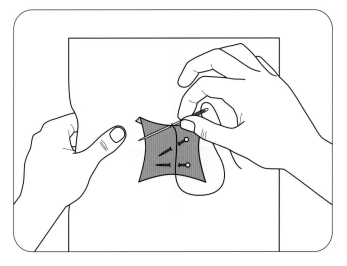

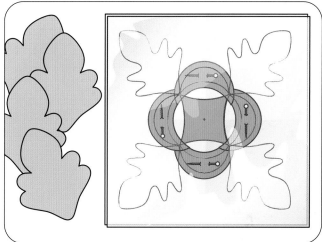

5 Pin the centre of the reel to the background fabric. Work turned-edge appliqué (see pages 182–83) all around the fabric shape, making sure that the stitches do not show on the right side.

6 Use the clear plastic film to position the reel sections around the centre of the reel. The ends of the sections will butt up against each other in line with the spokes of the centre of the reel, but there is no need to turn them under as they will be covered by the ends of the oak leaves. Appliqué the reel parts to the background.

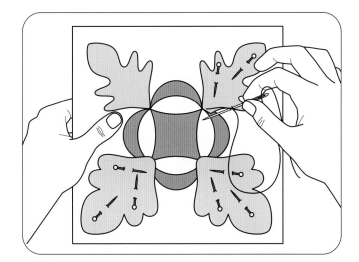

7 Position the leaves using the clear film again. The ends of the leaves need to be turned under and fit exactly against the spokes of the centre of the reel, as well as covering the joins between the reel sections. Appliqué the leaves to the background.

8 Once all the appliqué is finished, press the background from the back to remove the guide fold lines. Square up the block, keeping the Oak Leaf and Reel centred.

Hawaiian appliqué

Hawaiian appliqué is a technique in which a single symmetrical and intricate motif is applied to the background and then echo-quilted. It can be hand- or machine-quilted.

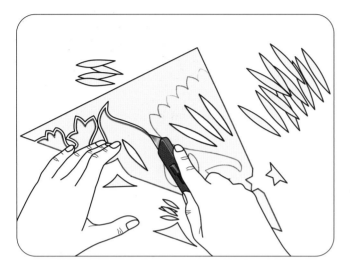

1 Cut a square of paper the same size as the motif. Fold it in half horizontally, then vertically, to make a small square, then diagonally through the folded corner to make a triangle. Trace a quarter-section of one of the templates on page 205 on to the triangle and cut around the outline, through all layers, with a sharp knife (protect the worksurface). Open out, then iron the motif flat.

2 Cut a square of plain fabric and of fusible webbing, both large enough to cover the entire motif. Iron the fusible webbing to the reverse of the fabric, leaving the backing paper in place. Lay the paper motif on the paper backing of the fusible webbing and fix in place with temporary adhesive spray. Trace around the outline of the motif with a fine marker or soft pencil.

3 Remove the paper template. Put the fabric with webbing backing on a cutting mat. Cut out the motif – use a rotary cutter on straight lines and scissors on intricate shapes. Cut some plain background fabric in a contrasting colour. Fold in half twice and once diagonally; press the folds to make guidelines for positioning.

4 Cut a piece of wadding (batting) the same size as the background fabric. Bond or pin it on the wrong side of the fabric. Peel off the fusible webbing's backing paper from the motif and position it in the centre of the background fabric, using the fold lines as a guide. Press the motif with a hot iron to bond it in place.

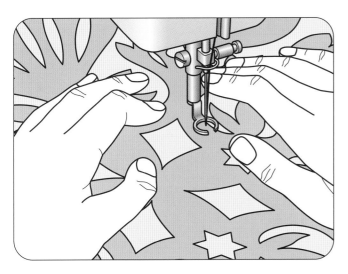

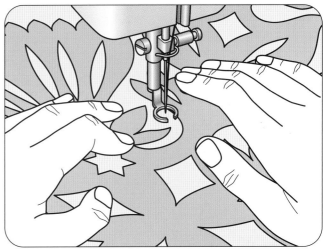

5 Using thread that matches the colour of the motif fabric, work zigzag stitch by machine all around the raw edges of the motif. Cut a piece of backing fabric the same size as the quilt top and tack (baste) it in position behind the quilt top, using one of the methods described on page 19.

6 Using thread to match the background fabric, work machine quilting all over the background fabric only. You can either echo-quilt (see page 41), following the outline of the motif in the traditional way, or work meander quilting (see page 47).

appliquéd quilts

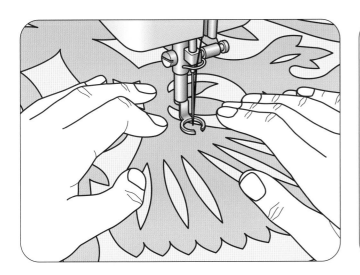

7 Using thread to match the motif fabric, work echo quilting to follow the outline of the motif within the area of the motif only.

8 Make up the finished quilt as described on pages 48–65.

Broderie perse

In the eighteenth and nineteenth centuries, chintz fabric was imported into Europe from the East, but it was very expensive. However, chintz motifs were easy to cut out and apply to a less expensive backing fabric. This was a way of extending the use of a small quantity of chintz. The technique was called broderie perse, or Persian embroidery.

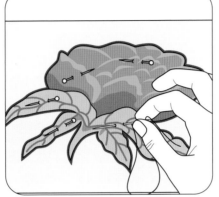

1 Choose a suitable motif from a piece of printed fabric. Cut it out carefully, leaving a border around 5mm (¼in) wide all around the edge. Choose a background fabric of approximately the same weight as the printed fabric.

2 Pin and then tack (baste) the cut-out motif in position on the background fabric.

3 Using thread to match the colours in the motif, slipstitch or blind stitch the motif to the background fabric. Turn under the edges of the motif as you work, as described in turned-edge appliqué on pages 182–83.

4 Press the finished piece from the reverse. You can also work broderie perse by machine using zigzag stitch, or by hand using blanket stitch or a similar embroidery stitch. The motifs can also be bonded to the background fabric with fusible webbing.

Working broderie perse

Choose a motif that will stand on its own and is not crossed by the stems or leaves of adjoining motifs. Cotton fabrics that are specially printed to use for broderie perse are now available.

Additional detail, or trailing stems that are impossible to cut out neatly, can be added with embroidery stitches.

Mola

The mola is a textile from the Kuna tribes of Panama. It is a blend of appliqué and embroidery and forms part of the women's dress. Traditionally it is made in cotton fabric in strong colours, with religious themes, stylized plants and animals, and even modern elements such as rockets and advertising slogans. Molas may be made into quilts.

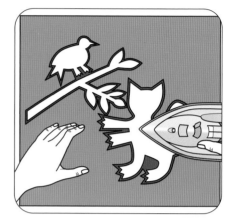

1 The mola is a type of reverse appliqué. First, cut each of the fabrics to the same size. Iron interfacing to the wrong side of the fabric that will be the bottom layer, and fusible webbing to the reverse of each of the other fabrics. Using the templates on pages 206–07, trace the main motifs on to the wrong side of the fabric that will be the top layer. Working with the top layer wrong side up, cut around each of the marked motifs, cutting not exactly on the outline but 5mm (¼in) outside it.

2 Place the top layer over the next layer down, both with the right side up. Position the motif templates in the centre of each cut-out shape. Draw around the templates on to the second layer. Working on the second layer of fabric only, cut out around each motif exactly on the marked line.

3 Peel the paper backing away from the fusible webbing on the reverse of the top layer of fabric. Place it over the second layer, aligning the cut-outs across both layers so there is a 5mm (¼in) border showing all around each. Bond the two layers together with a hot iron.

Working reverse appliqué

If you are working on a large project with lots of complex shapes over a period of time, only cut out the small section that you can work each time, otherwise the edges may begin to fray before you come to stitch them.

Note that if you are working a piece in many colours, all the different layers of fabric do not need to cover the entire area of the appliqué. This would be both bulky and a waste of fabric – you only place a layer of a different colour under the section of the appliqué where it needs to appear. However, you may want to cut through multiple layers at some points to vary the sequence of colours.

When cutting out a small motif, you may not need to cut out the central area – just clip around the edges so you can turn them under to create the shape.

4 Trace the outline of each of the motifs and colour block areas on to separate sheets of acetate. Cut out each outline to make a positive template and a negative guide to use for positioning. Choose a colour of fabric for each motif and colour block. Draw around each template on the reverse of the chosen fabric, making sure that each piece is aligned the correct way up.

5 Cut out each of the pieces in fabric. Position each piece on the fabric that will become the bottom layer, making sure none of them overlap. Use the bonded double layers made in step 3 on top to check positioning. When each piece is correctly aligned, peel off the backing and press to bond them all to the bottom layer.

6 Lay the acetate guides over the double-bonded layer and use them to mark out the colour block areas with a water-soluble marker. Remove the acetate and mark regular lozenge shapes across each colour block area. Cut out each of these lozenge shapes carefully with a sharp knife.

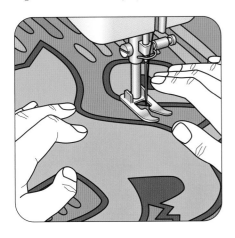

7 Remove the fusible webbing's backing paper from the reverse of the double-bonded layer. Place it over the bottom layer, aligning all the shapes carefully, and press into position with a hot iron. Using matching thread, work machine zigzag stitch around the raw edges of the top fabric.

8 Finish the mola by adding embroidered details to the main motifs (see pages 210–17 for embroidery stitches to choose from).

9 Press the finished design from the front, but use a pressing cloth. Add binding as described on pages 60–65.

Appliqué squares

Modern methods of appliqué mean that projects can even be constructed with little or no stitching involved.

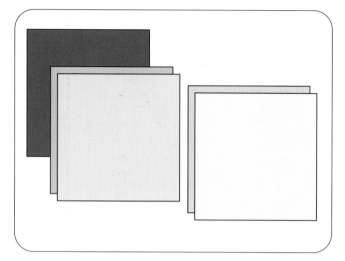

1 Cut five squares of contrasting fabric, all the same size as your finished block, in a range of shades: dark, medium-dark, medium, medium-light and light. The dark square is the backing. Layer the other four in pairs with a layer of fusible webbing between: medium-dark with medium; medium-light with light. Bond the pairs together with a hot iron.

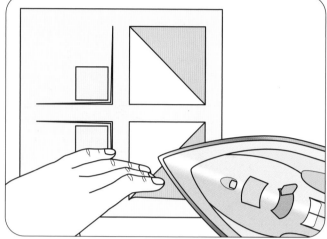

2 Working on the lightest pair (medium-light with light), cut a triangular flap in each quadrant. Fold the flaps back and secure in the corners with small squares of fusible webbing.

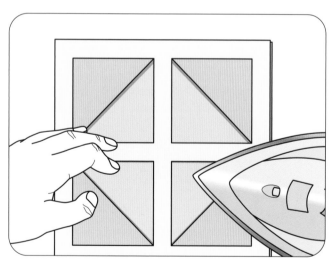

3 Using strips of fusible webbing, bond the section made in step 2 on top of the other bonded pair of squares, aligning the edges.

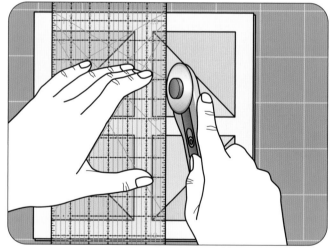

4 Measure 5mm (¼in) from the previous cut and cut a triangular flap in each quadrant of the bottom layer, being careful not to cut into the fold.

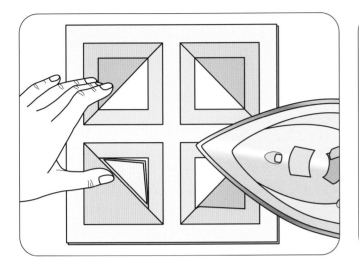

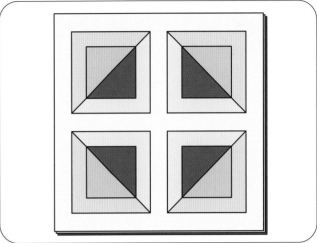

5 Fold these new flaps back and secure in the corners again with small triangles of fusible webbing.

6 Lay the completed sequence on top of the backing square and bond in position. Make a variety of blocks, using different sequences of colours, then bond to a backing fabric in the desired order.

7 A wide selection of variations on this basic theme is possible – try cutting the flaps on point, as shown here, or using striped fabric for a different effect.

templates

Oak Leaf and Reel

Copy each piece of the template to the size you need.

Hawaiian

Enlarge your chosen template to the size you need.

Mola

The templates are shown full size, but you can
reduce or enlarge them to the size you need.

embellished quilts

Quiltmakers have often added extra embellishments to their quilts by including embroidery, sequins and beads, or even painting or dyeing the fabric. Signature or friendship quilts feature signatures or names as part of the design, while crazy quilts are the ultimate expression of an embellished quilt.

techniques

There are hundreds of ways to embellish fabric, but perhaps the most popular is with embroidery. Beads, sequins and colouring the fabric in some way are also particularly common embellishment techniques.

Embroidery

A specialist embroidery book will feature hundreds more embroidery stitches than the ones featured here, but these basic ones will be used again and again.

Starting off

There are several ways of securing the thread when beginning to embroider.

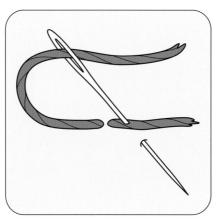

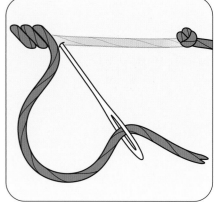

1 Overstitching – Bring the threaded needle up through the fabric, leaving a long end on the reverse. Hold the end in place as you begin stitching, until it is secured by the stitches, then cut off any excess.

2 Knot – Make a knot at the end of the thread, then take the needle down through the fabric. Work stitches over the thread on the reverse until it is secure, then cut off the knot and pull the tail to the back.

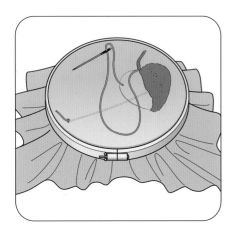

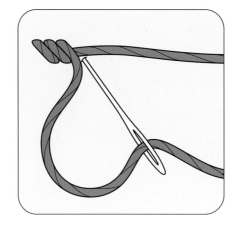

3 Waste knot – Make a knot at the end of the thread, then take the needle down through the fabric so the knot is about 15cm (6in) away from the working area. When you have finished stitching, cut off the knot and weave in the thread end on the reverse.

4 Tie-on – On the reverse, take a tiny stitch, leaving a short end. Make a small cross stitch through the tail. This method works best if the final embroidery will hide the small cross stitch.

Changing threads

If the thread runs out in the middle of a line of stitching, this method will hide the change to a new length of thread.

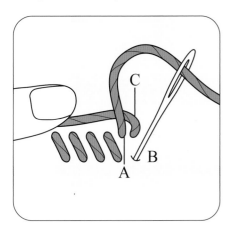

1 Come up at A with the old thread. Thread a new length in another needle and come up at C, holding the thread in position on the right side. With the old thread and needle, go down at B and fasten off. Continue stitching with the new thread.

Finishing off

At the end of a sequence of stitching, secure the thread firmly.

1 Take the needle and thread through to the reverse of the fabric. Weave the needle in and out of a few adjacent stitches and pull the thread through gently.

Running stitch

This simple stitch is similar to quilting stitch in appearance, but is worked in a different way. It is ideal for outlining and details.

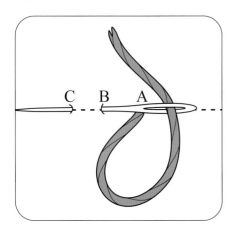

1 Come up through the fabric at A, back down through it at B, then up to the surface again at C. Don't pull the thread through the fabric yet.

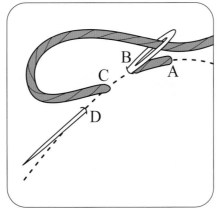

2 Continue by going back down through the fabric at D and coming up at E. Pull the thread through very gently to avoid causing gathers in the fabric.

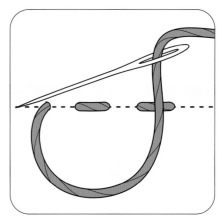

3 Keep working steps 1 and 2 along the line of the design, making the stitches smooth and even.

Stem stitch

Stem stitch, which dates back to Ancient Egypt and Peru, is another popular outlining stitch and creates a smooth line.

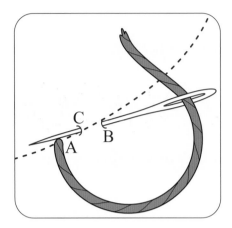 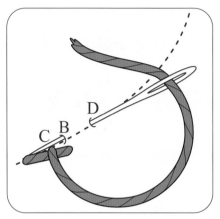 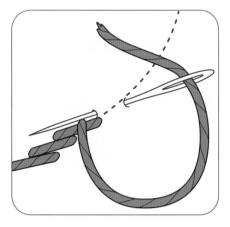

1 Come up through the fabric at A, back down through it at B, then up to the surface again at C. Keep the thread below the needle as you work.

2 Continue by going back down through the fabric at D and coming up just to the left of B. The stitches should be slightly diagonal, with each stitch overlapping the end of the previous one a little.

3 Keep working steps 1 and 2 along the line of the design, making the stitches smooth and even.

Backstitch

Backstitch creates a continuous line of stitches, which looks like machine stitching on the right side.

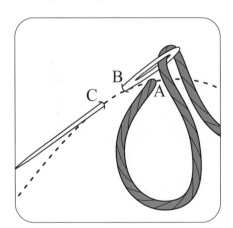 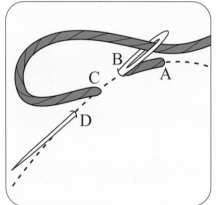 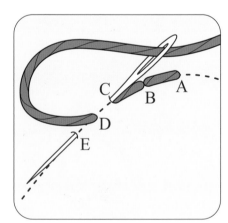

1 Working from right to left, come up through the fabric at A, go down into it again at B and up at C. Pull the thread through.

2 Go down into the fabric at B to make a backstitch, then up again at D ready for the next stitch. Pull the thread through.

3 Go down into the fabric at C again and up at E to form the next stitch. Keep repeating this sequence to create a continuous line of even stitches that touch each other.

Cross stitch

This stitch has been used for centuries in all kinds of ways, in many different scales and with several variations.

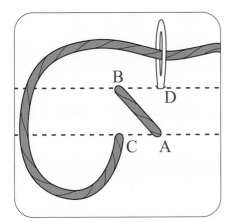

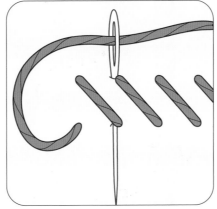

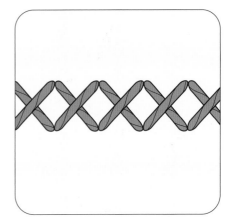

1 To make a single cross stitch, come up through the fabric at A, go down into it again at B, up to the surface at C and down again at D. It can also be worked so the top half of the stitch slants the other way.

2 To make a row of cross stitches, first work a row of even stitches that all slant in the same way. To work back down the row, start by putting the needle in at the top of the previous stitch.

3 Work diagonal stitches back down the row, slanting the other way, to form a line of even crosses.

French knot

A versatile stitch, which creates a small bead on the surface of the fabric. It can be used to add texture, highlight details or create a dotted line.

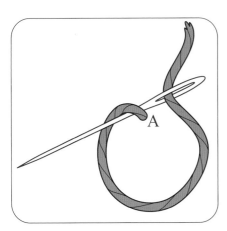

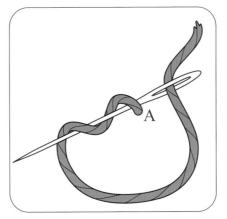

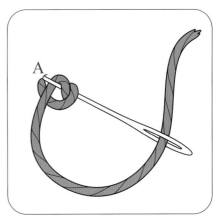

1 Come up through the fabric at A and wrap the thread around the needle once in an anticlockwise direction.

2 Keeping the needle away from the fabric, wrap the thread around the needle a second time in the same way.

3 Push the wraps together, and slide them to the end of the needle. Take the needle down near where it came out of the fabric, pulling the thread through to create a knot.

Fly stitch

This stitch can be worked as scattered single stitches to add texture across an area, or in vertical or horizontal rows to form a line.

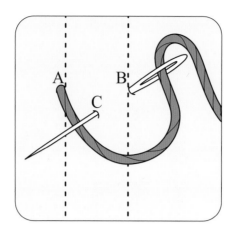

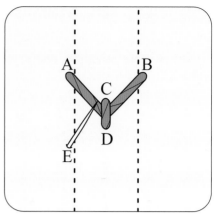

1 Come up through the fabric at A, go down into it at B and up to the surface at C. Keep the needle over the working thread.

2 Go down into the fabric again at D to form a short, straight stitch holding down the loop just made. Come up at E to begin the next stitch.

Feather stitch

This is a pretty, feathery stitch, which was once very popular for decorating English smocks. It can be used to create lines or as a filling stitch.

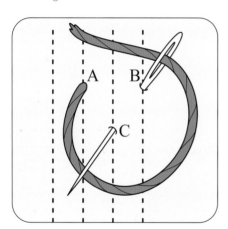

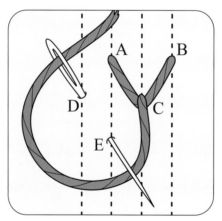

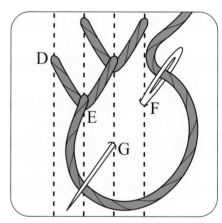

1 Come up through the fabric at A, go down into it at B and up to the surface at C. Loop the thread under the point of the needle from left to right.

2 Go down into the fabric at D, over to the left of C, and up at E. Loop the thread under the point of the needle from right to left.

3 Go back over to the other side to go down into the fabric at F and up at G. Loop the thread under the point of the needle from left to right. Continue in this way.

Herringbone stitch

This stitch is often used in both Greek and Indian embroidery and is a variation of cross stitch.

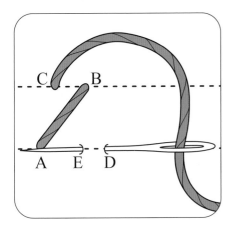

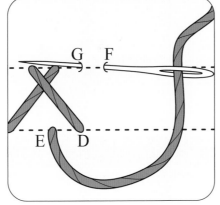

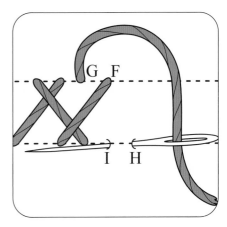

1 Come up through the fabric at A, go down into it at B and up to the surface again at C. Cross over the stitch just made and go back down into the fabric again at D and up at E. The threads will cross at the top.

2 Cross over the stitch just made again and go down into the fabric at F and up at G. The threads will cross at the bottom.

3 Cross over the stitch just made; go down at H and up at I. The threads will cross at the top. Continue repeating steps 1 and 2.

Blanket stitch

Although it can be used decoratively, blanket stitch is also used to finish raw edges. Buttonhole stitch is similar, but the uprights are worked next to one another.

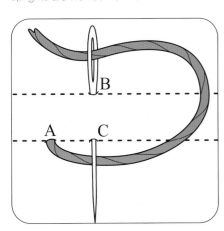

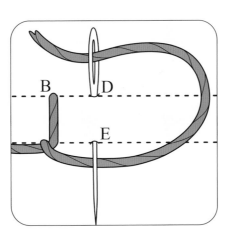

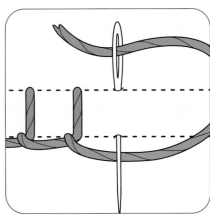

1 Come up through the fabric at A, go down at B and up again at C immediately to the right of A. Loop the thread under the point of the needle from left to right. Pull the thread through.

2 Go down into the fabric at D a short way to the right of B, and up at E. Loop the thread under the point of the needle again.

3 Continue working in this way along the line or edge, keeping the stitches evenly sized and spaced.

Chain stitch and lazy daisy stitch

A decorative looped stitch that can be
used to make a chain line, or worked in
a circle to make a flower.

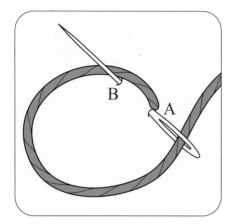

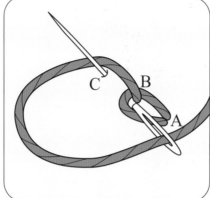

1 Come up through the fabric at A,
then go down into it again slightly to
the left of A and come up to the surface
again at B. Loop the thread under the
point of the needle from right to left.

2 Pull the thread through. Start the
next chain by going down into the
fabric again slightly to the left of B, inside
the first loop, and then up at C. Loop the
thread around the point again.

3 To make a flower, work the first
chain as in step 1 and pull the
thread through. Make a small stitch over
the loop to hold it in place. Make five
stitches in a circle.

Knotted insertion stitch

Also called knotted faggot stitch, this
decorative stitch is often used to join two
pieces of fabric.

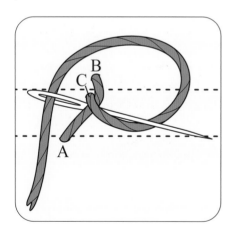

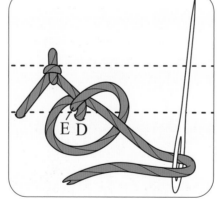

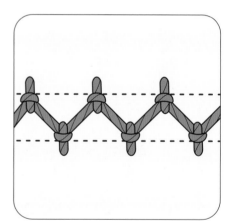

1 Come up through the fabric at A, go
back down through it at B and up
to the surface again at C. Lay the thread
over the slanting stitch, left to right. Slide
the needle under the stitch then over the
working thread. Pull the thread through.

2 Go down into the fabric at D, up at
E and pull through. Make a loop,
then slide the needle from left to right
behind both threads and through the loop
to make a knot. Repeat from B.

3 If you are using this stitch to join
two pieces of fabric, the dotted
lines show the edge of each piece.
Remember to hem the edges of the fabric
before working the stitch. Space the
edges about 5–10mm (¼–½in) apart.

Feathered chain stitch

Worked from top to bottom, this border stitch is a combination of chain stitch and feather stitch. Keep the column of stitching straight by drawing four parallel guidelines before you begin.

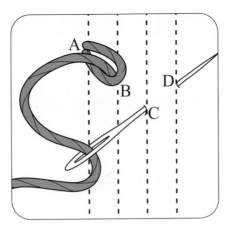

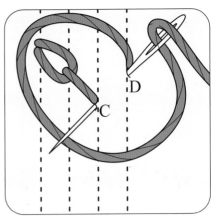

1 Come up through the fabric at A, make a loop and go down into the fabric right next to A, coming up to the surface again at B through the loop. Slanting the needle to the right, go down into the fabric at C and up at D.

2 Pull the thread through and go down into the fabric again right next to D, coming up to the surface at C. Loop the thread under the point of the needle.

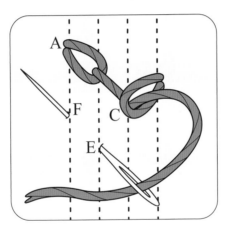

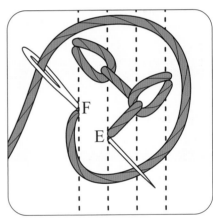

3 Slanting the needle to the left, go down into the fabric at E and up at F, making a straight stitch.

4 Pull the thread through and go down into the fabric again right next to F, coming up to the surface at E. Loop the thread under the point of the needle. Continue in this way.

Embroidering

Choose good-quality embroidery thread for your work – poor-quality thread may not be colourfast. Also, try to match the composition of the thread to the composition of the fabric.

Embroidery is easier to work if the fabric is held fairly taut: an embroidery frame will hold the area you are working on.

Embellishments

There are a few other kinds of embellishments that are used on quilts, which are perhaps less common than embroidery. Generally they are employed in quilts that are made for display rather than for day-to-day use.

Beads

Beading is a wonderful way to add texture, sparkle and colour to any kind of fabric. Beads come in a very wide range of sizes, colours and shapes, so it is relatively easy to find just the right type for a particular project.

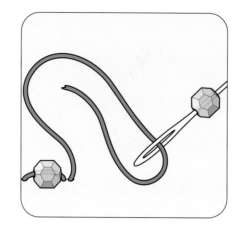

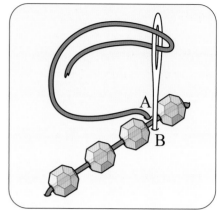

1 To sew on a single bead, come up through the fabric and the bead, then take the needle back down into the fabric close to the bead. Take a stitch under the fabric to the next bead position and repeat.

2 To sew on several beads at the same time, come up through the fabric and thread a few beads on to the needle. Go back down into the fabric at the end of the row of beads and take a small stitch to secure the thread. To couch the line of beads, come up at A, over the thread between two beads, and go back down at B. Repeat every three or four beads.

Sequins

Sequins come in a range of shapes and sizes, and may be plain or faceted, with a central hole for stitching. There are two ways of attaching them.

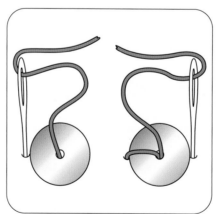

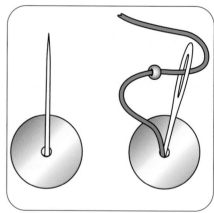

1 Using a thread that matches the sequin, come up through the central hole. Go over the sequin and back down through the fabric to one side. Repeat on the other side so the two stitches run straight across the sequin.

2 Using a thread that matches the sequin, come up through the central hole and then thread a small glass bead on to the needle – one that is bigger than the hole in the sequin. Take the thread over the bead, then take the needle back through the central hole.

Shisha mirrors

Shisha mirrors are small pieces of reflective mica that are used in embroidery, particularly in Eastern work.

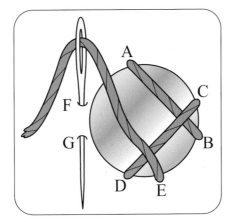

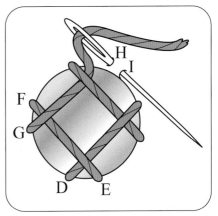

1 Place the mirror in position and bring the thread up from behind the fabric at A. Work the first four stitches over the mirror, as shown, creating a diamond-shaped grid to hold the mirror in place.

2 To keep the stitching symmetrical, slide the needle under the end of the first stitch each time you come to the end of a sequence.

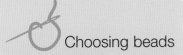 Choosing beads

Glass beads are heavier than plastic ones, but they will not melt if caught with a hot iron.

If the quilt is to be wash-able, made sure the beads are safe to wash too.

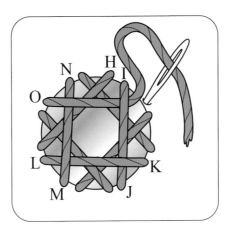

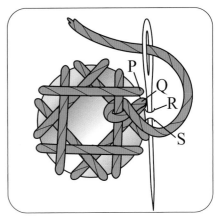

3 Work four more stitches over the first four in exactly the same way, but so the grid is rotated and set square this time.

4 Come up through the fabric very near to where the needle went in to complete the last stitch. Take the needle under and over the intersection of the vertical and diagonal stitch, then back down into the fabric just next to where you came out. Make a small stitch to take you a little further round the mirror. Repeat this sequence until all the edges of the mirror have been covered.

Fusing fabric

One of the latest techniques in textile art is to use a soldering iron to cut, bond and etch fabric. Most synthetic fabrics will begin to melt or scorch if a reasonable amount of heat is applied, and this can be used to create interesting effects. Different layers can be manipulated and attached to create three-dimensional shapes on the surface of a piece of fabric, or to add areas of texture. You can sew or embroider the finished fused fabric design into a quilt as if it were an ordinary piece of fabric. However, work of this nature may be delicate and only suitable for a quilt intended for display.

Using a soldering iron
This technique works best if there is a depth of fabric for the tip of the soldering iron to dig into. Choose a soldering iron with a pointed tip.

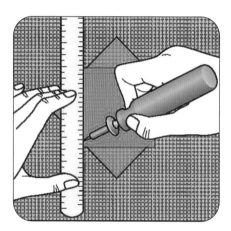 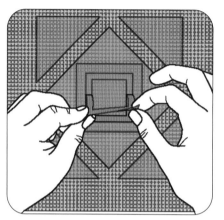 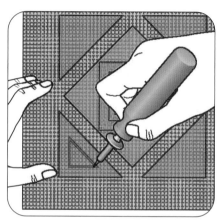

1 Layer several pieces of synthetic fabric and hold them in place with a metal ruler (work on a heat-resistant surface). To begin bonding, run the tip of the hot soldering iron along the edge of the ruler.

2 If you press quite deeply, you can cut right through some layers, but the melted edges will tend to hold the fabric layers together. When you have built up several layers, you can tear or cut away some areas to reveal the colours underneath.

3 You can also use the tip of the soldering iron to 'draw' a design on the surface of the fabric. The lines will create texture and a different colour, either from the burning effect of the iron or from the fabric revealed beneath. Freehand lines will tend to be lighter and less emphatic than those drawn along the straight edge of a ruler.

Tips for fusing fabric

Synthetic fabrics give off fumes when they melt, so do wear a mask and work near an open window.

Nylon organza is a good fabric to use for this technique: it is smooth and transparent and comes in a wide range of colours.

For the best control of the tip, hold the soldering iron like a fountain pen rather than like a knife.

Work on a heat-resistant surface and make sure there is somewhere to put the hot soldering iron when it is not in use: it will quickly cause damage if you are not careful.

Colouring fabric

You can create different effects, change the colour and add areas of pattern to fabric by using dye or paint. Fabric is very easy to dye, as long as you choose the correct type of dye for the composition of the fabric and follow the instructions carefully. Certain fabrics cannot be dyed and on others it is only possible to achieve a lighter shade of the dye colour.

Most manufacturers offer a wide range of colours, but you can also mix colours to get the exact shade you need.

Fabric paints are also available in many colours and for different types of fabric. Make sure the fabric will take the paint successfully by doing a test on a small scrap first. The colour is usually fixed by heat.

Painting with fabric paint

Fabric paints are great for adding extra colour and detail to a small area.

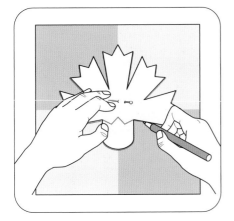

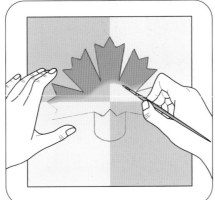

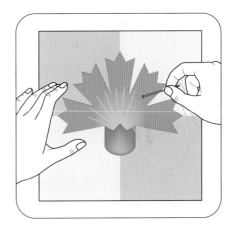

1 Make a template (see page 86) for the shape you wish to paint, place it on the fabric and draw around the outline with a suitable marker.

2 Paint within the outlines of the motif. For deep, rich colour, you may need more than one coat. You can add shading with another colour, just as you would when painting on paper.

3 Fix the colour following the manufacturer's instructions. Add embroidery or other embellishments to create any fine detail needed.

Using fabric dyes and paints

Weigh the fabric when dry to calculate quantity of dye required. Follow the manufacturer's instructions for mixing and fixing the colours. Keep utensils for dyeing separate from other items used in the home. Use rubber gloves, and protect clothes and worksurfaces.

Pre-wash fabrics thoroughly before dyeing or painting, to remove any finishes or stains that could prevent the colour from taking.

You can also use bleach to lighten the colour of fabric and to create the same fabric pattern in lighter tones, as seen in the Amoeba quilt on page 84.

Dip-dyeing

Dip-dyeing will give graded colour across a piece of fabric, running from dark to light. The darkest section will be that immersed in the dye.

1 Dissolve and mix the dye, according to the manufacturer's instructions, in a stainless-steel bowl, pan or sink.

2 Dip just one edge of the fabric into the dye and leave it to soak – the colour will gradually bleed up into the area of fabric above the waterline. When you are happy with the density and area of colour, remove the fabric and hang it to dry away from direct light or sunlight.

3 Rinse the fabric in cold water until water runs clear, then wash separately in hot water using normal washing detergent. For wool and silk, rinse in lukewarm water. Fix the dye as detailed in the manufacturer's instructions.

Tie-dyeing

The technique of tie-dyeing prevents the dye from reaching the fabric evenly – any part of the fabric that the dye can't reach will stay white or be much lighter.

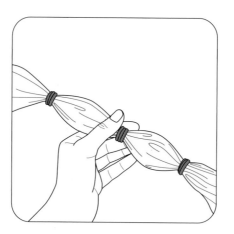 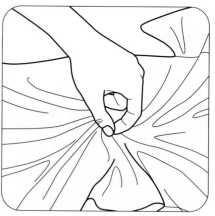

1 Dissolve and mix the dye, according to the manufacturer's instructions, in a stainless-steel bowl, pan or sink. Now either fold, pleat or twist the fabric, tying it in position securely with string or rubber bands.

2 To make the traditional circular design, lay the fabric flat and pinch the centre of where you want the circle to be. Twist the fabric into a spiral around the centre and secure with string or elastic. Immerse the fabric in the dye, then fix according to the instructions.

Redwork

Although embroidery has often been used to embellish quilts, it was rarely the main design element until redwork became popular in the late nineteenth century. Any plain outline stitch is acceptable for redwork: backstitch, stem stitch and split stitch (like stem stitch, but the thread comes up through the thread of the previous stitch each time) were all popular. Although the designs were usually stitched on white or cream cotton or calico (muslin) in red thread – hence the name – other thread colours were sometimes used, notably blue, green or black.

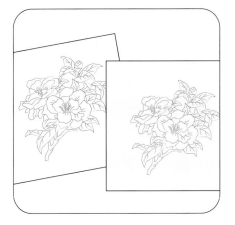

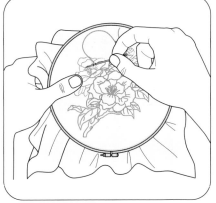

1 Select a design from the templates on pages 226–27. Transfer the design to a square of plain fabric using a suitable method (see pages 36–38).

2 Place the square of fabric in an embroidery hoop. Embroider along all the lines of the design using backstitch or stem stitch (see page 212).

3 Press the finished block. Make a selection of blocks featuring motifs with a similar theme and set them edge to edge, or with sashing, to make up the quilt top.

Friendship quilts

Sometimes called autograph quilts, album quilts or presentation quilts, friendship quilts were made to commemorate a special occasion or as a gift for someone moving away. They featured the people's signatures: sometimes these were just signed in ink, but often the names were then embroidered to preserve them.

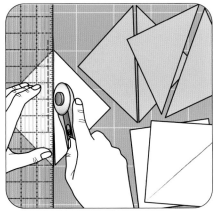

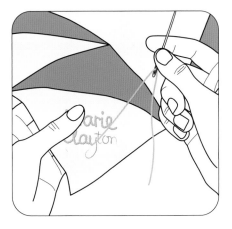

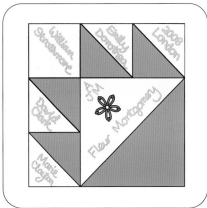

1 Make up the basic block – almost any design is fine, as long as it has enough plain space for the signatures.

2 Use a fine marker to write on the signatures. Embroider over each one using backstitch or stem stitch.

3 The finished block can be set with spacer blocks or with sashing to make up the quilt top.

Sashiko

Sashiko is traditionally worked in a special thick, white
thread on indigo fabric, in a range of geometric designs or
stylized motifs.

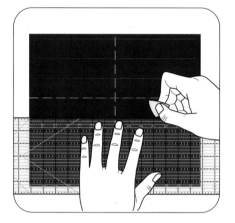

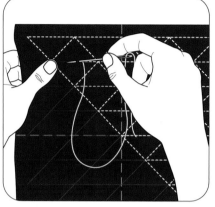

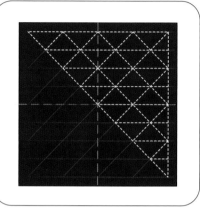

1 Plan out the design on the fabric,
using a suitable method (see pages
36–38). Layer the top and the backing
fabric – sashiko does not always need a
layer of wadding (batting).

2 Thread a needle with special
sashiko thread, or embroidery
thread, and stitch along the lines of the
design. Use larger stitches spaced more
widely apart than when quilting, but keep
the stitches and the spaces between
them even.

3 The final design is ready to make
up as a block in a quilt top, or as
a cushion cover, bag or wall hanging.

Creating a sashiko or kantha design

Although sashiko is commonly seen in white thread on indigo fabric,
it can also be done on red fabric and in blue or red on white or
cream. The special sashiko thread is also available in a wide range
of other colours.

Sashiko designs are simple but elegant. A measure of restraint in
using motifs is the key to creating the look.

Kantha embroidery (see page 45) is typically done in bright thread
to create a variety of traditional and stylized motifs on a pale fabric
background. Traditional thread colours are red, yellow, black and blue.

Crazy patchwork

This technique uses scraps of fabric in random shapes and sizes. Luxurious fabrics such as velvet, silk and satin are ideal. The scraps are embellished with embroidery, beads or sequins. The steps below use the foundation-piecing technique, but the scraps can also be machine- or hand-pieced.

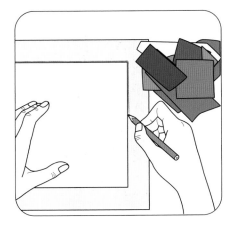

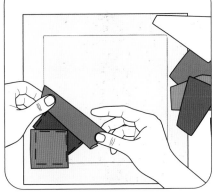

1 Draw an outline of the area you want to cover on the background fabric to use as a guideline as you work – the pieces should extend slightly over this line. Gather the scraps of fabric together so they are handy for making a selection.

2 Starting in one corner, tack (baste) the first piece of fabric to the background. Fold under the raw edge on the next piece, to prevent the edges fraying too much. Place the next piece with its folded edge covering the raw edge of the first piece, and tack in position. Continue in this way until the marked area is completely covered.

3 Secure the patches in place permanently by working a selection of hand embroidery stitches (see pages 210–17) along all the edges. Make sure you stitch through all the layers, and into the background fabric.

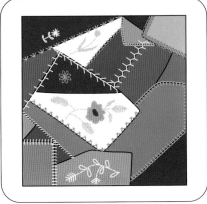

4 Remove all the tacking (basting) threads and add further decoration as required, such as embroidery motifs, beads, sequins or lace.

Working crazy patchwork

The more decoration that is added to a crazy patchwork design, the better the final effect will be. The Victorians used ribbons, lace, beads, buttons and masses of embroidery to achieve a luxurious look.

Contained crazy patchwork is a technique in which the scraps are made up into blocks and the blocks are then joined together into a quilt, sometimes with sashing added. This way of working was more popular in America – in Britain the scraps were more usually made up into one large piece of fabric.

templates.

Redwork

Reduce or enlarge your chosen template to the size you need.

Sashiko

Reduce or enlarge your chosen template to the size you need.

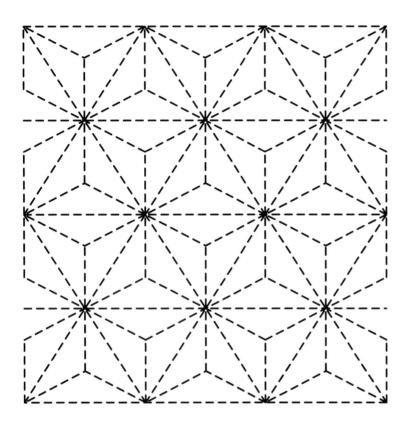

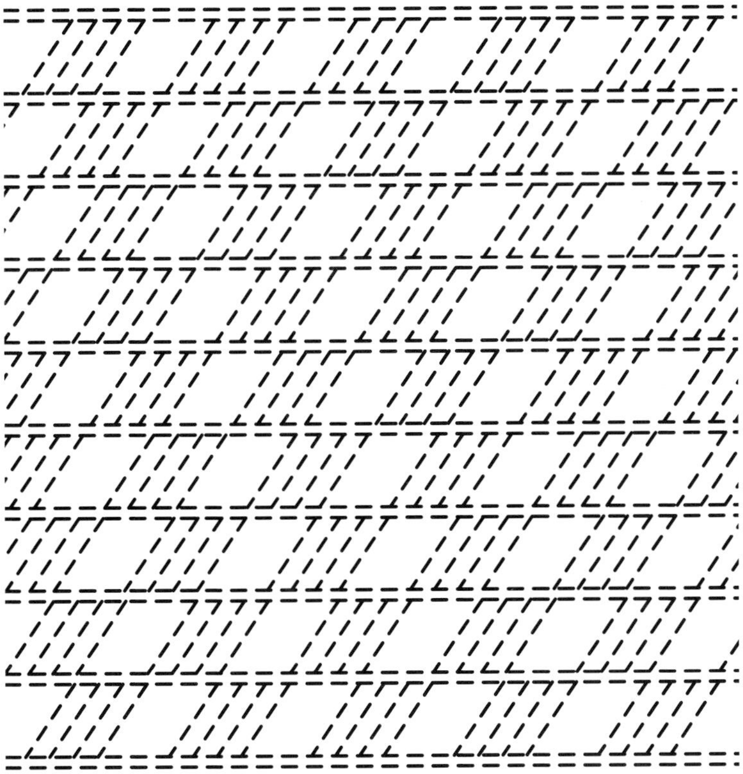

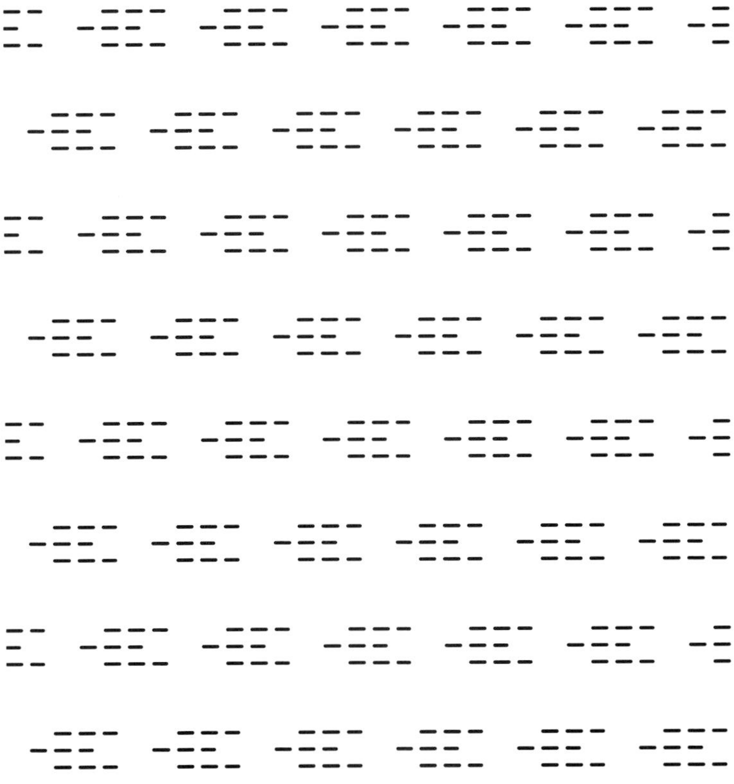

embellished quilts

folded quilts

As long as people have worked with fabric, they have also experimented with different ways of manipulating it. Folding not only gives extra layers for additional warmth, but can also be used to add interesting shapes and texture. Folded edges don't fray, so folding can even save time by cutting out steps in the process of stitching.

cathedral window

Cathedral Window can appear to be very complex, particularly when another square of contrasting fabric is inserted into the folded window. Since the patchwork is made up of several layers, it does not need wadding (batting) or a backing layer. There are also other ways to get a similar effect – see Japanese folded patchwork on pages 236–38, and Chinese Coin opposite.

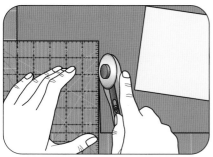

1 Cut four large squares of the main fabric, each approximately the same size as you wish the finished block to be.

2 Fold all four edges of each square over by 5mm (¼in) and finger-press in place. Try to keep the corners as neat and square as possible.

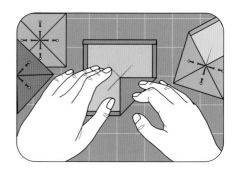

3 Fold one of the squares diagonally to find the centre point, then fold the opposite corners in to meet at the centre. Pin in place, then repeat with the other three squares.

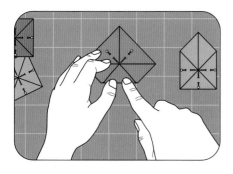

4 Fold opposite corners into the centre again and press. Make a small stitch in matching thread to hold down the points in the centre – note that this stitch will show.

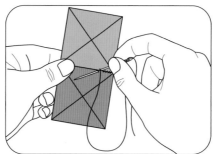

5 You will now have four folded units that are a quarter of the size of the original squares of fabric. Whipstitch these four units together – this seam won't show at the end.

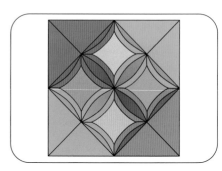

6 Cut four squares of contrasting fabric, each slightly smaller than one folded unit. Place these on point to cover the whipstitched seams that were made in step 5.

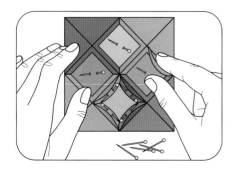

7 Roll the folded edges of the units over to cover the raw edges of the contrasting squares. Slipstitch along all the folded edges, but try to ensure that the stitches do not show on the finished item (shown right).

Secret Garden

This is the reverse of Cathedral Window; to make it, follow steps 1–3, then add the square of contrasting fabric to the middle of the folded square before continuing with steps 4 and 5. Omit step 6; when the edges of the main square are rolled back in step 7, the contrast fabric will show as an 'X' on each folded unit.

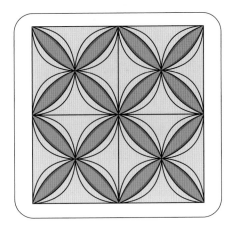

Chinese Coin

This is yet another variation of Cathedral Window – although some believe that Cathedral Window actually originated in China, so this would just be another way of working the technique using less fabric. It's best to use closely woven fabrics for Cathedral Window, which keep their shape well during the folding and ironing process.

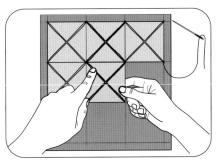

1 Cut squares of fabric and fold the points into the centre. Cut some small squares just a little smaller than the folded squares you have just made, and a large square of contrasting fabric to use as a backing.

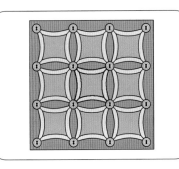

2 Place the large backing square with the right side facing upwards. Position rows of folded squares on top so that they all butt up to each other. Tack (baste) the folded squares in place at the corners only.

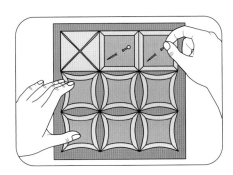

3 Place the small squares, right side up, on top of each of the folded squares and pin in place. Roll the edges of the folded squares over the top of the small squares, hiding the raw edges. Slipstitch in place.

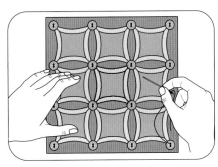

4 The squares that you folded in step 1 do not have turned-under edges, so at each corner where the points meet, there can be a tiny bit of raw edge showing, which can look untidy and begin to fray. Cover with a small circle of felt, a button or a bead.

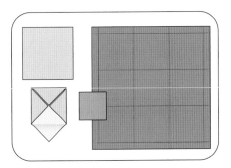

5 The completed design. Cathedral Window is also called Lucky Coin or Ancient Coin in China, because the final effect can resemble an overlapping series of old Chinese coins, which are round with a square hole in the centre.

folded log cabin

Log Cabin is one of the most popular traditional designs because it is so versatile. This folded construction technique can be used to make any of the block layouts and setting variations featured on pages 103–14 with the advantage that the folded edge covers the stitching in each round.

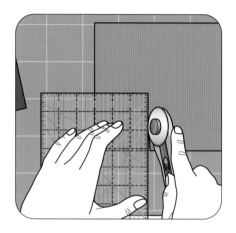

1 Cut a centre square – traditionally this is red. Cut strips slightly wider than the centre square in a range of light fabrics and dark fabrics.

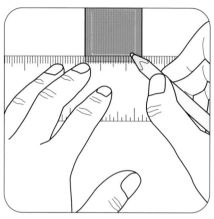

2 Measure and mark a seam allowance of 5mm (¼in) on each side of the centre square.

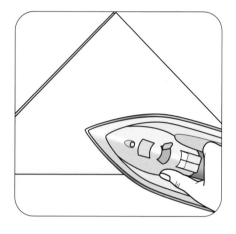

3 Fold the backing square in half diagonally, twice, and press to find the centre. Fold the strips in half lengthways and press.

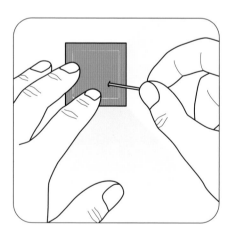

4 Place the centre square right in the centre of the backing square, using the fold lines made in step 3 as a guide, and pin in position.

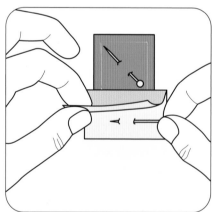

5 Line up the fold of the first strip with the seam line on one side of the centre square. Open out the strip and stitch along the fold line.

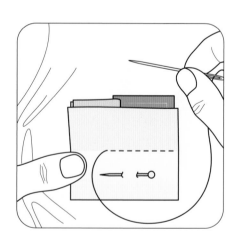

6 Fold the strip back. Turn the backing square round and add the next strip in the same way, making sure the previous strip is flat beneath.

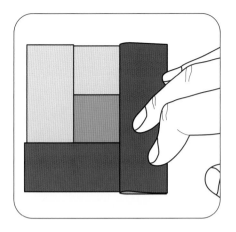

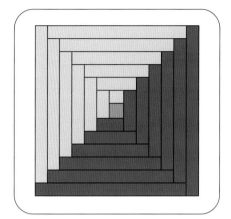

7 Keep working around the central square, following the correct order of light and dark for the block layout.

8 As you finish each round of strips, mark a new seam allowance around the edge as in step 2.

9 This technique can also be worked using machine stitching. Take care that each strip remains completely flat.

japanese folded patchwork

This technique gives a look similar to that of Cathedral Window, but because the construction is much less fiddly, it is possible to incorporate a square of wadding (batting) in each unit to make the finished quilt warmer. There are two different ways to make the folded units.

Circle-and-square

This method uses a square and a circle, and is slightly less wasteful of fabric than the two-circle method. The stitch holding the edges can be a very small running stitch, as shown here, or edges can be slipstitched in place so the stitching shows less.

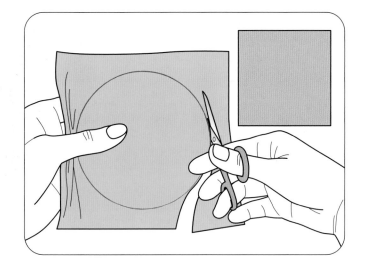

1 Cut a circle of fabric and a square in a contrasting colour. The square should be about the size of one finished unit, the circle big enough to cover the square plus a little extra. If you want to add wadding (batting), cut a square of wadding slightly smaller than the square.

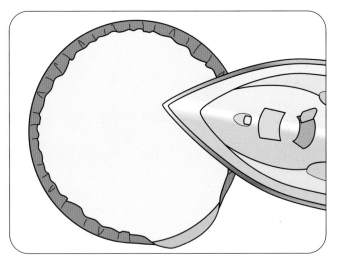

2 Fold over the edges of the circle to the wrong side and press in place. You will find it easier to keep the circle perfectly round if you use a thick paper template and press the edges over it as in English paper piecing (see page 90), then remove the paper.

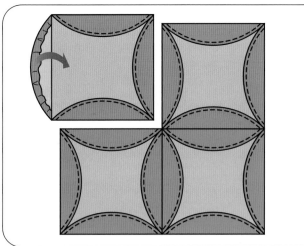

3 Place the wadding (batting), if used, on top of the wrong side of the circle, then place the square on top, right side up. Fold the edges of the circle over the square on all four sides to conceal the raw edges and stitch in place. Make three more units in the same way and whipstitch them together.

Two-circle

This method uses two circles and is really easy to work, although it is a little bit harder to incorporate the wadding (batting) in the units.

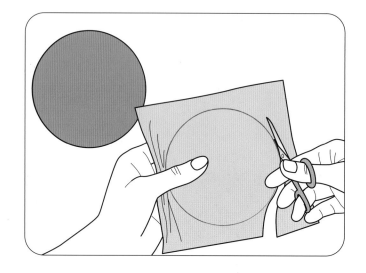

1 Cut two circles of fabric the same size, in contrasting colours. The circles should be big enough to cover the area of one unit, plus seam allowance. If you want to add wadding (batting), cut a square of wadding slightly smaller than the finished unit will be.

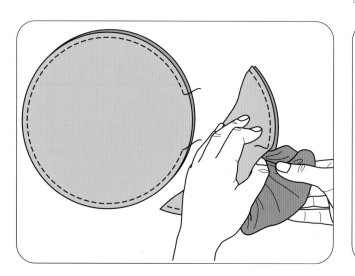

2 Place the two circles, right sides together, with edges aligned and stitch all round, leaving a small gap to turn through. Turn right side out, then push the square of wadding (batting) inside (if used) and pin in place in the centre. Slipstitch the gap in the edge closed.

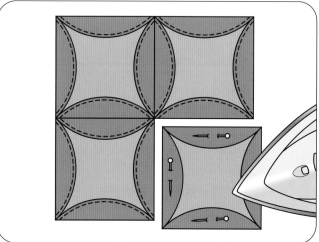

3 Fold over the edges of the circle on all four sides to make a square unit, then press and pin in place. Work either slipstitch or running stitch around the edges to hold them in position. Make three more units in the same way and whipstitch them together.

tucks

If you combine pintucks with strips of fabric in different colours, a whole range of new effects can be created. The pintucks can be spaced equally apart or can be irregular – and the strips between the tucks can also vary in width.

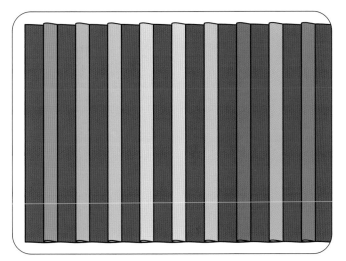

1 You can either make coloured tucks against a black background, as shown here, or black tucks with plain coloured strips between, as in the following steps.

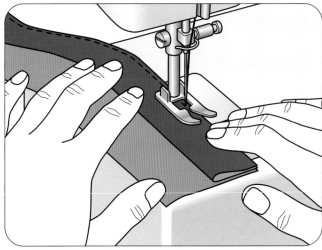

2 Cut strips of fabrics in various colours and a selection of strips in one colour. Fold the single-colour strips in half. Place one folded strip on the right side of a coloured strip, with raw edges aligned. Stitch the folded strip in place.

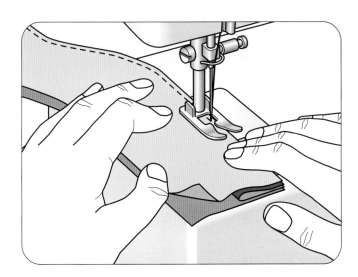

3 Place another coloured strip (right side down) on top of the folded strip, with raw edges aligned. Stitch the coloured strip in place.

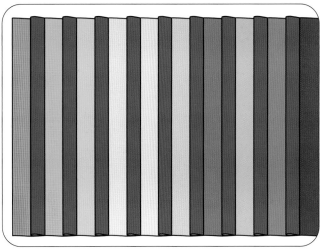

4 Carry on in this way until you have a piece of fabric with varying coloured stripes, separated by pintucks that are all in one colour.

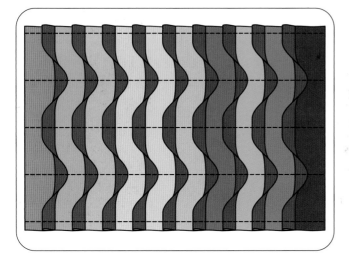

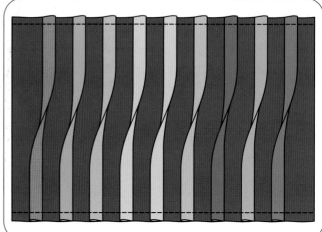

Wave tucks

Press all the tucks in one direction. Stitch down the edge of the block to hold the tucks flat, and in a straight line down the centre. Mark lines an equal distance between the centre line of stitching and the two edge lines. Stitch along each of these lines in turn, pressing each tuck in the opposite direction as you stitch it.

Twist tucks

This technique works best on narrow strips of tucked fabric. Press all the tucks in one direction, then stitch down one edge of the strip only, to hold them in place. On the opposite side of the strip, press the tucks the other way, so there is a twist in the middle of each, and stitch down this edge to hold all the tucks in position.

Making tucked fabric

British quilter Louise Mabbs has developed a quicker method of making pieces of tucked fabric. Cut all the strips of fabric, then just stitch them together flat, alternating coloured and black strips to make a striped piece of fabric. Decide if you want the colour or the black to be the tuck, and then just stitch the adjacent seams together.

Inserting straight tucks

This technique uses straight strips of a contrasting fabric, simply folded in half and inserted at intervals across the block.

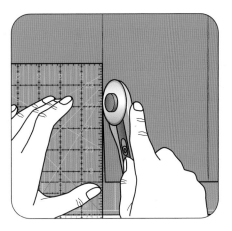

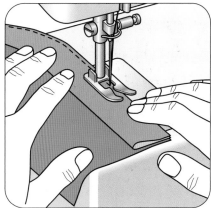

1 Mark straight lines across the background square, where you want to insert the tucks. Cut the square apart along the lines, using a rotary cutter and ruler.

2 Cut the strip of fabric for the tuck and press it in half lengthways. Lay it on the right side of the first section of the background square, with raw edges aligned. Stitch in place.

Working on the bias

Angled or curved cuts in the background square will be on the bias; mark notches at 5cm (2in) intervals on all the lines before cutting the square apart. Stretch the bias-cut background fabric as you sew in the tuck, while keeping the tuck at normal tension. Stretch the next layer of background fabric to match the notches on the first before stitching it in place. The seams will look puckered at first, but will relax into place.

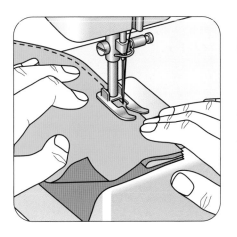

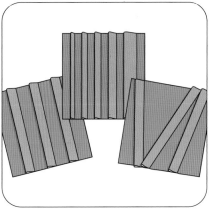

3 Lay the next section of background square on top, with the right side facing the tuck and raw edges aligned. Stitch in place.

4 Repeat the process to insert the other tucks. You can create different effects by varying the width of the tucks, or by placing them at an angle.

Inserting curved tucks

Tucks do not need to be inserted in straight lines – you can also create curves or shallow spirals.

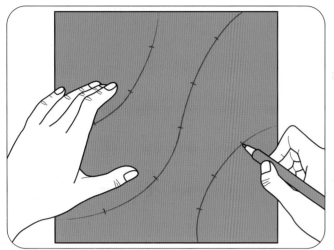

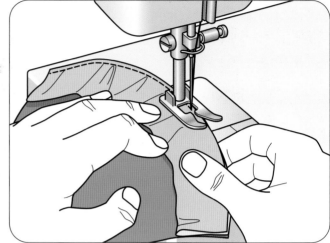

1 Mark freehand curving lines across the background square where you want to insert the tucks; mark notches at 5cm (2in) intervals on all the lines before cutting the square apart. Cut the square apart along the lines, using a rotary cutter.

2 Cut the strip of fabric for the tuck and press it in half lengthways. Lay it on the right side of the first section of the background square, with raw edges aligned. Stitch in place, remembering to stretch the background fabric and keep the tuck at the normal tension (see page 239).

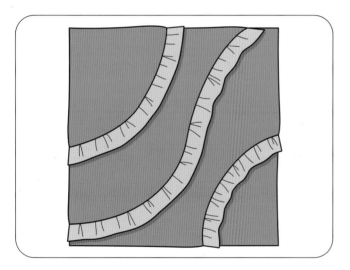

3 Lay the next section of background square on top, with the right side facing the tuck and raw edges aligned. Stretch this top piece gently so the notches align with those on the first section of background, then stitch in position. The seams will relax into place, causing the tucks to gather slightly.

Adding spirals

If you cover the surface of a block with a tuck stitched into
a spiral, it gives a wonderful three-dimensional flower effect.

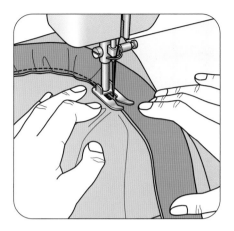 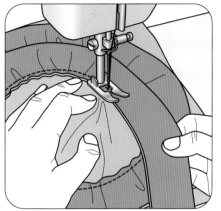 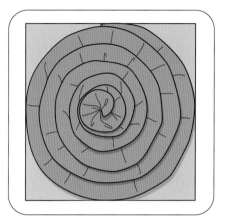

1 Make a very long strip of bias fabric
– join two sections (see page 64)
to achieve the correct length if necessary.
Press the strip in half and fold under at
one end. Mark the seam allowance on
the edge of the block. Beginning with the
turned-under end of the strip, align the
beginning of the long folded edge with
the marked line in the centre of one side
of the square. Start stitching the spiral
in place near the raw edge of the strip.

2 Ease the strip as you work so
that the folded edge lies as flat
as possible and the raw edge is slightly
gathered. This will ensure that the strip
lies flat and covers the raw edges of the
previous round.

3 At the centre, tuck the ends of the
strip under before stitching in place.
You can begin at the centre of the square
and work outwards in a spiral for a slightly
different effect.

Adding pleated strips

This uses exactly the same idea as the
spirals, but the strips of fabric are cut
straight, not on the bias, and pleated to
change direction, which will give a more
angular look.

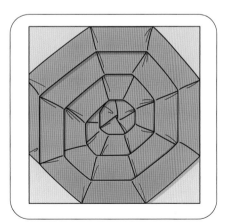 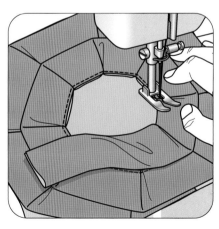

1 Here the spirals are pleated
outwards. Begin at the centre and
add pleats to change direction as you
work towards the edge.

2 In this block the strip is pleated
inwards. Start at the outer edge
and add pleats to change direction as
you work towards the centre.

folded quilts

folded pinwheel

This is based on a twist fold that is quite often used in origami, which has been adapted in different ways by several quiltmakers in order to work in fabric – this version was developed by the British fabric artist, Wendy Lowes. It gives a pinwheel effect that would be complicated to make using piecing – although piecing would offer the option of using several colours.

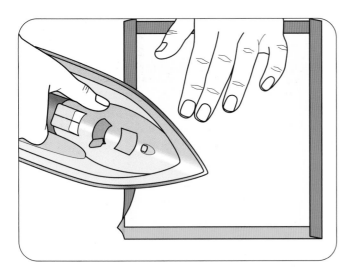

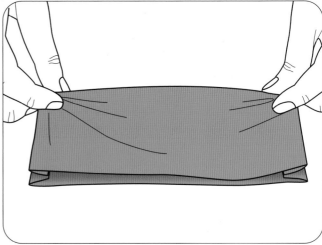

1 Cut a square of fabric twice the width and length of the finished block. Turn over 5mm (¼in) to the wrong side along all four edges; the easiest way to do this is to cut a square of thick paper with sides 1cm (½in) smaller than the fabric square, place it on top and press the edges of the fabric over it.

2 Fold the square in half, wrong sides facing. Finger-press – or use an iron – at the very ends of the fold only to make a little pinch mark in the centre of each side. Don't press all the way across the fold. Repeat in the other direction.

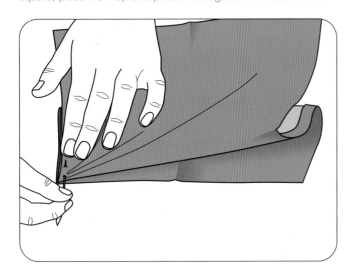

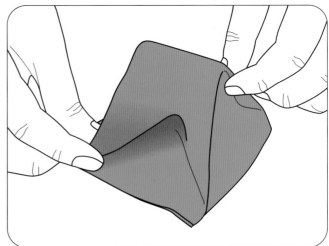

3 Lay the square flat again, then take one of the pinch marks just made and move it up so it aligns with the corner above. Insert a small pin parallel to the edge, to hold all the layers in place.

4 Repeat steps 3 and 4 with the other three pinch marks. You should now have a little dome of fabric standing up in the middle of the square.

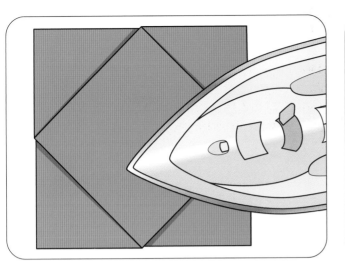
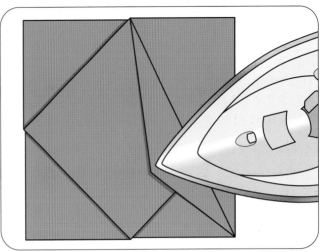

5 Gently press down the dome of fabric with the tips of your fingers – it will form a diamond in the centre of the square. Press the diamond flat with an iron.

6 Lift one corner of the diamond and fold it over to make a new fold line running from the point of the diamond to the opposite point of the square.

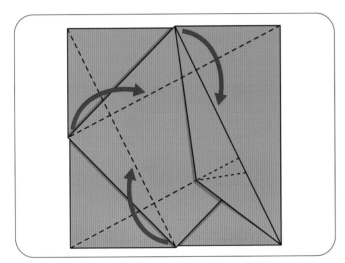
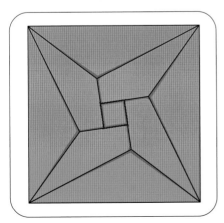

7 Repeat with the other three corners of the diamond. This origami-style diagram shows the first fold described in step 8 completed, with dotted lines and arrows showing the other three folds still to be made.

8 Tuck the end of the last fold under the first, to keep the pattern symmetrical. Make a tiny stitch at the eight points where the folds meet in the centre of the square, to hold them all in place.

9 The lines of the finished pinwheel provide a strong, graphic image in a single colour of fabric. When this block is folded in striped fabric, amazingly complex designs can be achieved.

suffolk puff

Suffolk puffs – called yo-yos in the USA – are puffy little circles of fabric that can be stitched together to make an openwork coverlet. They can also be used as embellishments. They normally don't contain wadding (batting), although there is no reason why a small piece should not be inserted in the circle before it is gathered.

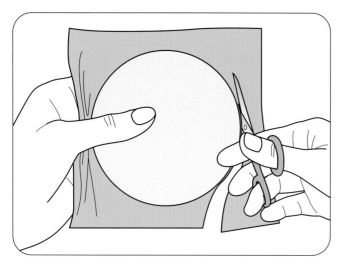

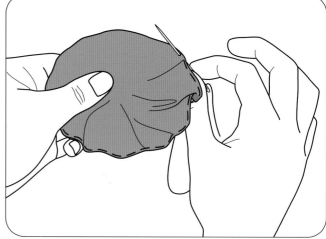

1 Cut out a circle of thick paper twice the size that the finished puff will be. Use this as a template to cut circles of fabric, remembering to add an extra 5mm (¼in) seam allowance all around.

2 Lay a fabric circle, right side down, with the template on top and press the seam allowance over the paper, gathering excess fabric as necessary to achieve a smooth edge. Remove the paper. Work a line of running stitches around the edge of the circle to hold the hem in place, but don't fasten off the end of the thread.

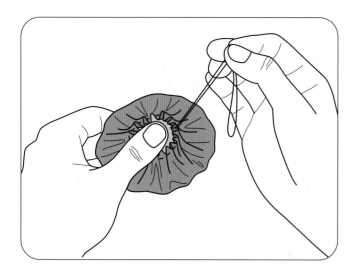

3 Pull the thread tight to gather the fabric edges into the centre, then fasten off the thread out of sight inside the hem. Even up the gathers all round, then firmly press the puff flat with your hand.

Using Suffolk puffs

If you are using the puffs as embellishment, you can either slipstitch them to the background around the edge, or use an embroidery stitch. If you are joining them together for a coverlet, keep them all the same way up and stitch the circles together only where they touch.

somerset patchwork

Somerset patchwork, a technique where small squares or rectangles of fabric are folded into triangles and stitched along one edge to a backing fabric, is better known as folded star or quill patchwork in the USA. As the technique consumes huge amounts of fabric, it is generally used to make smaller items such as tiny cushions or box tops, or to add an area of texture to a plain quilt.

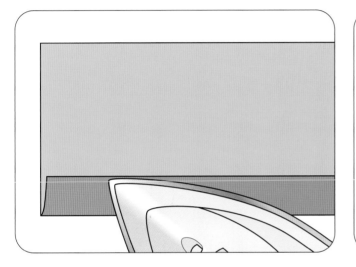

1 Cut a small rectangle of fabric, fold up the bottom long edge and press into place.

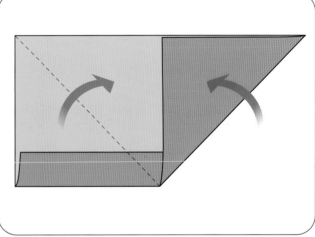

2 Find the centre of the folded edge and fold up from this point, so half the folded edge now runs vertically upwards from the centre point. Repeat on the other side to form a pyramid with a slit down the centre.

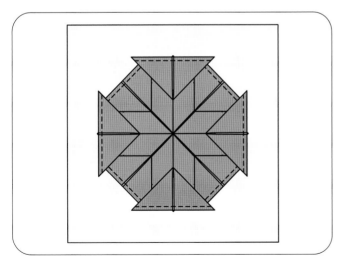

3 Arrange four folded points in a circle, with edges touching, and stitch to a backing fabric along the bottom edges. Add further concentric circles of points, with the tips aligning in straight rows towards the centre (make sure you cover the bottom raw edges of the previous line each time).

Spanish Points

The variation known as Spanish Points is made in a slightly different way to achieve a narrower triangle with no slit down the middle.

Begin as in step 1, but in step 2 fold over further so the first half of the folded edge is at a greater angle. When the second side is folded over in the same way, the layers of fabric will overlap each other completely. The top edge of the triangle will not be straight – it will have two little points with raw edges sticking up, which can either be snipped off or just concealed in a seam or by the following rows of points.

glossary

acetate – Flexible, totally clear film. Useful for transferring separate colour block areas of a motif to fabric.

album quilt – Quilt made of many different blocks, often with symbolic designs appliquéd on each block. If each block is signed, it is known as an autograph or signature quilt.

Amish quilt – The Amish people are a religious culture. Their antique quilts tend to use rich, jewel-like, solid colours with black as a background, often in striking geometric patterns, with wide, plain borders. Modern Amish quilts made for sale can use any fabric in any design, but retain the excellent quilting. The Amish quilt trade is generally found in Pennsylvania, Ohio or Indiana.

appliqué – A piecing process using small amounts of fabric or fabric motifs sewn on to a background fabric in a decorative design. Appliqué can be done by hand, machine or with fusible webbing, and is often combined with pieced blocks or placed in a border to frame a pieced quilt. Appliqué is a great technique for covering stains, rips or other problem areas.

backing – The bottom or back layer of a quilt, usually a plain fabric that has been pieced to the width of the quilt.

bagging a quilt – The method of sewing the wadding (batting) and backing to the outside edges of a quilt (right sides together), then turning the whole thing inside out as if it were a pillowcase. If you have laid out the layers correctly, the wadding will be in the middle, and you can just slipstitch the turn-through opening to close it and to finish.

Baltimore album quilts – An elegant form of intricate appliqué that was very popular in the mid-nineteenth century in Baltimore, Maryland, USA.

bargello quilting – A design layout with offset blocks of colour in a rising or falling, flame-like pattern.

basting – US term for tacking.

batik – A method of fabric dyeing in which areas of design are covered with wax or another resist substance to prevent dye from penetrating into that area. Indonesia is particularly famous for its batiks.

batting – US term for wadding or stuffing.

bearding – When fibres from the wadding (batting) pass through a quilt top and form a fuzz on the surface of the quilt; thought to be caused by static electricity. It is usually associated with cheap polyester wadding, but can also occur with other types.

betweens – Small, thin needles used for finishing quilting. Sizes range from 8–12, the smaller number being a longer-length needle.

bias – The diagonal direction across woven fabric, at a 45° angle to the warp and the weft threads. Fabric cut on the bias stretches and must be handled with great care. Bias binding allows binding to be curved without pleating.

bias binding – See Binding.

big stitch – A type of quilting in which embroidery or crewel thread is used in large stitches for a decorative effect.

binding – A strip of fabric sewn over the edges of a quilt to finish the raw edges and/ or decorate the edge. Normally a binding is sewn on to one side, then brought over the edges to the other side and slipstitched in place. Alternatively, a binding can be formed by folding the edge of the quilt top over to the front, or vice versa. Binding can be straight or cut on the bias.

blindstitch – A type of invisible stitching often used for appliqué.

blocks – Pieced quilt tops are constructed by sewing together smaller units called blocks in a certain layout.

border – A strip of fabric sewn to the outer edges of a quilt top to serve as a frame for the interior, or to enhance the design.

broderie perse – Literally, Persian embroidery. This is a type of appliqué first made popular in the early 1800s, when cotton was extremely expensive. Large images, such as animal or flower motifs, are cut from a printed fabric and appliquéd to a different background fabric.

calico – In the UK, a type of plain, unbleached cotton fabric. In the USA, cotton fabric with a small, repeat design, usually floral.

chain piecing or sewing – Feeding prepared pieces into the sewing machine one after the other continuously, without lifting the foot or breaking the thread. This allows you to sew many units without stopping after each one, saving both time and thread.

charm quilt – Quilt made of many small pieces of fabric, with no two pieces alike. The pattern is usually a one-patch design. Also known as a beggar's quilt, since to collect a variety of different fabrics the quilter often begged or exchanged fabric with friends. Millennium quilts are a type of charm quilt with 2,000 different fabrics, made to celebrate the end of the twentieth century.

cheater's cloth – Fabric printed with an all-over quilt block design to look like a pieced or appliquéd quilt top.

colour value – Usually described in terms of light and dark, the value determines how close a colour is to either white or black.

corded quilting – A type of quilting in which a narrow channel is stitched in a double layer of fabric and a length of cord or yarn is inserted between the layers to create a raised line. Also known as Italian quilting.

coverlet – A bedcover, which may be woven but is often made from a quilt top with backing but no wadding (batting) or quilting.

crazy quilt – A quilt assembled from irregular (often scrap) pieces, with no set pattern or overall design. A popular pattern during the Victorian period, when it was made with silks and velvets and embellished with much embroidery.

crossways grain – Also known as the cross-grain, weft or width. The crossways grain of a woven fabric is at right angles to the selvages and has more stretch than the lengthways threads.

directional print – Fabric with a printed pattern that has a definite direction or grain (nap). Care must be taken to match the direction when piecing.

ease – To make two pieces of different sizes fit together in the same seam. One piece may have to be stretched a little, or bunched up slightly, to get both pieces the same length.

echo quilting – Several lines of quilting stitches following the edge of a shape or block, thus echoing the shape.

English paper piecing/ English paper patchwork – A method of hand piecing using paper templates inside the block elements to guide where the edges are turned under. The papers are later removed.

fat quarter – A unit of measurement for fabric, made by cutting a half-yard in half again vertically, so usually measuring around 45 x 55cm (18 x 22in). This allows for cutting larger pieces than a regular quarter-yard would.

finger-pressing – Using your fingers to press a seam or press a fold into fabric, instead of an iron.

finished size – The final sewn size of a completed block without seam allowances.

foundation piecing – A method of assembling a block by sewing pieces to a foundation of plain fabric. Sewing on a foundation of paper is known as foundation paper piecing.

frameless quilting – Working without a frame when quilting, usually when stitching a small piece or a single block.

free-motion quilting – A type of machine quilting in which the feed dogs on the sewing machine are lowered or covered, allowing the quilter to move the quilt sandwich at will under the needle to create a design.

freezer paper appliqué – Freezer paper was originally a wrapping paper for meat (USA), with a light coating of wax on one side. It can be used as a template for appliqué by drawing the design on the paper side, cutting it out and ironing the template to the fabric, wax side down, using a very hot, dry iron.

fusible webbing or interfacing – Webbing or interfacing that can be ironed on to a fabric for easier appliqué, or to support the fabric.

fussy cutting – The selective cutting of fabric, based around specific parts of the pattern or design. The ultimate example of fussy cutting is the cutting out of individual fabric motifs for broderie perse.

grain – The direction of the lengthways (warp) and crossways (weft) threads of a fabric. The lengthways grain, parallel to the selvage, stretches least and should be used for borders whenever possible. The crossways grain, at right angles to the selvage, has slightly more give.

hanging tube – A tube sewn to the back top of a quilt to allow it to be hung. Also known as a hanging sleeve.

Hawaiian appliqué/ quilting – A special type of appliqué from the Hawaiian Islands, in which an intricate symmetrical design is cut from fabric in one piece and applied to a background fabric. It is often echo-quilted.

kantha quilt – Kantha is a type of embroidery done by the village women of West Bengal and Bangladesh. The embroidery stitches are worked on layers of fabric cut from old dhotis or faded saris, holding the layers together. The top and bottom layers of a kantha are always white or of a very light colour, so that the brightly coloured stitching is visible. The embroidery forms decorative motifs and often covers the entire piece so the surface has a delicate, rippled look.

kit quilt – A package that includes the pattern, directions and fabric for one quilt. Kit quilts were particularly popular in the first half of the twentieth century.

loft – A word usually used to describe the thickness and airiness of wadding (batting). High-loft wadding does not need much quilting and will give a puffy quilt. Low-loft wadding will allow fine quilting details to be appreciated.

long-arm quilting – Quilting using a (commercial) quilting machine with a very long bed to do the overall quilting.

meander quilting – Another term for stippling.

metallic needles – These are constructed specifically for use with metallic and monofilament threads. They are thin, with a sharp point to eliminate thread breakage, an elongated eye to make threading easier, and an elongated scarf (groove on the back of the needle, above the eye) to prevent shredding. Metallic machine embroidery needles are available in sizes 70/10 to 90/14.

Millennium quilt – A type of charm quilt with 2,000 different fabrics, made to celebrate the end of the twentieth century.

mitred corner – Corner (usually of a border) that is joined at a 45° angle, like a picture frame.

mola – Textile made from appliqué and reverse appliqué, worn by the Kuna Indians, a tribe living in the San Blas islands off the coast of Panama. May be made into a quilt.

motif – A single design element or a patch used for appliqué.

non-woven stabilizer – A fabric made by bonding fibres with adhesive or by needle-punching with a serrated needle so friction causes the fibres to cling together, instead of a fabric made by weaving. It is not particularly strong, but does not stretch and so is ideal as a stable foundation fabric.

on point – A square block that is set diagonally with the corners at top and bottom, side and side.

overlocker – A type of sewing machine that makes overcast seams and cuts off the excess automatically. Also known as a serger.

paper piecing – See English Paper Piecing/Foundation Piecing.

patchwork – An older term for piecing squares together, still used in England. Sometimes, pieced quilts are referred to as patchwork quilts.

penny squares – In nineteenth-century America, dry goods stores sold 15cm (6in) muslin (gauze) squares marked with a variety of designs for a penny each. These 'penny squares' are often seen incorporated into old redwork bedspreads and linens.

piecing – A process of sewing fabric pieces together by hand or machine to create a larger piece. Also referred to as patchwork.

pin-tack (pin-baste) – To use curved safety pins to temporarily hold together the three layers of a quilt in preparation for quilting.

pounce – A special powder – see Pouncing.

pouncing – A technique used to transfer lines and other markings to fabric in embroidery and tailoring. A pin, dressmaker's wheel or unthreaded sewing machine needle is used to make holes along the lines of the design on paper. The paper is then pinned to the fabric and fine chalk dust or special pounce powder (sometimes known as inking powder) is brushed through the holes. The powder can also be dabbed through the holes using a small piece of rolled-up felt.

Prairie Points – A simple, folded fabric triangle made in multiples and attached as a decorative edging finish on quilts and garments, with the point facing out.

Princess Feather – A traditional appliqué design widely worked in the nineteenth century. Its name is a reference to a feather worn by the then Princess of Wales.

quillow – A specially designed quilt that is a cross between a sleeping bag, a quilt and a pillow, which folds up into a carrying bag.

quilt – An item made from two layers of fabric with a layer of filling, such as wadding (batting), in between. The fabric at top and bottom can be single pieces, or can be pieced. In appliquéd quilts, usually only the top is appliquéd.

quilt sandwich – A term quilters use to describe a quilt top, wadding (batting) and backing layered together.

quilt top – The top layer of a quilt.

quilting stitch – A special type of running stitch that holds the layers of a quilt together permanently.

ralli quilt – A traditional type of quilt originating from rural Indian areas of Rajasthan and Gujarat on the Pakistan border. The quilt top is made of scraps of cotton fabric dyed to white, black, red and yellow or orange with green, dark blue or purple. Ralli quilts have layers of worn fabric or cotton fibres as wadding (batting), and the layers are held together by thick coloured thread stitched in straight lines.

redwork – Simple outline embroidery designs worked in running stitch, using red thread on cream or white cloth. Traditional motifs are animals, flowers, children's and kitchen themes. Redwork can be done in other colours, greenwork or bluework for example, but if done in black it is called black redwork because blackwork refers to a specific single-thread embroidery technique.

repeat – Measurement between the centres of identical motifs running in a straight line lengthways along printed or woven fabric. A half-drop repeat fabric is when the motifs are identical but staggered, so the motifs in one row crossways fall halfway between the motifs in the rows above and below.

reverse appliqué – An appliqué technique in which the motif is stitched to the underside of the background. The top fabric is then cut away inside the stitching line and the edges turned under to reveal the motif behind. Molas and Hawaiian quilts are made using reverse appliqué.

sampler quilt – A quilt made of different block patterns, usually as an exercise in piecing techniques.

sashiko quilting – Japanese style of precise quilting designs using embroidery thread; the stitches are large on top, but small on the reverse.

sashing – Strips of fabric sewn between pieced blocks to separate them when joining them together into a quilt top.

sawtooth – A zigzag design found in many quilt patterns.

scherenschnitte – A method of folding paper and then cutting intricate designs to transfer to fabric to make quilt blocks. See also Hawaiian Appliqué.

scrap quilt – A quilt of any design made with left over fabrics.

selvedge – The outer edges of a length of fabric. The selvedge is usually more tightly woven than the rest of the fabric and so is normally cut off and not used. There is often manufacturer's information on the selvedge.

serger – Another term for an overlocker.

set on point – Placing a square block at an angle, so it sits on one corner and forms a diamond shape.

setting – Arranging pieced or appliquéd blocks in a quilt top, often to create a secondary design with the juxtaposition of colours or tones.

setting block – A block used with pieced or appliquéd blocks in a quilt top. Can be a solid block or another pieced block. May vary in size, especially along the edges of the quilt top.

sharps – Small, thin needles with a really sharp point that pierces the thread of woven fabrics. Better for joining pieces than for quilting; a good choice for sewing straight stitches. Available in sizes 60/8 to 90/14.

signature (or autograph) quilt – A quilt made from blocks that have been signed, sometimes with the signature embroidered over. These were popular fundraiser quilts in the early twentieth century, particularly with the Red Cross and some church groups.

stab stitch – A stitch used in quilting and embroidery, in which the needle and thread are taken through the layers of fabric at a right angle and in only one direction at a time.

stash – Collection of fabrics used for quilting.

stencil – A type of template used to mark quilting patterns on a quilt top. The design is cut out of a piece of plastic or cardboard, and marking is done by drawing through the openings.

stippling – Closely spaced quilting stitches following an irregular design with no crossing lines, used to fill background space and create surface texture. Also called meander quilting.

stitch in the ditch – Quilting in the 'ditch' created by the seams of the pieces in a block. The quilting pattern will therefore outline the block pattern.

straight grain – The straight, lengthways (warp) grain along a piece of fabric. See also Bias.

strip piecing – Cutting and sewing strips of fabric before cutting individual shapes.

strippy quilt – A type of quilt widely made in the second half of the nineteenth century, with vertical strips of alternating fabrics. Strippies were usually quilted with a separate design on each strip.

summer quilt – A quilt that has a top and a back, but no wadding (batting).

superstition block – A block deliberately wrongly orientated or made of a different fabric, since 'only God can make something perfect'.

tacking – Long stitches that may be used to hold the top, wadding (batting) and backing of a quilt together while the quilting is being done; they are removed when the quilt is completed. In the USA, tacking is called basting. A quilt can also be tacked with safety pins. Fusible wadding is also available, which does not need tacking in place.

template – A shape used as a pattern for piecing or appliqué patches, or for tracing lines to be quilted. Can be purchased or cut from cardboard or template plastic.

tied quilt – A quilt in which knotted strings or ties are used to hold the three layers of the quilt together.

top – Another term for a quilt top.

trapunto – A quilting design in which areas of the design are padded from the back to bring them into relief.

turkey red – A type of brilliant red fabric or thread that was dyed with the first colourfast red dye. It was popular for quiltmaking towards the end of the nineteenth century.

wadding – A layer in the centre of a quilt between the top and the backing, giving warmth and thickness. Wadding (known in the US as batting) can be cotton, polyester, blends, silk or wool.

warp/ weft – The woven threads in fabric. Warp threads are long and run from top to bottom along the length of the material, parallel to the selvage. Weft threads run from side to side and are therefore shorter.

watercolour quilt – A technique that uses small squares of floral print fabrics to build up a subtle and diffused design.

wholecloth quilt – A quilt in a plain coloured fabric, depending on the quilting pattern alone for interest.

WIP – Work in progress.

WOW – White on white.

resources

UK RESOURCES

The Quilters' Guild of The British Isles

St Anthony's Hall, Peasholme Green,
York YO1 7PW.
Tel: +44 (0)1904 613242
www.quiltersguild.org.uk
E-mail: admin@quiltersguild.org.uk
Organization for quiltmakers in Britain
and worldwide.

Creative Quilting

30–32 Bridge Road, Hampton Court
Village, East Molesey, Surrey KT8 9HA.
Tel: +44 (0)20 8941 7075
www.creativequilting.co.uk
E-mail: isabelle@creativequilting.co.uk
Fabrics and wadding, books,
haberdashery and craft supplies.

The Cotton Patch

1283–1285 Stratford Road, Hall Green,
Birmingham B28 9AJ.
Tel: +44 (0)121 702 2840
www.cottonpatch.co.uk
Patchwork and quilting fabrics, books,
wadding, haberdashery and
quilt design software.

Quilters' Haven

68 High Street, Wickham Market,
Suffolk IP13 0QU.
Tel: +44 (0)1728 746275/746314
www.quilters-haven.co.uk
E-mail: quilters-haven@btinternet.com
Patchwork and quilting fabrics, books,
wadding, haberdashery and
quilt design software.

Pelenna Patchworks

5 Bevans Terrace, Pontrhydyfen,
Port Talbot SA12 9TR.
Tel: +44 (0)1639 898444
www.pelennapatchworks.co.uk
E-mail: sales@pelennapatchworks.co.uk
Online quilting and patchwork supply
shop, for fabrics, tools and haberdashery.

Sew Creative

Wroxham Barns, Tunstead Road,
Hoveton, Norfolk NR12 8QU.
Tel: +44 (0)1603 781665
www.sewcreativequilts.co.uk
E-mail: sales@sewcreativequilts.co.uk
Patchwork and quilting fabrics,
embroidery materials, beads, books.

Rio Designs

Flint Cottage, Treacle Lane, Rushden,
Buntingford, Herts SG9 0SL.
Tel: + 44 (0)1763 288234
www.riodesigns.co.uk
E-mail: sales@riodesigns.co.uk
Supplier of software for quilters with help
and support available seven days a week
until early evening.

Creative Beadcraft

Unit 2, Asheridge Business Centre,
Asheridge Road, Chesham,
Bucks HP5 2PT.
Tel: +44 (0)1494 778818
www.creativebeadcraft.co.uk
E-mail: beads@creativebeadcraft.co.uk
Beads and beading supplies.

Beads Direct

Unit 10, Duke Street, Loughborough,
Leicestershire LE11 1ED.
Tel: +44 (0)1509 218028
www.beadsdirect.co.uk
E-mail: service@beadsdirect.co.uk
Beads and beading supplies.

US RESOURCES

American Quilter's Society

PO Box 3290, Paducah,
KY 42002-3290.
Tel: +1-270-898-7903
www.americanquilter.com
Organization for quiltmakers in America
and worldwide.

The Appliqué Society

PO Box 89, Sequim,
WA 98382-0089.
Tel: 1-800-597-9827
www.theappliquesociety.org
E-mail: tas@theappliquesociety.org
International society for all those interested
in appliqué.

Quilts, Inc.

7660 Woodway, Suite 550, Houston,
TX 77063.
Tel: +1-713-781-6864
www.quilts.com
E-mail: shows@quilts.com
Organizers of annual International Quilt
Festivals in Houston and Chicago (open to
the public), as well as two annual trade
shows for quilting and soft crafts.

International Machine Quilters' Association

PO Box 419, Higginsville,
MO 64037-0419.
Tel: +1-660-584-8171
www.imqa.org
E-mail: Admin@IMQA.org
Organizers of the annual Machine Quilters'
Showcase in Overland Park, Kansas.

The Electric Quilt Company

419 Gould Street, Suite 2,
Bowling Green,
OH 43402-3047.
Tel: +1-419-352-1134
www.electricquilt.com
(Sales) 1-800-356-4219
E-mail: sales@electricquilt.com
(Tech Support) +1-419-352-1134
(General Information)
E-mail: customerservice
@electricquilt.com
Quilt design software company, with
distributors in the US, Canada, Europe,
Great Britain, Japan, Australia, New
Zealand and South Africa.

QuiltSOFT

5441 Brockbank Place, San Diego,
CA 92115.
Tel: +1-619-583-2970
www.quiltsoft.com
E-mail: tech@quiltsoft.com
Quilt design software company.

Fusion Beads

3830 Stone Way N, Seattle,
WA 98103.
Tel: +1-206-782-4595 (store).
Toll free tel: +1-888-781-3559.
For customers outside US & Canada:
Tel: +1-206-781-9500.
www.fusionbeads.com
E-mail: orders@fusionbeads.com
E-mail: suppport@fusionbeads.com
Beads and beading supplies.

acknowledgements

With many thanks to the quilters who lent their work to be photographed: Rose Epton-Peter, Avril Horn, Gwen Jones, Sally Manning, Doreen Plumridge, Marion Stanway and Sinéad Hurley. Thank you to Maggi McCormick-Gordon for teaching me much of what I know about quilting, and to my mother, Joan Clayton, for teaching me how to sew.

I would also like to thank everyone at Collins & Brown for their help and support, particularly Miriam Hyslop, Caroline King and Gemma Wilson. Thank you to Kuo Kang Chen for the excellent illustrations, Debi Treloar and Holly Jolliffe for the beautiful photography, Louise Leffler for the stylish design and Fiona Corbridge for her thorough but sympathetic editing of the text.

And finally, a big thank you to Janome for supplying the sewing machine and all its accessories.

Picture credits

Pages 1, 2 and 119 (ph Debi Treloar)
"Evenings in the Garden" (2000)
Made by Rose Epton-Peter
Inspired by Stourhead Gardens in Wiltshire.
100% hand-dyed cotton and silk, Seminole patchwork strips machine pieced in random folded Log Cabin style, machine quilted.

Pages 4 and 198 (ph Debi Treloar)
"Liberty Rose Garden" (2005)
Made by: Doreen Plumridge
100% Liberty lawn, hand pieced, hand appliqué, broderie perse spacer units, machine quilted.

Pages 5 and 177 (ph Debi Treloar)
"Double Wedding Ring" (1997)
Made by: Doreen Plumridge and Florence Suttie.
100% cotton, hand pieced with some machine stitching, hand quilted.

Page 6 (ph Debi Treloar)
"Grass II: Meadow" (2004)
Made by Rose Epton-Peter
One of a series of "Grass" quilts
100% hand-dyed cotton, computer designed and foundation-pieced blocks, free-motion machine quilted.

Page 9 (ph Debi Treloar)
"Amiss Amish" (2001)
Made by: Rose Epton-Peter
100% cotton, alternative arrangement of Jacob's Ladder block, machine pieced, free-motion machine quilted.

Pages 10 and 65 (ph Debi Treloar)
Kaffe Fassett Quilt (2003)
Made by: Rose Epton-Peter, designed by Kaffe Fassett
100% Kaffe Fassett cotton, machine pieced, machine quilted.

Pages 51, 56 and 149 (ph Debi Treloar)
"Thank Christmas it's Finished" (1999–2004)
Made by: Avril Horn
100% cotton, various sampler blocks with hand and machine stitching, specially-designed pieced border.

Pages 66 and 69 (ph Debi Treloar)
Wholecloth Cot Quilt (2004)
Made by: Gwen Jones
100% cotton, hand quilted in a mixture of solid colour thread and variegated thread.

Page 71 (ph Debi Treloar)
"Dawn", "Midday", "Evening", "Night" (2001)
Made by: Rose Epton-Peter
Miniature strippy wallhangings inspired by the bleak Dorset heathland.
100% cotton, some hand-dyed, machine strip-pieced, machine quilted.

Page 84 (ph Holly Jolliffe)
"Amoeba" (1998)
Made by: Doreen Plumridge
100% Liberty lawn with some pieces bleached to a lighter tone, machine pieced, hand quilted.

Page 99 (ph Holly Jolliffe)
"From the Desert to the Sea" (2002)
Made by: Rose Epton-Peter
100% cotton batik, machine strip-pieced blocks, free-motion machine quilted.

Page 102, 151 and 165 (ph Holly Jolliffe)
Sampler Quilt (2003)
Made by: Marion Stanway
100% cotton, all scissor-cut, hand-stitched piecing, machined sashing, hand quilted.

Page 111 (ph Holly Jolliffe)
"Liberty Chain" (1986)
Made by Doreen Plumridge
100% Liberty lawn, machine pieced Log-Cabin style, hand quilted.

Page 115 (ph Debi Treloar)
"Cabin Fever" (2004)
Made by: Rose Epton-Peter
100% cotton, some hand-dyed, offset Log Cabin blocks, foundation pieced, machine quilted.

Page 178 (ph Debi Treloar)
Thai cushion (1995)
Maker unknown
40/60% polycotton, reverse appliqué and turned-edge appliqué.

Page 181 (ph Holly Jolliffe)
"Liberty Garden Pond" (1999)
Made by: Doreen Plumridge
100% Liberty lawn with 'paving' pieces bleached to a lighter tone, hand pieced, hand appliqué, hand quilted, ruched border.

Page 208 (ph Debi Treloar)
"Rice Crackers" (2003)
Made by: Rose Epton-Peter
Inspired by rice paddy fields.
100% cotton, some hand dyed, machine-pieced blocks, machine-couched acrylic yarn embellishments, free-motion machine quilted.

Page 230 (ph Michael Wicks)
"Op Art Twist"
Made by: Wendy Lowes (2006).
100% cotton, folding blocks.

Page 235 (ph Holly Jolliffe)
"Microwave" (2002)
Made by: Rose Epton-Peter
Inspired by the waves on the sea shore.
100% hand-dyed cotton, miniature offset Log Cabin blocks, foundation pieced, machine quilted.

Page 237 (ph Holly Jolliffe)
Japanese Folded Quilt (2008)
Made by: Sinéad Hurley
100% cotton, folded blocks, quilt-as-you-go.

Front cover (ph Catherine Gratwicke)
"Collection" (2014)
Made by: Jane Brocket
Fabric from the Lotta Jansdotter 'Echo' collection.
Featured in Quilt Me (2014) by Jane Brocket.

Back cover (ph Catherine Gratwicke)
"Wisteria" (2014)
Made by: Jane Brocket
Barkcloth and assorted printed cottons.
Featured in Quilt Me (2014) by Jane Brocket.

index

album quilts 223, 248
Amish Bars 72
Anabaptists 9, 74
antique quilts 24
Anvil 135
appliquéd quilts 7, 24, 69, 74, 178–207, 248
  bias strip appliqué 193
  broderie perse 30, 199
  fabrics 191
  Folk Art 180–3
  freezer paper appliqué 185–6, 249
  fused appliqué 187
  hand applique 180–6
  Hawaiian appliqué 196–7, 205, 250
  history of 8
  inlay appliqué 190
  machine appliqué 192
  Mola 200–1, 206–7, 249, 250
  Oak Leaf and Reel 194–5, 204
  peaks and valleys 184
  reverse appliqué 8, 188–9, 200, 250
  shadow appliqué 191
  squares 202–3
  techniques 180–203
autograph quilts 223
Axehead, Double 159

Baby Blocks 150–1
back stitch 18, 62, 101, 212, 223
backing 32–3, 250
bagging 59, 248
Baltimore album quilts 248
Barbara Bannister Star 153
Barn Raising 105
Basket 168
Basket of Flowers 169
basketweave 77, 99
basting (tacking) 19, 248, 250
batik 248
beads and beading 58, 218, 219, 248
Bengal 8, 45
bias strips 63–4, 193, 248

binding 60–5, 193, 248
blanket stitch 45, 215
Blazing Star 153
block patterns: curves 158–65
  mosaics 146–51
  representational 168–71
  squares/triangles 124–5
  stars 152–7
  strips 98–123
  templates 172–7
Block Puzzle 151
block shapes, Log Cabin 110–12
blocks 48, 248
  joining 49, 53
  orientation 50
  sashing 52, 53
  setting patterns 50
  sizes 49
  spacer 50
  squaring up 49
bobbin holders 22
bobbins 25
borders 54–7, 72, 78–9, 248
boutis 69
Bow Tie 113, 142–3
Box or Formal Garden 127
Box Kite 133
Brick 100–1
broderie perse 30, 199, 248
Broken Dishes 128–9
Broken Pinwheel 131
Broken Star 155
Butterfly 161
Buzzard's Roost 129

Cabin in the Cotton 109, 114
Cake Stand 169
calico 223, 248
Calico Puzzle 133
Card Basket 157
Carpenter's Wheel 155
Cathedral Window 232–3, 236
Chain and Hourglass 121
chain piercing 248
chain stitch 215
charm quilts 248, 249
cheater's cloth 248
chevron patterns 57, 77
  Chevron Log Cabin 112

Double Chevron 120
  Seminole 118–20
  Single Chevron 120
Chimneys and Cornerstones 109
Chinese Coin 75, 233
Churn Dash 133
circle-and-square 236
clamshell 77, 82, 158–9, 173
colour: colouring fabric 221–2
  using colour 28–9, 248
constructing a quilt 48–65
cording 42, 68, 69, 248
corners 55, 80–1, 249
cornerstones 55
cotton 26, 199, 223
Country Farm 157
Courthouse Steps 106
coverlets 248
crazy patchwork 225
crazy quilts 248
Cross, Double 139
cross stitch 43, 44, 45, 213
crosses, feathered 82
Crosses and Losses 139
crossways grain 248
Crow's Foot 135
crow's foot stitch 45
curves 158–65
  curved lines 46
  curved seams 92
  inserting curved tucks 242
  stitching curved (bias) seams 164
cutting 86, 88
  tools 14–15

designs, enlarging and transferring 38
diagonal patterns: diagonal inwards 77
  diagonal lines 76
  diagonal outwards 77
  diagonal trellis 76
diamond patterns 172
  Diamond Grandmother's Flower Garden 147
  Diamond Log Cabin 112
  Diamond Star 103
  Diamonds 120

Light and Dark Diamonds 104
  Little and Large Diamonds 114
  Scintillating Diamond 104
dimensional quilting 43
directional print 248
displaying quilts 63
Double Axehead 159
Double Cross 139
Dove 163
Dresden Plate 161
Drunkard's Path 162–3, 173
dyes and paints 221

ease 248
echo quilting 41, 248
Eight-Pointed Star 154–5
embellished quilts 208–29
embroidery 74, 210–17, 225
English paper piecing 90, 150, 248–9
enlarging designs 38
equilateral triangle 172
  Equilateral Triangle Log Cabin 110
Evergreen 141
exploding star 82

fabric 191
  colouring 221–2
  fusing 220
  ironing and pressing 24
  and needles 23
  preparation 26
  printed 248
  storage 25
  types of 26–7
fabric paint 221
Falling Timbers 163
Fan 160–1, 174
Fancy Stripe 129
fat quarters 31, 249
feather stitch 214
  feathered chain stitch 216
feathered designs 82, 83
feet, sewing machine 22
filling grids or patterns 41
finger-pressing 48, 244, 249
floral patterns 30

Flutter Blades 130
fly stitch 214
Flying Geese 57, 74
Flying Geese Pineapple block 108
Folded Log Cabin 234–5
Folded Pinwheel 244–5
folded quilts 230–47
   Cathedral Window 232–3, 236
   Folded Log Cabin 234–5
   Folded Pinwheel 244–5
   Japanese folded patchwork 236–8
   Somerset Patchwork 247
   Suffolk Puff 246
   tucks 239–43
folded star 247
Formal Garden (Box) 127
foundation piecing 96, 249
Four-Patch 98, 101, 124–5, 130, 142, 143
   Double Four-Patch 125, 163
   Four-Patch and Squares 125
   Four-Patch Rectangles 57
Four-Pointed Star 152–3, 175
frames 17
free-motion quilting 47
freezer paper appliqué 185–6, 249
French-fold binding 61
French knots 44, 213
friendship quilts 223
Friendship Star 126–7
Fruit Basket 169
fused appliqué 187
fusible webbing 249
fusing fabric 220
fussy cutting 249

geometric patterns 30
grain, fabric 27, 248, 249, 250
Grandmother's Flower Garden 146–7
Granny's Choice 143
grid templates 76–7

half-buttonhole stitch 45
Half-Log Cabin 112
hand quilting 36–45
hand stitches, basic 18–19
hanging tube 249

Hawaiian appliqué 9, 196–7, 205, 249, 250
hearts 82
herringbone stitch 43, 215
hexagon patterns 77, 172
   Hexagon Log Cabin 110
   Hexagon Star 147
   Hexagon Tile 147
history 8–9
Hole in the Barn Door 105, 133
hoops 17
hope chest 9
Hovering Hawks 139

in-the-ditch 41
Indian Hatchet 143
inlay appliqué 190
Inner City Block 151
interfacing 249
Irish Chain 122–3
irons 24, 48

Jacob's Ladder 138–9
Japanese folded patchwork 236–8
Josephine's Knot 164–5, 174
Justice 113

kantha 8, 45, 224, 249
Kimono 171
King's Cross 117
kit quilt 249
Kite 171
Kite Tails 149
knots 39, 44, 210
   French knots 213
   knotted insertion stitch 215
Kuna tribes 200

Laced Star 153
large quilts, working on 47
lazy daisy stitch 215
leaves 83
Lemon Star 155
LeMoyne Star 155
Light and Dark Diamonds 104
lighting 25
Lilies 135
Lily 155
linen 26
Little and Large Diamonds 114
Little Red Schoolhouse 170–1
loft 249

Log Cabin 98, 102–14, 234
   block shapes 110–12
   combination setting patterns 113–14
   Log Cabin Courthouse Steps 106
   Log Cabin Pineapple 108
   Log Cabin Star 104
London Stairs 101
long-arm quilting 249
lover's knot 83

machine quilting 9, 20–3, 46–7, 97
   long-arm quilting 68, 249
   machine appliqué 192
   machine piecing 91–7
Maltese Barn Raising 105
Maple Leaf 134–5
marking 12–13, 36, 86, 87
matelassage 69
mats and rulers 88
meander stitch 47, 249
measuring and marking tools 12–13
medallion designs 68, 69
Mennonite quilts 74
Mennonite tack 45
Methodist knot 44
Mexican Cross 114
Milky Way 127
Millennium quilts 249
Mitred Triangle block 117
Mola 200–1, 206–7, 249, 250
Monkey Wrench 137
mosaics 146–51
motifs 41, 82–3, 180, 187, 199, 200, 249
Mrs Taft's Choice 145

needles 17, 20, 22, 249
Nine-Patch 98, 121, 126, 132, 144
Nine-Patch Star 127
Nocturne 165
North Star 153

Oak Leaf and Reel 194–5, 204
Ocean Wave 147
Octagon Log Cabin 112
Octagon Pineapple block 108
Ohio Star 156–7
Old Star 145

origami 244
outline 41
overlocker 249
overstitching 210
paper patterns 87
patchwork 7, 8, 16, 249
   crazy patchwork 225
   Shell patchwork 159
   see also pieced quilts
patterns, fabric 30–1
patterns, paper 38, 87
Peace and Plenty 129
peaks and valleys 184
penny squares 249
pentagons 172
   Pentagon Log Cabin 112
perforated patterns 38
pieced quilts 8, 84–177, 249
   chain piecing 92, 248
   foundation piecing 96, 249
   hand piecing 89–90
   joining pieced units 93
   machine piecing 91–7
   marking and cutting 86–7
   quilt-as-you-go 97
   ripping seams 94
   rotary cutting 88
   string piecing 100, 101
   templates 172–7
   triangle squares 95
Pine Tree 140–1
Pineapple basic block 108
pins 17
pintucks 239
Pinwheels 105, 130–1
   Broken Pinwheel 131
   Double Pinwheel 131
   Pinwheel Triangles 117
piqûre de Marseilles 69
pleated strips 243
Postage Stamp 148–9
Prairie Points 57, 249
presentation quilts 223
pressing 24, 48, 107, 113, 185
Princess Feather 249
printed fabric 31, 248

quarter-triangles, stitching 157
quill patchwork 247
quillow 249
quilt-as-you-go 97
quilt sandwiches 250
quilting stitch 40, 250

Rail Fence 98–9, 101
Railroad 139
ralli quilts 44, 250
Redwork 223, 226–7, 250
representational 168–71
reverse appliqué 188–9, 200, 250
reversible quilts 33
right-angled triangles 172
   Right-Angles Triangle Log Cabin 110
rings 83
ripping seams 94
Robbing Peter to Pay Paul 143
rolling 47
Roman Stripe 116–17
rotary cutting 14, 88, 101
Rough Sea 137
running stitch 18, 44, 211

sampler quilts 50, 250
sashiko 8, 45, 224, 228–9, 250
sashing 52, 250
Sawtooth 144–5, 250
   Sawtooth Four-Patch 145
   Sawtooth Rows 145
scale 31
scherenschnitte 250
Schoolhouse 170–1, 175
Scintillating Diamond 104
scrap quilts 75, 250
seams: curved seams 92, 164
   joining seamed pieces 89
   ripping seams 94
   single straight seams 89
   working with bias seams 150
Secret Garden 233
selvedges 250
Seminole 57, 118–20
sequins 218
setting blocks 50, 250
shadow appliqué 191
Shells 159
Shisha mirrors 219
Shoofly 132–3
silk 27
slipstitch 18, 62, 236
Snail's Trail 136–7
Snake in the Hollow 161
software programs 15
soldering iron 220

Somerset Patchwork 247
Southern Belle 129
Space Flight 114
spacer blocks 50
Spanish Points 247
spirals 243
split bars 73
split stitch 223
squares 57, 124–45
   appliqué squares 202–3
   Square in a Square in a Square 114
   square swirl 83
stained-glass appliqué 193
stars 152–7
   Barbara Bannister Star 153
   Blazing Star 153
   Broken Star 155
   Diamond Star 103
   Eight-Pointed Star 154–5
   exploding star 82
   Four-Pointed Star 152–3, 175
   Friendship Star 126–7
   Hexagon Star 147
   Laced Star 153
   LeMoyne Star 155
   Lily 155
   Log Cabin Star 104
   North Star 153
   Ohio Star 156–7
   Old Star 145
   Star of Bethlehem 155
   Trailing Star 131
   Variable Star 157
   Virginia Star 155
stem stitch 212, 223
stencils 16, 250
Steps 103, 120
steps pattern 77
stippling 41, 47, 250
stitches: back stitch 18, 62, 101, 212, 223
   blanket stitch 45, 215
   chain stitch 215
   cross stitch 43, 44, 45, 213
   crow's foot stitch 45
   embroidery 225
   feather stitch 214
   feathered chain stitch 216
   fly stitch 214
   French Knot 44, 213
   half-buttonhole 45
   hand appliqué 183

hand stitching 18–19
   herringbone 43, 215
   knotted insertion stitch 215
   lazy daisy stitch 215
   machine stitching 97
   meander stitch 47, 249
   Mennonite tack 45
   overstitching 210
   quilting stitch 39, 40, 250
   running stitch 18, 44, 45, 101, 211
   size of 37
   slipstitch 18, 62, 236
   split stitch 223
   stem stitch 212, 223
   whipstitch 18
   zigzag 192
storage 25
Straight Furrow 103
straight grain 250
straight lines 36, 46
straight tucks 241
Streak of Lightning 103
string piecing 100, 101
strippy quilts 70–5, 250
strips 91, 98–123
stuffed quilting 43
Suffolk Puff 246
Sunshine and Shadow 104
synthetic fabrics 27

tacking (basting) 19, 248, 250
Tall Pine Tree 141
templates 16, 36, 76–83, 86–7, 172–7, 204–7, 226–8, 250
texture patterns 31
Thick and Thin 109
thread 17, 20, 23, 25, 183
   changing 211
   colours 224
   embroidery 217
   strengthening 73
   tension 21
tie-dying 222
ties 44
tissue paper 37
tools 12–17
Totem Poles 113
tracing wheels 38
Trailing Star 131
transferring designs 38
trapunto 8, 42, 43, 68, 250
travelling 40
Tree of Paradise 141

triangles 124–45, 172
   equilateral triangle 172
   Equilateral Triangle Log Cabin 110
   Mitre Triangle 117
   Pinwheel Triangle 117
   right-angled triangle 172
   Right-Angles Triangle Log Cabin 110
   stitching quarter-triangles 157
   Triangle Block 117
   triangle squares 95
Trip Around the World 149
tucks 239–43
tulips 83
Tumbling Blocks 150–1
Turtle 165
twist tucks 240
two-circle 238

utility quilting 44–5

Variable Star 157
Vine of Friendship 163
Virginia Star 155

wadding 32–3, 250
wave tucks 240
Wedding Ring 166–7, 175
Wheel of Fortune 137
whipstitch 18
wholecloth quilts 68–9, 250
Windmill 130
Windmill Blades 108
window templates 87
wine glass 77
Wonder of the World 163
wool 26
workplace 25
woven fabric 27

yosegire 8
yo-yos 246

Marie Clayton has been sewing since she was a child, but only discovered the joys of quilting and patchwork a few years ago. She has written several sewing books, including *The Needlecrafter's Companion* and the *Ultimate Sewing Bible and First Dressmaking*.

Also in this series:

978-1-91023-176-0

978-1-84340-563-4

978-1-90844-901-6

978-1-84340-450-7

978-1-84340-574-0

978-1-84340-672-3

978-1-90939-718-7

978-1-90939-798-9

978-1-90939-797-2

PAVILION

Whatever the craft, we have the book for you – just head straight to Pavilion's crafty headquarters.

Pavilioncraft.co.uk is the one-stop destination for all our fabulous craft books. Sign up for our regular newsletters and follow us on social media to receive updates on new books, competitions and interviews with our bestselling authors.

We look forward to meeting you!

www.pavilioncraft.co.uk

Published in the United Kingdom in 2016 by
Collins & Brown
1 Gower Street
London
WC1E 6HD

An imprint of Pavilion Books Company Ltd

Copyright © Collins & Brown 2009

Distributed in the United States and Canada by Sterling Publishing Co., Inc.
1166 Avenue of the Americas, New York, NY 10036

ISBN 9781910231777

A CIP catalogue for this book is available from the British Library.

10 9 8 7 6 5 4 3 2 1

Reproduction by Mission, Hong Kong
Printed in Singapore

This book can be ordered direct from the publisher at
www.pavilionbooks.com